HENRY STEDMAN has been writing guidebooks for over ten years and walking for a lot longer. He is the author or co-author of half a dozen titles including Trailblazer's guides to *Kilimanjaro*, *Hadrian's Wall Path* and *Dolomites Trekking – Alta Via 1 & Alta Via 2*, as well as *The Bradt Guide to Palestine* and the *Rough Guides* to both *Indonesia* and *Southeast Asia*.

When not trekking or travelling, Henry lives in Hastings, editing other people's guidebooks and putting on weight.

Coast to Coast
First edition 2004; this third edition: 2008

Publisher
Trailblazer Publications
The Old Manse, Tower Rd, Hindhead, Surrey, GU26 6SU, UK
Fax (+44) 01428-607571, info@trailblazer-guides.com
www.trailblazer-guides.com

British Library Cataloguing in Publication Data
A catalogue record for this book is available from the British Library

ISBN 978-1-905864-09-6

© **Trailblazer 2004, 2006, 2008**
Text and maps

Editor: Anna Jacomb-Hood
Proof-reading: Laura Stone
Layout: Anna Jacomb-Hood
Illustrations: pp62-3: Nick Hill, pp65-6: Rev CA Johns
Photographs (flora): C1 Row 3 left and centre, C2 Row 2 centre,
C3 Row 1 centre and right, © Charlie Loram; all others © Bryn Thomas
All other photographs: © Henry Stedman (unless credited)
Cartography: Nick Hill
Index: Anna Jacomb-Hood and Jane Thomas

The maps in this guide were prepared from out-of-Crown-
copyright Ordnance Survey maps amended and updated by Trailblazer.

Warning: hill walking can be dangerous
Please read the notes on when to go (p25) and on outdoor safety (pp52-4).
Every effort has been made by the author and publisher to ensure that the information
contained herein is as accurate and up to date as possible. However, they are unable
to accept responsibility for any inconvenience, loss, or injury sustained by anyone
as a result of the advice and information given in this guide.

Printed on chlorine-free paper from farmed forests by
D2Print (☎ +65-6295 5598)

Coast to Coast
PATH

ST BEES TO ROBIN HOOD'S BAY
planning, places to stay, places to eat,
includes 109 large-scale walking maps

HENRY STEDMAN

TRAILBLAZER PUBLICATIONS

Acknowledgements

Thanks, firstly, to Charlie Loram, the original series editor, for all the work he did before I even put pen to paper or foot to path. Also at Trailblazer I'm grateful to Anna Jacomb-Hood, Nick Hill, Laura Stone and Jane Thomas. I'd also like to thank Jim Manthorpe for updating the previous edition of my book.

On the path, thanks are due to Rachel Dunckley in Borrowdale for her advice, companionship and hospitality in Borrowdale; Hazel Wilkinson at Honister; Dave, John, Stefan and Bernard at Ennerdale and beyond; Bob Forber at Patterdale; Merilyn Green and Ted Wiles at Danby Wiske and beyond for all their advice, recommendations and company; Judy Balco and Malcolm Hoskin (Canada) at Danby Wiske; Andre Volmer (Ger) from Keld to Robin Hood's Bay; and as ever to Bryn, for keeping me in work.

Thanks also to the readers who wrote to us with suggestions, in particular: Peter Stott, Godfrey Cole, Denis and Frances Shaw, Mary Schafer, Sally and Martin Fielding, Alice Sin and Bill Paul.

A request

The author and publisher have tried to ensure that this guide is as accurate and up to date as possible. Nevertheless things change. If you notice any changes or omissions that should be included in the next edition of this book, please write to Trailblazer (address on p2) or email us at info@trailblazer-guides.com. A free copy of the next edition will be sent to persons making a significant contribution.

Updated information will shortly be available on the Internet at
www.trailblazer-guides.com

Front cover: On the trail between Helvellyn and Patterdale in the Lake District.
© Henry Stedman

CONTENTS

INTRODUCTION

The Coast to Coast path runs between St Bees on the Irish Sea coast and Robin Hood's Bay on England's north-eastern shore. It was devised in the early 1970s by the legendary fell walker, guidebook writer and illustrator, Alfred Wainwright. At first glance it doesn't appear to be anything special. At 191½ miles (307km) it is not the longest path in the country and certainly doesn't, as some people mistakenly think, span England at its widest point. It makes no claim to being technically demanding or especially tough either (though we can safely predict that those who attempt it will find it sufficiently challenging, and I've been told by several American Coast to Coast veterans to make it clear that this is a trek, or a hike, and *not* a mere walk). Nor does it, unlike the long-distance paths that run alongside Hadrian's Wall or Offa's Dyke, follow any ancient construction or border. In fact, it's not even an official National Trail.

In truth, the Coast to Coast is but one route out of an infinite number that could be devised by joining the various footpaths and byways to form a single, unbroken route across England. It's just a testing, long-distance path from one side of northern England to another that provides those who complete it with a quick snapshot of the country.

But what a snapshot that is! Around two-thirds of the walk are spent in the national parks of the Lake District, the Yorkshire Dales and the North Yorkshire Moors. These parks encompass some of the most dramatic scenery in the country, from its highest fells to its largest lakes, its most beautiful woods and its bleakest, barest moors. The walk also passes through areas alive with some of Britain's rarest wildlife, including red squirrels and otters, and even skirts around the eyrie of England's only golden eagle.

Furthermore, where man has settled on the trail he has, on the whole, worked in perfect harmony with nature to produce some of England's finest villages, from elegant Grasmere to exquisite, refined Egton Bridge. The trail itself is a further example of the harmony between man and nature. The paths and bridleways that make up the trail have existed for centuries and as such, though man-made, do not feel or look like an imposition on the landscape but are very much part of it. It is a subtle distinction, and an important one.

While these paths and villages continue to thrive, in other places where man once lived and worked, nature has been allowed to reclaim the upper hand yet again: the poignant, overgrown ruins of mills and mines, of ancient Iron Age villages and mysterious stone circles are all silent witnesses to a bygone age. They punctuate the path and provide absorbing highlights along the way.

All this, and all within a trail that takes around a fortnight to complete. It's true that the Coast to Coast may not be the longest, most difficult or most recognized of long-distance trails in England. But few, if any, can match it for beauty or splendour.

About this book

This guidebook contains all the information you need. The hard work has been done for you so you can plan your trip from home without the usual pile of books, maps, guides and tourist brochures. It includes:

● All standards of accommodation from campsites to B&Bs and luxurious hotels
● Walking companies if you want an organized tour and baggage carriers if you just want your luggage carried
● Itineraries for all types of walkers
● Answers to all your questions: when to go, degree of difficulty, what to pack, and how much the whole walking holiday will cost

When you're all packed and ready to go, there's comprehensive public transport information to get you to and from the Coast to Coast path and 109 detailed maps and town plans to help you find your way along it. The route guide section includes:

● Walking times
● Reviews of campsites, bunkhouses, hostels, B&Bs, guesthouses and hotels
● Cafés, pubs, tearooms, takeaways, restaurants and shops for buying supplies
● Rail, bus and taxi information for all the villages and towns along the path
● Street plans of the main towns: St Bees, Grasmere, Shap, Orton, Kirkby Stephen, Reeth, Richmond and Robin Hood's Bay
● Historical, cultural and geographical background information

Minimum impact for maximum insight

Man has suffered in his separation from the soil and from other living creatures ... and as yet he must still, for security, look long at some portion of the earth as it was before he tampered with it.   **Gavin Maxwell**, *Ring of Bright Water*, **1960**

Why is walking in wild and solitary places so satisfying? Partly it is the sheer physical pleasure: sometimes pitting one's strength against the elements and the lie of the land. The beauty and wonder of the natural world and the fresh air restore our sense of proportion and the stresses and strains of everyday life slip away. Whatever the character of the countryside, walking in it benefits us mentally and physically, inducing a sense of well-being, an enrichment of life and an enhanced awareness of what lies around us.

All this the countryside gives us and the least we can do is to safeguard it by supporting rural economies, local businesses, and low-impact methods of farming and land-management, and by using environmentally sensitive forms of transport – walking being pre-eminent.

In this book there is a detailed and illustrated chapter on the wildlife and conservation of the region and a chapter on minimum-impact walking, with ideas on how to tread lightly in this fragile environment; by following its principles we can help to preserve our natural heritage for future generations.

PART 1: PLANNING

About the Coast to Coast path

HISTORY

The Coast to Coast path owes its existence to one man: Alfred Wainwright. It was in 1972 that Wainwright, already renowned for his exquisitely illustrated guides to walking in the Lake District, trekked across England on a path of his own devising. It was an idea that he had been kicking around for a time: to cross his native land on a route that, as far as he was aware, would 'commit no offence against privacy nor trample on the sensitive corns of landowners and tenants'. The result of his walk, a guidebook, was originally printed by his long-time publishers, *The Westmoreland Gazette*, the following year. It proved hugely successful. Indeed, a full twenty years after the book was first published, a spin-off television series of the trail was also made in which Wainwright himself starred, allowing a wider public to witness firsthand his wry, abrupt, earthy charm.

Wainwright reminds people in his book that his is just one of many such trails across England that could be devised, and since Wainwright's book other Coast to Coast walks have indeed been established. Yet it is still *his* trail that is by far and away the most popular, and in order to distinguish it from the others, it is now commonly known as Wainwright's Coast to Coast path.

The route has been amended slightly since 1973 mostly because, though careful to try to use only public rights of way, in a few places Wainwright's original trail actually intruded upon private land. Indeed, even today the trail does in places cross private territory, and it is only due to the largesse of the landowners that the path has remained near-enough unchanged throughout its 191½ miles.

Though the trail passes through three national parks, crosses the Pennine Way and at times joins with both the Lyke Wake Walk and the Cleveland Way, it is not itself one of the 15 national trails in the UK, though there are some who are campaigning for it to be included in order that it may enjoy greater protection and maintenance than it has received heretofore. Whether that ever arises remains to be seen. What is certain is that the path is one of the most popular of Britain's long-distance trails, with around 9500 people attempting it every year.

HOW DIFFICULT IS THE COAST TO COAST PATH?

The Coast to Coast path is a long, tough walk but there's no need for crampons, ropes or any other climbing paraphernalia. So, despite the presence of some fairly steep ascents and descents, all of them are 'walkable', and no mountaineering or climbing skills are necessary. All you need is some suitable clothing, a bit of money, a rucksack full of determination and a half-decent pair of calf muscles.

PLANNING YOUR WALK

That said, the most common complaint I've received about this book, particularly from American readers, is that it doesn't emphasize how tough it can be. So let us be clear: **the Coast to Coast is a lengthy and in many places tough trek**. The Ramblers' Association of Great Britain officially describe the walk as 'challenging' and they're not wrong.

The Lake District, in particular, contains many up-and-down sections that will test you to the limit; however, there are plenty of tearooms and no shortage of accommodation in this section should you decide to take a break. The topography of the eastern section, on the other hand, is less dramatic, though the number of places with accommodation drops too, and for a couple of days you may

---

❑ **Mr Coast to Coast – Alfred Wainwright**

The popular perception of the man who devised the Coast to Coast path is that of a gruff, anti-social curmudgeon with little time for his fellow men, though one who admittedly knew what he was doing when it came to producing guidebooks. It's an unflattering portrait, but one that the man himself did little to destroy. Indeed, many say that he deliberately cultivated such a reputation in order to make himself unapproachable, thus allowing him to continue enjoying his beloved solitary walks without interruptions from the cagoule-clad masses who trudged the fells in his wake.

Yet this unflattering and rather dull two-dimensional description disguises a very complex man: artist, father, divorcé, pipe smoker, accountant, part-time curator at Kendal Museum, TV personality, romantic and cat-lover.

Alfred Wainwright was born in Blackburn on 17 January 1907, to a hardworking, impoverished mother and an alcoholic father. Bright and conscientious, his early years gave little clue to the talents that would later make him famous, though his neat handwriting – a feature of his guidebooks – was frequently praised by his teachers. Leaving school to work in accounts at the Borough Engineer's Office in Blackburn Town Hall, he regularly drew cartoons to entertain his colleagues. When, in December 1931, he married Ruth Holden, it seemed that Wainwright's life was set upon a course of happy – if humdrum – conformity.

Wainwright, however, never saw it like that. In particular, he quickly realized that his marriage had been a mistake and felt stifled and bored with his home life; feelings that not even the arrival of a son, Peter, could erase. His wife, though loyal, good and obedient, left Wainwright unfulfilled and any trace of romantic love that had been in the marriage at the beginning quickly drained away.

To escape the misery at home, Wainwright threw himself into his new-found hobby, fellwalking. He first visited the Lakes in 1930 and soon after was making detailed notes and drawings on the walks he made. Initially, these visits were few and far between, but a move to Kendal ten years later to take up a position as an accounting assistant allowed Wainwright to visit the Lakes virtually every weekend. Yet it wasn't until the early 1950s that Wainwright struck upon the idea of shaping his copious notes and drawings into a series of walking guides.

The idea wasn't a new one: guides to the Lakes had existed since at least the late 18th century and previous authors had included such literary luminaries as William Wordsworth. Where Wainwright's guides differed, however, was in their detail and the unique charm of their production.

For Wainwright was a publisher's dream: his writing was concise and laced with a wry humour, his ink sketches were delightful, and every page was designed and laid

find yourself walking 15 miles or more in order to reach a town or village on the trail that has somewhere to stay.

Regarding safety, there are few places on the regular trail where it would be possible to fall from a great height, save perhaps for the cliff walks that book-end the walk (though I've never heard of it happening before, particularly as there's a fence or wall between you and the cliffs for most of the way now). On some of the high-level alternatives (see p95 and p112), however, there is a slightly greater chance of being blown off a precipice, though again it's highly unlikely.

The greatest danger to trekkers is, perhaps, the chance of becoming lost or disorientated, particularly in the Lake District where there is a distinct lack of

down by the author himself, with the text justified on both sides (and without hyphens!) around the drawings. As a result, all the publisher really needed to do was crank up the printing press, load in the paper, and hey presto! They had another best-seller on their hands.

His first seven books, a series of guides to the Lakeland fells, took fourteen years to produce and by the end he had built up quite a following amongst both walkers and those who simply loved the books' beauty. Further titles followed, including one on the Pennine Way (a walk that he seemed to have enjoyed rather less than the others, possibly because at one point he had needed to be rescued by a warden after falling in a bog). As an incentive to walkers, however, he offered to buy every reader who completed the entire walk a pint, telling them to put it on his bill at the Border Hotel at the end of the Pennine Way. The Coast to Coast was the follow-up to the Pennine Way, with the research starting in 1971 and the book published in 1973. It was a project that Wainwright seemed to have derived much greater enjoyment from (though, unfortunately, there was no offer of a free drink this time!).

While all this was going on, however, Wainwright's private life was in turmoil. Though his homelife with Ruth remained as cold as ever, Wainwright had found the love of his life in Betty McNally, who had visited him in his office on official matters sometime in 1957. For Wainwright, it was love at first sight, and he began courting Betty soon after. They married eventually in 1970, and by all accounts this union provided Wainwright with the contentment and happiness he had so signally failed to find in his first marriage. She also accompanied Wainwright on his forays into television, where his gruff, no-nonsense charm proved a big hit.

At the time of their marriage Wainwright, already 63, promised Betty ten happy years. In the event, he was able to provide her with 21, passing away on Sunday, January 20, 1991. His last wish, fulfilled two months later by Betty and his long-time friend Percy Duff, was to have his ashes scattered on Hay Stacks. At the end of his autobiography, *Ex-Fellwanderer*, he sums his life up thus:

I have had a long and wonderful innings and enjoyed a remarkable immunity from unpleasant and unwelcome incidents. ... I never had to go to be a soldier, which I would have hated. I never had to wear a uniform, which I also would have hated. ... I was never called upon to make speeches in public nor forced into the limelight; my role was that of a backroom boy, which suited me fine. I never went bald, which would have driven me into hiding. ... So, all told, I have enjoyed a charmed life, I have been well favoured. The gods smiled on me since the cradle. I have had more blessings than I could ever count.

signposting, and especially in bad weather. A compass is thus pretty vital, as is dressing for inclement weather, or at least carrying a spare set of clothes with you. Not pushing yourself too hard is important too, as this will lead only to exhaustion and all its inherent dangers. In case all this deters you from the walk because it sounds too difficult or dangerous, bear in mind that a seven-year-old girl has completed the walk with her father in 13 days!

Route finding

(See the box on p68 for more details on this.) Waymarking varies along the path. Once over the Pennines and into Yorkshire the trail is fairly well signposted and finding your way shouldn't be a problem. In the Lakes, on the other hand, there are no Coast-to-Coast signposts and you may have to rely on the maps and descriptions in this book to find your way. For much of the time the path is well-trodden and obvious, though of course there are situations where there are a number of paths to choose from, and other occasions where the ground is too boggy and no path is visible at all. Foggy conditions are another problem, particularly in the Lake District. In these instances a compass is essential to help you find the correct path.

In the Lakes in particular there are a number of high-level alternatives to the main route, and fit trekkers should, if the weather allows, seriously consider taking them. Though harder, the rewards in terms of the views and sense of achievement make it all worthwhile.

HOW LONG DO YOU NEED?

I've heard about an athlete who completed the entire Coast to Coast path in just 37 hours. I've read about a walker who did it in eight days. I know somebody who did it in ten. But excepting these superhuman achievements, for most people, the Coast to Coast trail takes a minimum of fourteen days.

Indeed, even with a fortnight in which to complete the trail, many people still find it fairly tough going, and it doesn't really allow you time to look around places such as Grasmere or Richmond which each deserve a day in themselves. So, if you can afford to build a couple of rest days into your itinerary, you'll be glad you did.

Of course, if you're fit there's no reason why you can't go a little faster if that's what you want to do, though you will end up having a different sort of trek to most of the other people on the route. For where theirs is a fairly relaxing holiday, yours will be more of a sport as you compete against the clock and try to reach the finishing line as quickly as possible. There's nothing wrong with this approach, though you obviously won't see as much as those who take their time. Nevertheless, *chacun à son goût*, as the French probably say. However, what you mustn't do is try to push yourself too fast. That road leads only to exhaustion, injury or, at the absolute least, an unpleasant time.

When deciding how long to allow for their trek, those intending to camp and carry their own luggage shouldn't underestimate just how much a heavy pack can slow you down. On pp32-3 there are some suggested itineraries covering different walking speeds. If you've only got a few days, don't try to walk it all; concentrate, instead, on one area such as the Lakes or North York Moors. You can always come back and attempt the rest of the walk another time.

Practical information for the walker

ACCOMMODATION

The route guide (Part 4) lists a fairly comprehensive selection of places to stay along the full length of the trail. You have three main options: camping, staying in hostels/bunkhouses, or using B&Bs/hotels. Few people stick to just one of these options the whole way, preferring, for example, to camp most of the time but spend every third night in a hostel, or perhaps take a hostel where possible but splash out on a B&B every once in a while.

The table on pp28-9 provides a quick snapshot of what type of accommodation is available in each of the towns and villages along the way, while the tables on pp32-3 provide some suggested itineraries. The following is a brief introduction as to what to expect from each type of accommodation.

Camping

It's possible to camp all along the Coast to Coast path, though few people do so every night. You're almost bound to get at least one night where the rain falls relentlessly, soaking equipment and sapping morale; it is then that most campers opt to spend the next night drying out in a hostel or B&B somewhere. There are, however, many advantages with camping. It's more economical, for a start, with most campsites charging somewhere between £2 and £7; one or two charge nothing at all. There's rarely any need to book, except possibly in the very high season, and even then you'd be highly unlucky not to find somewhere. There's also the freedom that carrying your accommodation with you brings, allowing you to stop for the night pretty much where and when you like.

The campsites vary: some are just the back gardens of B&Bs or pubs; others are full-blown caravan sites with a few spaces put aside for tents. Showers are usually available, occasionally for a fee though more often than not for free. Note that the youth hostels on the Coast to Coast path no longer accept campers. Note, too, that some of the bigger towns such as Richmond and Grasmere do not have recognized campsites, with the nearest being around three miles away.

Wild camping (ie camping not in a regular campsite; see p49) is also possible along the route but please do not make camp in a field without first gaining permission from the landowner. Some recommended wild campsites include Grisedale Tarn (between Grasmere and Patterdale), Innominate Tarn (by Hay Stacks on the high route between Ennerdale Bridge and Borrowdale), Angle Tarn (between Patterdale and Shap) and Sunbiggin Tarn (on the way to Kirkby Stephen).

Remember that camping is not an easy option; the route is wearying enough without carrying your accommodation around with you. Should you decide to camp, therefore, we advise you to consider employing one of the baggage-carrying companies mentioned on pp20-1 (though this does, of course, mean that it will cost more and that you lose a certain amount of freedom, as you'll have to agree at least a day before with the company your destination for the night – and stick to it – so that you and your bag can be reunited every evening.)

Bunkhouses/camping barns

The term 'bunkhouse' or 'camping barn' can mean many different things. In most cases it's nothing more than a draughty old barn in a farmer's field with a couple of wooden benches to sleep on; sleeping bags are thus necessary.

While not exactly the lap of luxury, a night in a bunkhouse/camping barn is probably the nearest non-campers will get to sleeping outside, while at the same time providing campers with a shelter from the elements should the weather look like taking a turn for the worse.

Most of the better bunkhouses/camping barns, especially those maintained by the YHA, provide a shower and simple kitchen with running water and perhaps a kettle, though little in the way of pots, pans, cutlery or crockery.

Hostels

Youth hostels are plentiful along the Coast to Coast path and if you haven't visited one recently – and thus the words 'youth' and 'hostel' still conjure up images of cold, crowded dorms, uncomfortable beds, lousy food and strict staff who take a sadistic pleasure in treating you like schoolchildren – we advise you to take a second look. The YHA (Youth Hostel Association) has in fact got some of the most interesting accommodation on the path, from two pretty country houses at Grasmere to a former shepherd's bothy at Black Sail (the most isolated accommodation on the route), some former workers' cottages at Osmotherley and an old corn mill at Robin Hood's Bay.

Each hostel comes equipped with a whole range of facilities, from drying rooms to washing machines, televisions to pool tables and fully equipped kitchens for guests to use. Many also have a shop selling a selection of groceries, snacks and souvenirs and some are even connected to the internet (though for some peculiar reason, the YHA always charges a fortune to use the internet at their hostels). All offer breakfast and/or dinner, some offer a packed lunch, and a couple even have a licence to sell alcohol. They are also good places to meet fellow walkers, swap stories and compare blisters.

Weighed against these advantages is the fact that beds are still arranged in dormitories thereby increasing your chances of sharing your night with a heavy snorer; however, many now have rooms with two to four beds and some are en suite. The curfew (usually 11pm) is annoying, too. A couple of the hostels also suffer from a shortfall in adequate washing facilities, with only one or two showers to be shared between 15 to 20 people. Nor is it possible to stay in hostels every night on the trail, for there are some areas where hostels don't exist and when they do they are occasionally at least a mile or two off the path.

❏ Should you book your accommodation in advance?

When walking the Coast to Coast path, it's essential that you have your night's accommodation booked by the time you set off in the morning, particularly if you're planning to stay in a hostel, bunkhouse, B&B or guesthouse. Nothing is more deflating than to arrive at your destination at the end of a long day only to find that you've then got to walk on a further five miles or so, or even take a detour off the route, because everywhere in town is booked.

That said, there's a certain amount of hysteria regarding the booking of accommodation, with many websites, B&Bs and other organizations insisting that you have to start booking at least six months in advance if you wish to have any chance of getting accommodation on the route. Whilst it's true that the earlier you book the more chance you'll have of getting precisely the accommodation you require, booking so far in advance does leave you vulnerable to changing circumstances: booking a full six months before setting foot on the trail is all very well if everything goes to plan, but if you break your leg just before you're due to set off or, God forbid, there's another outbreak of foot and mouth, all you're going to end up with is a lot of lost deposits. By not booking so far in advance, you give yourself the chance to shift your holiday plans to a later date should the unforeseen arise.

In my experience, the situation is not as bad as some suggest, at least not outside the high season (by 'high season' I mean the summer period coinciding with the long school holidays in the UK – from the middle of July to the first week of September). Outside this period, and particularly in April/May or September, as long as you're flexible and willing to take what's offered – with maybe even a night or two in a youth hostel if that's all there is – you should get away with booking just a few nights in advance, or indeed often just the night before. The exceptions to this rule are at the weekends, when everywhere is busy and it's essential you find somewhere as soon as you can, and in places such as Danby Wiske or Blakey Moor where accommodation is very limited.

In summary, therefore, my advice is this. Firstly, it's always worth phoning ahead to book your accommodation. If you are staying in **B&Bs** and walking in high season, this should be done two to three months in advance, particularly if you have a preference for specific B&Bs. If, on the other hand, you're not too bothered which B&B you stay in, are trekking in April/May or September, and don't mind the occasional possibility of having to walk a mile or two off the route to get a room, you can probably get away with booking your accommodation by ringing around a night or two before. If you can book at least a few nights in advance, however, so much the better, and at weekends it's essential you book as soon as you can.

If you're planning on staying in **youth hostels** the same applies though do be careful when travelling out of high season as many hostels close for a couple of days each week and shut altogether from around November to Easter. Once again, it's well worth phoning at least one night before, and well before that if it's a weekend, to make sure the hostel isn't fully booked or shut. **Campers**, whatever time of year, should always be able to find somewhere to pitch their tent, though ringing in advance can't hurt and will at least confirm that the campsite is still open.

If you are travelling in April/May or September, at the beginning or end of the walking season, you may find many shut for two or three days per week, or that they have been taken over by school groups and walkers are shut out. Even in high season most are not staffed during the day and walkers have to wait until 5pm before checking in. Furthermore, it is rumoured that most youth hostels will save your booked bed only until 6pm – though to be fair, I never came across this rule on the route and if it does exist it doesn't seem to be rigidly enforced. And finally, the cost of staying in a hostel, once breakfast has been added on, is in most instances not that much cheaper (around £12-17 for members) than staying in a B&B, especially if you are walking with someone.

Booking a hostel Despite the name, anybody of any age can join the YHA. This can be done at any hostel, or by contacting the **Youth Hostels Association of England and Wales** (☎ 0870-770 8868, 🖳 www.yha.org.uk). The cost of a year's membership is £16 for an adult, less for anyone under 18.

Having secured your membership, youth hostels are easy to book, either online or by phone through the contact details above. If you are booking only a few days in advance it may be better to ring each hostel direct; if you haven't actually booked in advance hostel staff will reserve a bed at the next stop on the path for you. Since non members have to pay £3 more per night it is worth joining if you expect to stay in a hostel for more than six nights in a year.

Bed and breakfast

Bed and Breakfasts (B&Bs) are a great British institution and many of those along the Coast to Coast are absolutely charming, with buildings often three or four hundred years old. There's nothing mysterious about a B&B; as the name suggests, they provide you with a bed in a private room, and breakfast – a hearty, British-style cooked one (see opposite) unless you specify otherwise beforehand – though they range in style enormously. Most B&Bs have both en suite rooms and rooms with shared facilities, though even with the latter the bathroom is never more than a few feet away. These rooms usually contain either a double bed (known as a double room), or two single beds (known as a twin room). Family rooms are for three or more people. Solo trekkers should take note: single rooms are not so easy to find so you'll often end up occupying a double room, for which you'll have to pay a single supplement (see below).

Since July 2007 there has been a ban on **smoking** in all enclosed places open to the public in England. While places to stay are able to designate rooms for smokers, do check this if it's important to you; see also box p19.

Some B&Bs provide an evening meal (see p18); if not, there's nearly always a pub or restaurant nearby or, if it's far, the owner will usually give you a lift to and from the nearest place with food. Always let the owner know if you have to cancel your booking so they can offer the bed to someone else.

B&B rates B&Bs in this guide start at around £20 per person for the most basic accommodation to over £40 for the most luxurious en suite places in a popular tourist haunt like Grasmere. Most charge around £25-30 per person. A typical single supplement is between £5 and £10. An evening meal (usually around £12-15) is often provided, but you may need to book in advance.

Guesthouses, hotels, pubs and inns

The difference between a B&B and a guesthouse is minimal, though some of the better **guesthouses** are more like hotels, offering evening meals and a lounge for guests. **Pubs and inns** also offer bed and breakfast accommodation, and tariffs are no more than in a regular B&B. **Hotels** do usually cost more, however, and some might be a little incensed with a bunch of smelly trekkers turning up and treading mud into their carpet. Most on the Coast to Coast walk, however, are used to seeing trekkers and welcome them warmly. Prices in hotels start at around £35 per person. When booking say if you want a room designated for smokers, see opposite.

Others

In addition to the accommodation types listed above there are also **holiday cottages**, stationary **caravans** and even one or two **adventure centres** along the route, though these tend to cater more to people staying for at least a few days rather than just one night.

FOOD AND DRINK

Breakfast

Stay in a B&B/guesthouse/hotel and you'll be filled to the gills with a cooked English breakfast. This usually consists of a bowl of cereal followed by a plateful of eggs, bacon, sausages, mushrooms, tomatoes, and possibly baked beans or black pudding, with toast and butter, and all washed down with coffee, tea and/or juice. Enormously satisfying the first time you try it, by the fourth or fifth morning you may start to prefer the lighter continental breakfast which most establishments now offer.

Alternatively, and especially if you are planning an early start, you might like to request a packed lunch instead of this filling breakfast and just have a cup of coffee before you leave.

The youth hostels mentioned in this guide offer breakfast; usually it is a good meal but they charge an additional £4-5.

Lunch

Your B&B host or youth hostel can usually provide a packed lunch at an additional cost, though of course there's nothing to stop you preparing your own (but do bring a penknife if you plan to do this). There are some fantastic locally made cheeses and pickles that can be picked up along the way, as well as some wonderful bakers still making bread in the traditional way (the bakery at Reeth springs to mind here; see p166). Alternatively, stop in a pub (see 'Evening meals' overleaf).

Remember, too, to plan ahead: certain stretches of the walk are devoid of eating places (the stretch from Patterdale to Shap for example) so read ahead about the next day's walk in Part 4 to make sure you never go hungry.

Cream teas

Never miss a chance to avail yourself of the treats on offer in the tearooms of Cumbria and Yorkshire. Nothing relaxes and revives like a decent pot of tea, and the opportunity to accompany it with a jam and cream scone (a combination known as a cream tea) or a cake or two is one that should not be passed up.

Evening meals

If you don't book a meal at your B&B you may find that in many of the villages, the pub is the only place to eat out. **Pubs** are as much a feature of the walk as moorland and sheep, and in some cases the pub is as much of a tourist attraction as any stone circle or ruined abbey. Most of them have become highly attuned to the desires of walkers and offer both lunch and evening meals (with often a few regional dishes and usually a couple of vegetarian options), some locally brewed beers, a garden to relax in on hot days and a roaring fire to huddle around on cold ones. The standard of the food varies widely, though portions are usually large, which is often just about all walkers care about at the end of a long day.

That other great British culinary institution, the **fish 'n' chip shop**, can also be found along the route. Larger towns also have Chinese and Indian **takeaways**; these are usually the last places to serve food in the evenings, staying open until at least 11pm.

Self-catering

There is a grocery shop of some description in most of the places along the route, though most of these are small (and often combined with the post office)

❑ **Information for foreign visitors**

● **Currency** The British pound (£) comes in notes of £100, £50, £20, £10, £5 and coins of £2 and £1. The pound is divided into 100 pence (usually referred to as 'p', pronounced pee) which come in silver coins of 50p, 20p 10p and 5p and copper coins of 2p and 1p.

● **Rates of exchange** Up-to-date exchange rates can be found at 🖳 www.xe.com/ucc.

● **Business hours** Most **shops** and main **post offices** are open at least from Monday to Friday 9am-5pm and Saturday 9am-12.30pm. Many choose longer hours and some open on Sundays as well. However, some also close early one day a week, often Wednesday or Thursday. **Banks** are usually open 10am-4pm Monday to Friday.

New licensing laws came into effect in November 2005. Since then **pub** opening hours have become more flexible and every landlord has to apply for a licence for the hours he/she wants to open – up to 24 hours a day seven days a week – so each pub may have different opening hours. However, most pubs on the Coast to Coast route continue to open between 11am and 11pm and some still close in the afternoon.

● **National (Bank) holidays** Most businesses are shut on 1 January, Good Friday (March/April), Easter Monday (March/April), the first and last Monday in May, the last Monday in August, 25 December and 26 December.

● **School holidays** School holiday periods in England are generally as follows: a one-week break late October, two weeks around Christmas and the New Year, a week mid-February, two weeks around Easter, and from late July to early September.

● **Travel/medical insurance** The European Health Insurance Card (EHIC) entitles EU nationals (on production of the EHIC card) to necessary medical treatment under the UK's National Health Service while on a temporary visit here. However, this is not a substitute for proper medical cover on your travel insurance for unforeseen bills and for getting you home should that be necessary. Also consider cover for loss and

and whether you'll be able to find precisely what you went in for is doubtful. If self-catering, therefore, your menus will depend on what you can find. The path is quite trekker-friendly, however, in that a couple of these small stores sell Camping Gaz (which you can also pick up in the bigger towns such as Grasmere, Kirkby Stephen and Richmond). Part 4 goes into greater detail about what can be found where.

Drinking water

There are plenty of ways of perishing on the Coast to Coast trail but given how frequently it rains and how damp the north of England is, thirst probably won't be one of them. Be careful, though, for on a hot day in some of the remoter parts of the Lake District after a steep climb or two you'll quickly dehydrate, which is at best highly unpleasant and at worst mightily dangerous. Always carry some water with you and aim in hot weather to drink three or four litres per day. Don't be tempted by the water in the multitude of streams that you come across. If the cow or sheep faeces in the water don't make you ill, the chemicals from the pesticides and fertilizers used on the farms almost certainly will. Using iodine or another purifying treatment will help to combat the former though there's little you can do about the latter. It's a lot safer to fill up from taps instead.

theft of personal belongings, especially if you are camping or staying in hostels, as there will be times when you'll have to leave your luggage unattended.

● **Weights and measures** In September 2007 the European Commission announced they would no longer attempt to ban the pint or the mile: so milk can continue to be sold in pints, as can beer in pubs, and road distances will still be given in miles. Most food is now sold in metric weights (g and kg) but the imperial weights of pounds (lb) and ounces (oz) can also be displayed. However, the population remains split between those who are happy with centigrade, kilograms and metres and those who still use fahrenheit, pounds and feet and inches.

● **Time** During the winter, the whole of Britain is on Greenwich Meantime (GMT). The clocks move one hour forward on the last Sunday in March, remaining on British Summer Time (BST) until the last Sunday in October.

● **Smoking** A ban on smoking in public places came into force in July 2007. The ban relates not only to pubs and restaurants, but also to B&Bs, hostels and hotels. These latter have the right to designate one or more bedrooms where the occupants can smoke, but the ban will be in force in all enclosed areas open to the public – even if they are in a private home such as a B&B. Should you be foolhardy enough to light up in a no-smoking area, which includes pretty well any indoor public place, you could be fined £50, but it's the owners of the premises who suffer most if they fail to stop you, with a potential fine of £2500.

● **Telephone** The international access code for Britain is +44, followed by the area code minus the first 0, and then the number you require. To call a number with the same area code as the phone you are calling from you can omit the code. It is cheaper to phone at weekends and after 6pm and before 8am on weekdays. Mobile phone reception is quite unreliable except when in the vicinity of urban areas. In hilly country head for high ground where a weak signal can often be picked up.

● **Emergency services** For police, ambulance, fire and mountain rescue dial ☎ 999.

MONEY

Banks are few and far between on the Coast to Coast path. There's a NatWest at Shap, a Barclays and an HSBC at Kirkby Stephen, and Richmond has branches of all the major banks, but apart from these places there's nothing. The **post office** thus provides a very useful service. You can get cash (by debit card with a PIN number, or by cheque with a debit card) for free at a post office counter if you bank with certain banks/building societies (see ⌨ www.postoffice.co.uk for a full list). A number of post offices also play host to the village **cashpoint/ ATM** (usually a Link machine). These machines are useful for people who cannot get cash from the counter but a number of these are privately operated and charge £1.25-1.75 whatever amount is withdrawn. Another way of getting money in your hand is to use the **cashback** system: find a store that will accept a debit card and ask them to advance cash against the card. A number of the local village stores, such as those in Reeth and Robin Hood's Bay, will do this, though you'll usually have to spend a minimum of £5 with them first.

With few local stores, pubs or B&Bs accepting credit or debit cards, and few places where you can get money out along the way, it is essential to carry plenty of cash (I usually reckon on £100 per person) with you, though keep it safe and out of sight (preferably in a moneybelt). A chequebook could prove very useful as a back-up, so that you don't have to keep on dipping into your cash reserves. **Travellers' cheques** can be cashed only at banks, foreign exchanges and some of the large hotels.

OTHER SERVICES

Internet access is available at Grasmere Youth Hostel, Patterdale YH, Kirkby Stephen library and Richmond library. In addition, *The White Swan* at Danby Wiske also offers an internet service (and by the time your read this the *Blue Bell Inn* will probably have replaced their computer that got nicked). Most small villages have a **post office** that doubles as the local store, and nearby you'll usually find a **phone box**.

There are **outdoor equipment shops** and **pharmacies** in the larger towns of Grasmere, Kirkby Stephen and Richmond and **tourist information centres** at Kirkby Stephen, Ullswater (near Patterdale), Reeth and Richmond.

WALKING COMPANIES

It is, of course, possible to turn up with your boots and backpack at St Bees and just start walking without planning much other than your accommodation (about which, see the box on p15). The following companies, however, are in the business of making your holiday as stress-free and enjoyable as possible.

Baggage carriers

There are several baggage-carrying companies serving the Coast to Coast route, from national organizations such as Sherpa to companies that consist of little more than one man and his van. With all these services you can book up to the last moment, usually up to around 9 o'clock the previous evening, though it's cheaper if you book in advance. All stipulate a maximum weight per bag of around 15-20kg. The cost is around £5-8 to take your bag to your next destination. Nearly all these services offer an accommodation-booking service as well.

Two of the better known are Sherpa and Packhorse. **Sherpa Van** (☎ 01748 826917; 🖥 www.sherpavan.com) is a nationwide company, set up by Sherpa Expeditions (see p22), that serves all the major walking trails in Britain, delivering luggage from one place to another from April to October.

Packhorse (☎ 017683 71777; 🖥 www.cumbria.com/packhorse) based at Kirkby Stephen, are a reliable and thoroughly organized outfit who quite rightly receive regular recommendations from their customers. In addition to transporting your luggage, the company also offers a daily passenger service between St Bees and Robin Hood's Bay, allowing passengers to travel along with the luggage, and hop off wherever they want, for £5.75 a stage or £6 if booked less than six weeks in advance (phone Packhorse for approximate times).

One bus departs Kirkby Stephen at 8.30am, arriving at St Bees at 10.15am, before travelling via the pick-up points back to Kirkby Stephen. A second bus also leaves Kirkby Stephen at 8.30am, stopping at the drop-off points before reaching Robin Hood's Bay at 3.30pm, then travelling directly back to Kirkby Stephen to arrive at 5.45pm. (In other words, the buses stop at the various drop-off points only when travelling from west to east.)

The cost of travelling directly from Kirkby Stephen to St Bees or Robin Hood's Bay to Kirkby Stephen is £21 per person. As if that wasn't enough help they also have a secure parking lot in Kirkby Stephen, where one can leave a car for the duration of the walk (£2.65 per day).

This service has two important consequences for trekkers. Firstly, it means that, should you be attempting the walk from west to east and need to miss out a stage for some reason, you can get the Packhorse bus to pick you up and drive you to the end of the next stage. The second important consequence is that you can use Kirkby Stephen as your base, hitching a lift on the Packhorse van to St Bees and the start of the walk, and another at the end of the walk back from Robin Hood's Bay. Thus you can leave your car in Kirkby Stephen (which is better than the alternative of leaving it in St Bees and travelling all the way back from the east coast to pick it up again). Or you can buy a return train ticket from your home to Kirkby Stephen, which may be cheaper than having to buy one ticket to St Bees, and another from Robin Hood's Bay.

Other companies offering a similar service include **Northwest Walks**, another company with a fantastic reputation for reliability and punctuality, **Coast to Coast Holiday & Baggage Services** and **Brigantes Walking Holidays** (see p22 for details of all these companies).

Self-guided holidays

Self-guided basically means that the company will organize accommodation, baggage transfer, transport to and from the walk and various maps and advice, but leave you on your own to actually walk the path. In addition to these, don't forget the specialist Coast to Coast websites (see box p38) that can also book accommodation and provide details of the walk.

● **Brigantes Walking Holidays** (☎ 01729 830463; 🖳 www.brigantesenglish walks.com; Rookery Cottage, Kirkby Malham, Skipton, North Yorkshire BD23 4BX) Primarily a baggage-transfer service although they can arrange a self-guided package too.

● **Coast to Coast Holiday & Baggage Services** (☎ 01642 489173; 🖳 www .coasttocoast-holidays.co.uk; 60 Durham Rd, Redcar, Cleveland TS10 3RY) Organizes walks from 11 to 17 days.

● **Contours Walking Holidays** (☎ 017684 80451, 🖳 www.contours.co.uk; Gramyre, 3 Berrier Rd, Greystoke, Cumbria, CA11 OUB) Offers seven different itineraries covering the Coast to Coast, from the strenuous to the simple and from 12 to 18 days.

● **Discovery Travel** (☎ 01904 632226, 🖳 www.discoverytravel.co.uk; Opsa House, 5a High Ousegate, York YO1 8ZZ) Offers a standard 15-day Coast to Coast walk as well, unusually, as the walk from east to west.

● **Explore Britain** (☎ 01740 650900, 🖳 www.xplorebritain.com; 6 George St, Ferryhill, Co Durham, DL17 0DT). Offers 14-, 17- and 18-day treks along the entire C2C, as well as dividing the walk into two, with a seven-day walk from St Bees to Kirkby Stephen, and an eight-day walk from Kirkby Stephen to Robin Hood's Bay.

● **HF Holidays** (☎ 020 8905 9556, 🖳 www.hfholidays.co.uk; Imperial House, Edgware Rd, London, NW9 5AL) Not cheap, but an extremely reliable and frequently recommended company that offers the Coast to Coast in its entirety (18 nights, from £995) as well as from St Bees to Keld and also from Keld to Robin Hood's Bay (9-10 nights, from £525).

● **Northwest Walks** (☎ 01257 424889, 🖳 www.northwestwalks.co.uk; 16 Langham Rd, Standish, Wigan WN6 0TF) It may be one of the smallest companies serving the route – essentially, it's a one-man operation – but it's also the one with the best reputation. Organizes 7- to 11-day walks along half of the path, or 14-18 days along the complete trail.

● **Packhorse** (☎ 017683 71777, 🖳 www.cumbria.com/packhorse; Chestnut House, Crosby Garrett, Kirkby Stephen, Cumbria CA17 4PR) They offer ten itineraries ranging from 6 to 8 nights (for those wishing to do half the trail only) and 13 to 17 nights (for the whole trail).

● **Sherpa Expeditions** (☎ 020 8577 2717, 🖳 www.sherpa-walking-holidays.co.uk; 131a Heston Rd, Hounslow, Middlesex, TW5 0RF) Offer two types of treks, for eight (half trail; St Bees to Kirkby Stephen or Kirkby Stephen to St Bees) and 15 (whole trail) days.

Group/guided walking tours

If you don't trust your map-reading skills or simply prefer the company of other walkers as well as an experienced guide, the following companies will be of interest. Packages nearly always include meals, accommodation, transport arrangements, minibus back-up and baggage transfer.

Have a good look at each company's website before booking as each has its own speciality and it's important to choose one that's suitable for you.
● **Footpath Holidays** (☎ 01985 840049, 🖥 www.footpath-holidays.com; 16 Norton Bavant, Near Warminster, Wiltshire, BA12 7BB) Runs hotel-based guided walking tours. There is no specific Coast to Coast itinerary, though they have run them in the past and do offer various itineraries in the Lake District and the Yorkshire Dales.
● **HF Holidays (see opp**osite) Offers the Coast to Coast in its entirety (15 days, 5/year, from £1365) as well as St Bees to Keld and Keld to Robin Hood's Bay (9 nights, 1/year each, from £789).
● **Northwest Walks** (see opposite) As already mentioned, the reputation of this company is sky high. At the time of writing charges were £975 for a 15-day walk along the entire trail, undertaken around five times a year from west to east in groups of around ten people.
● **Ramblers Countrywide Holidays** (☎ 01707 386800, 🖥 www.cw.ramblers holidays.co.uk; Lemsford Mill, Lemsford Village, Welwyn Garden City, AL8 7TR) No specific Coast to Coast itinerary but this walking specialist does offer packages to Grasmere and the Lakes as well as a Highlights of Wainwright walk.
● **Sherpa Expeditions** (see opposite) Run two to three 15-day Coast to Coast treks a year costing from £920.

TAKING DOGS ALONG THE COAST TO COAST PATH

The Coast to Coast is a dog-friendly path, though it is extremely important that dog owners behave in a responsible way. Dogs should always be kept on leads while on the footpath to avoid disturbing wildlife, livestock and other walkers. Dog excrement should be cleaned up and not left to decorate the boots of others; take a pooper scooper or plastic bag if you are walking with a dog.

It is particularly important to keep your dog on a lead when crossing fields with livestock in them, especially around lambing time (see box p51) which can be as early as February or as late as the end of May. Most farmers would prefer it if you did not bring your dog at all at this time.

In addition, in certain areas on the Coast to Coast trail (particularly between Shap and Kirkby Stephen) there are notices ordering owners to keep their dogs on a lead to protect endangered ground-nesting birds, particularly between March and June; dogs can frighten them off and possibly cause them to desert their nests.

Remember when planning and booking your accommodation that you will need to check if your dog will be welcome. Youth hostels do not permit them unless they are for assistance and some inns and hotels charge extra for a dog. Note, too, that your dog needs to be extremely fit to complete the Coast to Coast path. You may not believe it when you watch your mutt haring around the fields, but they do have a finite amount of energy too, so make sure your dog is up to the task of walking for ten or twenty miles a day.

Budgeting

England is not a cheap place to go travelling, and while the north may be one of the cheaper parts of it, the towns and villages on the Coast to Coast route are more than used to seeing tourists and charge accordingly. You may think before you set out that you are going to try to keep your budget to a minimum by camping every night and cooking your own food, but it's a rare trekker who sticks to this rule. Besides, the B&Bs and pubs on the route are amongst the Coast to Coast's major attractions, and it would be a pity not to sample the hospitality in at least some of them.

If the only expenses of this walk were accommodation and food, budgeting for the trip would be a piece of cake. Unfortunately, in addition to these there are all the little **extras** that push up the cost of your trip: for example beer, cream teas, stamps and postcards, internet use, buses here and there, baggage carriers, phone calls, laundry, film, souvenirs, entrance fees. It's surprising how much these add up!

CAMPING

You can survive on as little as £10-12 per person if you use the cheapest campsites, don't visit a pub, avoid all the museums and tourist attractions in the towns, cook all your own food from staple ingredients ... and generally have a pretty miserable time of it. Even then, unforeseen expenses will probably nudge your daily budget up. Include the occasional pint, and perhaps a pub meal every now and then, and the figure will be nearer £15 per day.

HOSTELS, BUNKHOUSES AND CAMPING BARNS

The current charge for staying in a **YHA hostel** is £12-17 per night for members. Whack on another £4-5 for breakfast and an evening meal (£7-10), though you can use their self-catering facilities for both. There is also lunch (£4-5) to consider, which means that, overall, it will cost £25-35 per day, or £40-45 to live in a little more comfort, enjoy the odd cream tea and beer and go out for the occasional meal.

There are a few bunkhouses and camping barns along the Coast to Coast. They vary in quality and price (expect to pay around £6).

B&BS, GUESTHOUSES AND HOTELS

B&B prices start at around £20 per person per night but can be twice this. Add on the cost of food for lunch and dinner and you should reckon on about £40 minimum per day. Staying in a guesthouse or hotel will cost more. Remember that there is often a supplement of £5-10 for single occupancy of a room.

When to go

SEASONS

Britain is a notoriously wet country and the north of England is an infamously damp part of it. Rare indeed are the trekkers who have managed to walk the Coast to Coast path without suffering at least one downpour on the way; three or four per trek are more likely, even in summer. That said, it's equally unlikely that you'll spend a fortnight in the area and not see any sun at all, and even the most cynical of walkers will have to admit that, during the walking season at least, there are more sunny days than showery ones. That **walking season**, by the way, starts at Easter and builds to a crescendo in August, before steadily tailing off in September. By the end of September few indeed are the trekkers on the trail, and in October many places close down for the winter.

Spring

Find a couple of dry weeks in springtime and you're in for a treat. The wild flowers are beginning to come into bloom, lambs are skipping in the meadows, the grass is green and lush and the path is not yet badly eroded. Of course, finding a dry fortnight in spring (around the end of March to mid-June) is not easy but occasionally there's a mini-heatwave during this season. Another advantage with walking at this time is that there will be few trekkers and finding accommodation is relatively easy. Easter is the exception, the first major holiday in the year when people flock to the Lake District and other national parks.

Summer

Summer, on the other hand, can be a bit *too* busy and, in somewhere popular like the Lakes over a weekend in August, little short of insufferable. Still, the chances of a prolonged period of sunshine are of course higher at this time of year than any other, the days are much longer and the heather is in bloom at this time, too, turning the hills a fragrant purple. If you crave the company of other trekkers summer will provide you with the opportunity of meeting hundreds of them, though do remember that you must book your accommodation well in advance. Despite the higher than average chance of sunshine, take clothes for any eventuality – it will still rain at some point.

Autumn

September is a wonderful time to walk, when many of the tourists have returned home and the path is clear. I think that the weather is usually reliably sunny, too, at least at the beginning of September, though I admit I don't have any figures to back this claim. The B&Bs and hostels will still be open, at least until the end of the month. By then the weather will begin to get a little wilder and the nights will start to draw in. The walking season is almost at an end.

PLANNING YOUR WALK

Winter

A few people trek the Coast to Coast in winter, putting up with the cold temperatures, damp conditions and short days for the chance to experience the trail without other tourists. Much of the accommodation will be closed too. But whilst it may also be a little more dangerous to walk at this time, particularly if taking one of the high-level routes through the Lakes, if you find yourself walking on one of those clear, crisp, wintry days it will all seem worth it.

RAINFALL

At some point on your walk, it will rain; if it doesn't, it's fair to say that you haven't really lived the full Coast to Coast experience properly.

The question, therefore, is not whether you will be rained on, but how often. But as long as you dress accordingly and take note of the safety advice given on pp52-4, this shouldn't be a problem.

Do, however, think twice about tackling some of the high-level alternatives if the weather is very inclement, and don't do so on your own.

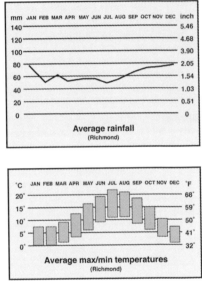

Average rainfall
(Richmond)

Average max/min temperatures
(Richmond)

DAYLIGHT HOURS

If walking in autumn, winter or early spring, you must take account of how far you can walk in the available light. It won't be possible to cover as many miles as you would in summer. Remember, too, that you will get a further 30-45 minutes of usable light before and after sunrise and sunset depending on the weather. In June, because the path is in the far north of England, those coming from the south may be surprised that there's enough light for walking until at least 10pm. Conversely, in late spring, late autumn and winter you will be equally amazed how quickly the nights draw in.

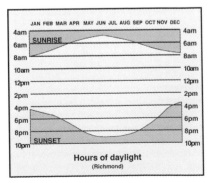

Hours of daylight
(Richmond)

ANNUAL EVENTS

Thanks largely to its popularity with tourists, Grasmere has over the past few years become something of a mecca for those interested in those peculiarly Lakeland sports such as fell running, and Cumberland and Westmoreland wrestling.

The annual **Grasmere Lakeland Sports and Show**, the origins of which date back around 300 years, takes place at the end of August. Other sports featured include tug-of-war, hound-trailing and the more recent addition of mountain-biking. If you are in the Lakes at this time, don't miss the opportunity of witnessing this unique event.

As you'd probably expect, Grasmere also hosts an annual **Art and Book Festival** at one of Wordsworth's old houses, Dove Cottage (or at a hotel very nearby). The festival usually takes place in January, is residential and consists of lectures, surgeries and workshops. For further information about these and other events see 🖳 www.lakelandgateway.info and click on Events.

The villages of Swaledale, which include Keld, Muker, Thwaite, Gunnerside and Reeth, hold an annual music festival; the **Swaledale Festival** (🖳 www.swaledale-festival.org.uk) usually takes place at the end of May to early June.

The festival has an annual theme (eg stringed instruments), and in addition to the music there are all kinds of other activities from art exhibitions and guided walking trails to craft workshops; information can be found and tickets bought on the dedicated website 🖳 www.swaledale-festival.org.uk.

Richmond Live is a pop music festival usually held over one weekend in July or August; for details visit the website 🖳 www.richmondlive.org.

Robin Hood's Bay hosts a **folk music weekend**, usually on the first or second weekend of June. For something a bit different, if you happen to be in the village in winter don't miss the **Victorian weekend** at the beginning of December, where the town turns out in 19th-century costume. It's all good fun, with quizzes, recitals, concerts and demonstrations, and it's all in aid of charity too. Further information about these is available on 🖳 www.robin-hoods-bay.co.uk – click on What's on.

In addition to the events outlined above, all kinds of **agricultural shows** take place annually in towns and villages on the Coast to Coast trail. These shows are an integral and traditional part of life all over rural England and particularly in the Lake District. Too numerous to list here, details of all the shows can be found by looking at the websites of the places concerned, of which you'll find a number in the box on p38.

PLANNING YOUR WALK

VILLAGE AND

Place name (Places in brackets are a short walk off the Coast to Coast path)	Distance from previous place§ approx miles/km	Cash Machine/ ATM	Post Office	Tourist Information Centre (TIC) Point (TIP)
St Bees		✔	✔	TIP
Sandwith	5/8			
Moor Row	3/5		✔	
Cleator	1/1.5			
Ennerdale Bridge	5/8 (via Dent)	✔	✔	
			(limited hours)	
Seatoller	13/21			Information barn
Borrowdale	1.5/2.5 (to R'thwaite)			
(Longthwaite, Rosthwaite, Stonethwaite)				
Grasmere	9.5/15 (from R'thwaite)	✔	✔	TIP
Patterdale	10/16 (direct valley route)		✔	TIC at Glenridding
Shap	16/25.5	✔	✔	
(Orton)	8/13		✔	
Kirkby Stephen	20/32 (from Shap)	✔	✔	TIC
Keld	13/21			
(Thwaite)	2/3			
(Muker)	3.5/5.5 (from Keld)			
(Gunnerside)	2.5/4 (from Muker)		✔	
Reeth	4/6.5 (from Gunnerside)	✔	✔	TIC
	11/17.5 (from Keld on official high path)			
Marrick	3/5			
Richmond	7.5/12	✔	✔	TIC
Colburn	3/5			
Catterick Bridge	2.5/4			
Bolton-on-Swale	2/3.5			
Danby Wiske	6/10			
Oaktree Hill	2/3.5			
Ingleby Cross/Arncliffe	6.5/10.5		✔	
(Osmotherley)	3/5 (from Ingleby Cross)		✔	
Clay Bank Top (Urra and Great Broughton)	12/19 (from Ingleby Cross)			
Blakey Ridge	9/14.5			
Glaisdale	10/16		✔	
Egton Bridge	2/3			
Grosmont	1.5/2.5	✔	✔	TIP
Littlebeck	3.5/5.5			
Hawsker	7.5/12			
Robin Hood's Bay	4.5/7.5		✔	

TOTAL DISTANCE 190.5 miles/307km

TOWN FACILITIES

Eating Place ✔=one; ✔✔=a few ✔✔✔=4 +	Food Store	Campsite	Hostels YHA/ H (IndHostel)/ B (Barn or Bunkhouse)	B&B-style accommodation ✔=one; ✔✔=a few ✔✔✔=4+	Place name (Places in brackets are a short walk off the Coast to Coast path)
✔✔	✔	✔		✔✔✔	**St Bees**
			B		**Sandwith**
✔	✔			✔	**Moor Row**
	✔			✔	**Cleator**
✔✔		✔	B/ YHA (5miles/8km)	✔✔	**Ennerdale Bridge**
✔		✔	B/YHA (1mile/1.5km)	✔✔	**Seatoller**
✔	✔	✔	B/YHA	✔✔✔	**Borrowdale**
					(Longthwaite, Rosthwaite, Stonethwaite)
✔✔✔	✔		YHA/H	✔✔✔	**Grasmere**
✔		✔	YHA	✔✔✔	**Patterdale**
✔✔✔	✔	✔		✔✔✔	**Shap**
✔✔	✔	✔		✔✔	**(Orton)**
✔✔✔	✔	✔	YHA	✔✔✔	**Kirkby Stephen**
	✔	✔		✔✔	**Keld**
✔				✔	**(Thwaite)**
✔	✔			✔✔	**(Muker)**
✔✔				✔	**(Gunnerside)**
✔✔✔	✔	✔	YHA (1¼miles/2km)	✔✔✔	**Reeth**
	✔	✔		✔	**Marrick**
✔✔✔	✔		B (2miles/3km)	✔✔✔	**Richmond**
		✔			**Colburn**
		✔		✔	**Catterick Bridge**
					Bolton-on-Swale
✔		✔		✔✔	**Danby Wiske**
		✔	B	✔	**Oaktree Hill**
✔				✔✔✔	**Ingleby Cross/Arncliffe**
✔✔	✔	✔	YHA	✔✔	**(Osmotherley)**
✔		✔		✔	**Clay Bank Top** (Urra and Great Broughton)
✔		✔		✔✔	**Blakey Ridge**
✔	✔			✔✔	**Glaisdale**
✔✔				✔✔	**Egton Bridge**
✔	✔	✔		✔✔✔	**Grosmont**
		✔		✔	**Littlebeck**
✔		✔		✔	**Hawsker**
✔✔✔	✔	✔	YHA (1mile/1.5km)	✔✔✔	**Robin Hood's Bay**

§ DISTANCE Distances are between places directly on the official Coast to Coast path

Itineraries

Most people tackle the Coast to Coast from west to east, mainly because this will allow them to walk 'with the weather at their back' (because most of the time the winds blow off the Atlantic from the west, so by walking from west to east you will have the wind blowing with you rather than against you). It is usual for people to attempt it in one go, though a number of companies (see pp22-3) offer the chance of tackling it in two stages, dividing the walk at Kirkby Stephen or Keld.

Part 4 of this book has been written from west to east (though there is of course nothing to stop you from tackling it in the opposite direction, and there are advantages in doing so – see opposite). To help you plan your walk look at the **planning map** (see opposite inside back cover) and the **table of village/town facilities** (on pp28-9), which gives a run-down on the essential

---

❏ HIGHLIGHTS

The best day and weekend walks on the Coast to Coast

The following suggested trails are for those who cannot, for whatever reason, complete the entire path in one go. They are, in my opinion, the best parts of the Coast to Coast path, and are all described in more detail in Part 4. However, because the Coast to Coast path is so varied and encompasses so many different landscapes and experiences, it is fair to say that none of them by themselves, fully capture the glory of the path. Nevertheless, they are all, in their own way, delightful. They are listed in the order in which they are reached on the trail if walking west to east. Public transport to and from the start and end of the walks is generally good; see pp43-5 for details of public transport.

Day walks

● **Ennerdale Bridge to Borrowdale** 14¹/₂ miles/23km (p84) The first truly gorgeous stretch of the Coast to Coast, combining the glories of Ennerdale Water with the tribulations of Loft Beck. Lengthy, slightly precarious if the weather closes in, and arduous too, particularly if taking the High Stile alternative, this is nevertheless a worthy, brutal introduction to the delights and rigours of Coast to Coast walking.

● **Borrowdale to Grasmere** 9¹/₂ miles/15km (p99) A walk of contrasts, this trail takes you from quiet, relatively 'untouristy' Rosthwaite to 'Wordsworth-ville', the ever-popular Grasmere. Not an easy walk, it can be a spectacular one if the day is clear and the high-level alternative is taken, with views to fells near and far.

● **Grasmere to Patterdale** 10 miles/16km (p109) Just a simple up-and-down, though the 'down' can be complicated by detours up St Sunday or Helvellyn which provide better views. Simply splendid.

● **Patterdale to Shap** 16 miles/25.5km (p119) One of the longest stages on the Coast to Coast trail. Not a classic, perhaps, though perfectly pleasant, and one of the most varied too as you leave the Lakes for a long trek by Haweswater, followed by

information you will need regarding accommodation possibilities and services. You could follow one of the suggested itineraries (see boxes pp32-3) which are based on preferred type of accommodation and walking speeds. There is also a list of recommended linear day and weekend walks below which cover the best of the Coast to Coast path, all of which are well served by public transport. The public transport map is on p43 and the services table on pp44-5.

Once you have an idea of your approach turn to Part 4 for detailed information on accommodation, places to eat and other services in each village and town on the route. Also in Part 4 you will find summaries of the route to accompany the detailed trail maps.

WHICH DIRECTION?

There are a number of advantages in tackling the path in a west to east direction, not least the fact that the prevailing winds will, more often than not, be behind you. If you are walking alone but wouldn't mind some company now and again you'll find that most of the other Coast to Coast walkers are heading in your direction too. However, there is also something to be said for leaving

---

a trudge through sheep and cattle fields to Shap Abbey. Complete this without too much trouble and you should have no trouble completing the entire trail.

● **Ingleby Cross/Osmotherley to Clay Bank Top/Blakey Ridge** 12-21 miles/19-33.5km (p194) Relive one of the longest and most arduous days on the walk as you tackle the Yorkshire Moors. Lightweights can duck out at Clay Bank Top, having prearranged accommodation at one of the nearby villages. Tough trekkers can carry on to Blakey Ridge and the splendid Lion Inn.

● **The Esk Valley: Glaisdale to Grosmont** 3^1/2 miles/5.5km (see p214) Not so much a trek as a pub crawl, this path takes you along the Esk Valley following the course of the river through woodland and along country tracks, with inn-laden villages en route. Grosmont, at the end of the trail, has trains and buses to return you to Scarborough, Whitby, or the beginning of the trail.

● **Grosmont to Robin Hood's Bay** 15^1/2 miles/25km (p220) Not a classic, with a lot of walking on roads by the standards of the Coast to Coast, but mentioned here because of the unmissable delights of Little Beck Woods, the pleasant sweetness of the villages at the start and finish, the windswept cliff-top tramp at the end, and the fact that you can pretend you've done the entire Coast to Coast path when you arrive in Robin Hood's Bay.

Weekend walks

In addition to the walk described below, a number of the day walks can be combined to make a two-day trek, particularly those in the Lake District.

● **Kirkby Stephen to Reeth** 26 miles/42km (p144) Anybody who manages to scramble over the Pennines and negotiate the boggy ground down to the old mining village of Keld deserves a reward of some sort, and picturesque Swaledale is just that. As an encore, masochists can take the higher, 'official' route over the moors to Reeth. These days, however, most people seem to settle for a gentle stroll down the dale, passing through or near the villages of Muker, Gunnerside and Thwaite on their way to Reeth.

PLANNING YOUR WALK

CAMPING

Night	Relaxed pace Place	Approx Distance miles/km	Medium pace Place	Approx Distance miles/km	Fast pace Place	Approx Distance miles/km
0	St Bees		St Bees		St Bees	
1	Egremont	11/17.5	Ennerdale Br	14/22.5	Ennerdale Br	14/22.5
2	Ennerdale Br	7/11	Borrowdale§	14.5/23	Borrowdale§	14.5/23
3	Seatoller	13/21	Grasmere*	9.5/15	Patterdale	19/30.5
4	Grasmere*	11/17.5	Patterdale	10/16	Shap	16/25.5
5	Patterdale	10/16	Shap	16/25.5	K. Stephen	20/32
6	Shap	16/25.5	Kirkby Stephen	20/32	Reeth	24/38.5
7	Orton	8/13	Keld	13/21	Applegarth	8/13
8	Kirkby Stephen	13/21	Reeth	11/17.5	Danby Wiske	17/27
9	Keld	13/21	Applegarth	8/13	Osmotherley	12/19
10	Reeth	11/17.5	Danby Wiske	16.5/26.5	Blakey Ridge	20/32
11	Applegarth	8/13	Osmotherley	12/19	Grosmont	13.5/21.5
12	Danby Wiske	16.5/26.5	Blakey Ridge	20/32	R. Hood's Bay	15.5/25
13	Osmotherley	12/19	Grosmont	13.5/21.5		
14	Clay Bank Top§	11/17.5	R. Hood's Bay	15.5/25		
15	Blakey Ridge	9/14.5				
16	Grosmont	13.5/21.5				
17	Littlebeck	3.5/5.5				
18	R. Hood's Bay	12/19				

* No campsite but alternative accommodation is available
§ See note opposite

STAYING IN B&Bs

Night	Relaxed pace Place	Approx Distance miles/km	Medium pace Place	Approx Distance miles/km	Fast pace Place	Approx Distance miles/km
0	St Bees		St Bees		St Bees	
1	Cleator	9/14.5	Ennerdale Br	14/22.5	Ennerdale Br	14/22.5
2	Ennerdale Br	5/8	Borrowdale§	14.5/23	Borrowdale§	14.5/23
3	Borrowdale§	14.5/23	Grasmere	9.5/15	Patterdale	19.5/31
4	Grasmere	9.5/15	Patterdale	10/16	Shap	16/25.5
5	Patterdale	10/16	Shap	16/25.5	K. Stephen	20/32
6	Shap	16/25.5	K. Stephen	20/32	Reeth	24/38.5
7	Orton	8/13	Keld	13/21	Richmond	10.5/17
8	K. Stephen	13/21	Reeth	11/17.5	Ingleby Cross	23/37
9	Keld	13/21	Richmond	10.5/17	Blakey Ridge	21/33.5
10	Reeth	11/17.5	Danby Wiske	14/22.5	Grosmont	13.5/21.5
11	Richmond	10.5/17	Osmotherley	12/19	R. Hood's Bay	15.5/25
12	Danby Wiske	14/22.5	Clay Bank Top§	11/17.5		
13	Ingleby Cross	9/14.5	Grosmont	22.5/36		
14	Clay Bank Top§	12/19	R. Hood's Bay	15.5/25		
15	Blakey Ridge	9/14.5				
16	Glaisdale	10/16				
17	Littlebeck	7/11				
18	R. Hood's Bay	12/19				

§ See note opposite

STAYING IN HOSTELS/CAMPING BARNS/BUNKHOUSES

Night	Relaxed pace Place	Approx Distance miles/km	Medium pace Place	Approx Distance miles/km	Fast pace Place	Approx Distance miles/km
0	St Bees		St Bees		St Bees	
1	Sandwith	3/5	Sandwith	3/5	Sandwith	3/5
2	Ennerdale Br*	12/19	Ennerdale Br	15.5/25	Ennerdale Br	15.5/25
3	Black Sail	8.5/13.5	Borrowdale§	10.5/17	Borrowdale§	10.5/17
4	Borrowdale§	5.5/9	Grasmere	10/16	Patterdale	20/32
5	Grasmere	10/16	Patterdale	10/16	Shap*	16/25.5
6	Patterdale	10/16	Shap*	16/25.5	K. Stephen	20/32
7	Shap*	16/25.5	K. Stephen	20/32	Reeth [Grinton]	25.5/41
8	Orton*	8/13	Keld*	13/21	Applegarth	9.5/15
9	K. Stephen	13/21	Reeth [Grinton]	12.5/20	Osmotherley	28.5/46
10	Keld*	13/21	Applegarth	9.5/15	Blakey Ridge*	20/32
11	Reeth [Grinton]	12.5/20	Danby Wiske*	16.5/26.5	Grosmont*	13.5/21.5
12	Applegarth	9.5/15	Osmotherley	12/19	R. Hood's Bay	15.5/25
13	Danby Wiske*	16.5/26.5	Clay Bank Top§*	11/17.5		
14	Osmotherley	12/19	Glaisdale*	19/30.5		
15	Clay Bank Top§*	11/17.5	R. Hood's Bay	19/30.5		
16	Blakey Ridge*	9/14.5				
17	Glaisdale*	10/16				
18	Littlebeck*	7/11				
19	R. Hood's Bay	12/19				

* No camping barns, bunkhouses or hostels but alternative accommodation is available
§ See note below

PLANNING YOUR WALK

the Lake District – many people's favourite part of the British Isles, let alone the favourite part of the path – until the end of the walk.

SUGGESTED ITINERARIES

The itineraries in the boxes opposite and above are based on different accommodation types – camping, hostels/bunkhouses/camping barns, and B&Bs – with each one divided into three alternatives depending on your walking speed (relaxed, medium and fast). They are only suggestions so feel free to adapt them. **Don't forget** to add your travelling time before and after the walk.

Note: Borrowdale refers to Longthwaite, Rosthwaite & Stonethwaite and Clay Bank Top includes Urra & Great Broughton.

SIDE TRIPS

The Coast to Coast path is long enough and few walkers upon it will be tempted by side trips that involve yet more walking. Yet the path cuts through possibly the richest trekking territory in England, and there are plenty of opportunities for short (or long) diversions off the trail should you wish. Such side trips are beyond the scope of this book but a quick glance at an Ordnance Survey map will give you some idea of the alternative trails and side trips available.

Wainwright's series of guides to Lakeland fells describes other walks around the Lake District in further detail. Certainly an ascent of some of the hills in the area gives an entirely different perspective of the Lakeland landscape. Old favourites include Great Gable, Striding Edge on Helvellyn, High Street and England's highest mountain Scafell Pike (978m).

What to take

Deciding how much to take can be difficult. Experienced walkers know that you should take only the bare essentials but at the same time you must ensure you have all the equipment necessary to make the trip safe and comfortable.

KEEP IT LIGHT

Experienced backpackers know that there is some sort of complicated formula governing the success of a trek, in which the enjoyment of the walk is inversely proportional to the amount carried. Carrying a heavy rucksack slows you down, tires you out and gives you aches and pains in parts of the body that you never knew existed. It is imperative, therefore, that you take time packing and that you are ruthless when you do: if it's not essential, don't take it.

HOW TO CARRY IT

If you are using one of the baggage-carrier services, you must contact them beforehand to find out what their regulations are regarding the weight and size of the luggage you wish them to carry. Even if you are using one of these services, you will still need to carry a small **daypack** with you filled with those items that you will need during the day: water bottle/pouch, this book, sunscreen, sun hat, wet-weather gear, some food, camera, money and so on.

If you have decided to forego the services of the baggage carriers, you will have to consider your **rucksack** even more carefully. Ultimately its size will depend on where you are planning to stay and how you are planning to eat. If you are camping and cooking for yourself you will probably need a 65- to 75-litre rucksack, which should be large enough to carry a small tent, sleeping bag, cooking equipment, crockery, cutlery and food. Those not carrying their home with them should find a 40- to 60-litre rucksack sufficient.

When choosing a rucksack, make sure it has a stiffened back and can be adjusted to fit your own back comfortably. Don't just try the rucksack out in the shop: take it home, fill it with things and then try it out around the house and out for a short walk. Only then will you be certain that the rucksack is properly adjusted; make sure the hip belt and chest strap (if there is one) are fastened tightly as this helps distribute the weight with most of it being carried on the hips. Put a small daypack inside the rucksack, as this will be useful to carry things in when leaving the main pack at the hostel or B&B.

One reader wrote in with the eminently sensible advice of taking a **waterproof rucksack cover**. Most rucksacks these days have them 'built in' to the sack, but you can also buy them separately for less than a tenner. Lining your bag with a bin liner is another sensible, cut-price idea. For further protection, it's also a good idea to keep everything wrapped in plastic bags inside the rucksack. That way, even if it does pour with rain, everything should remain dry.

FOOTWEAR

Boots and socks

Only a decent pair of strong, durable trekking **boots** are good enough to survive the rigours of the Coast to Coast path. Don't be tempted by a spell of hot weather into bringing something flimsier: the bogs and marshes on the trail never dry out and there are few things less agreeable in life than walking along a trail with saturated socks and boots. Make sure, too, that your boots provide good ankle support for the ground is rough and stony and twisted ankles are commonplace. Make sure your boots are waterproof as well: these days most people opt for a synthetic waterproof lining (Gore-Tex or similar), though a good quality leather boot with dubbin should prove just as reliable in keeping your feet dry.

In addition, many people bring an extra pair of shoes or trainers to wear off the trail. This is not essential but if you are using one of the baggage-carrying services and you've got some room in your luggage why not?

If you haven't got a pair of the modern hi-tech walking **socks** the old system of wearing a thin liner sock under a thicker wool sock is just as good. Bring a few pairs of each.

CLOTHES

In a country notorious for its unpredictable climate, it is imperative that you pack enough clothes to cover every extreme of weather, from burning hot to bloomin' freezing. Modern hi-tech outdoor clothes come with a range of fancy names and brands but they all still follow the basic two- or three-layer principle, with an inner base layer to transport sweat away from your skin, a mid-layer for warmth and an outer layer to protect you from the wind and rain.

A thin lightweight **thermal top** of a synthetic material is ideal as the base layer as it draws moisture (ie sweat) away from your body. Cool in hot weather and warm when worn under other clothes in the cold, pack at least one thermal top. Over the top in cold weather a mid-weight **polyester fleece** should suffice. Fleeces are light, more water-resistant than the alternatives (such as a woolly jumper), remain warm even when wet, and pack down small in rucksacks; thus they are ideal trekking gear. Over the top of all this a **waterproof jacket** is essential. 'Breathable' jackets cost a small fortune (though prices are falling all the time) but prevent the build-up of condensation.

Leg wear

Many walkers find trekking trousers an unnecessary investment. Any light, quick-drying trouser should suffice. Jeans are heavy and dry slowly and are thus not recommended. A pair of waterproof trousers *is* more than useful, however, while on really hot sunny days you'll be glad you brought your shorts. Thermal **longjohns** take up little room in the rucksack and could be vital if the weather starts to get really cold. **Gaiters** are not necessary but, again, those who bring them are always glad they did, for they provide extra protection in boggy ground and when the vegetation around the trail is dripping wet after bad weather.

Underwear

Three or four changes of underwear is fine. Any more is excessive, any less unhygienic. Because backpacks can cause bra straps to dig painfully into the skin, women may find a **sports bra** more comfortable.

Other clothes

Don't leave home without both a **sun hat** and **gloves** – you'd be surprised how cold it can get up on the fells even in summer.

TOILETRIES

Once again, take the minimum. **Soap**, **towel**, a **toothbrush** and **toothpaste** are pretty much essential (although those staying in B&Bs will find that most provide soap and towels anyway). Some **toilet paper** could also prove vital on the trail, particularly if using public toilets (which occasionally run out).

A **plastic trowel** is also useful for digging holes when defecating outdoors (see p48). Other items: **razor**; **deodorant**; **tampons/sanitary towels** and a high-factor **sun-screen** should cover just about everything.

FIRST-AID KIT

A small first-aid kit could prove useful for those emergencies that occur along the trail. Suggestions for what should be in this kit include: **aspirin** or **paracetamol**; **plasters** for minor cuts; **moleskin**, **Second Skin** or some other treatment for blisters; a **bandage** for holding dressings, splints, or limbs in place and for supporting a sprained ankle; **elastic knee support** for a weak knee; a small selection of different-sized **sterile dressings** for wounds; **porous adhesive tape**; **antiseptic wipes**; **antiseptic cream**; **safety pins**; **tweezers**; and **scissors**.

GENERAL ITEMS

Essential items are a **map**, **torch**, **water bottle/pouch**, **spare batteries**, **penknife**, **whistle** (see p52 for details of the international distress signal), some **emergency food** and a **watch** (preferably with an alarm to help you make an early start each day). Those with weak knees may need a **walking pole** or **sticks**. If you know how to use it properly a **compass** is extremely handy and in the Lakes it becomes essential. Some people find a **mobile phone** invaluable too, though note that in the Lakes reception is usually available only on the fells.

Useful items include a **book** for evenings or train/bus journeys, some **plastic bags** to put rubbish in, a pair of **sunglasses**, **binoculars** and a **camera**.

CAMPING GEAR

Both campers and those intending to stay in the various bunkhouses en route will find a sleeping bag essential. A two- to three-season bag should suffice for summer. In addition, campers will need a decent bivvy bag or tent, a sleeping mat, fuel and stove, and cutlery/pans, a cup and a scrubber for washing up.

MONEY

Cash machines (ATMs) are infrequent along the Coast to Coast path, with none between Richmond and Grosmont, though their numbers are growing as post offices and shops along the trail install them. Banks are even rarer, with only Kirkby Stephen, Shap and Richmond boasting any. Not everybody accepts **debit** or **credit cards** as payment either – though most B&Bs and restaurants now do. As a result, you should always carry a fair amount of cash with you, just to be on the safe side. A **cheque book** from a British bank is useful in those places where credit cards are not accepted. See also p20 and p28. Crime on the trail is thankfully rare but it's always a good idea to carry your money in a **moneybelt**.

MAPS

The hand-drawn maps in this book cover the trail at a scale of 1:20,000 and this large scale, combined with the notes and tips written on the maps, should be enough to stop you losing your way. That said, these maps are designed to be used in conjunction with a 'regular' map of the region – ie one with contours, which could prove invaluable should you need to abandon the path and find the quickest route down because of, for example, bad weather. They also help you to identify local features and landmarks and devise possible side trips.

Unfortunately, the two Outdoor Leisure strip maps produced by the Ordnance Survey (☎ 08456 050505, 🖳 www.ordnancesurvey.co.uk) that covered the entire trail at a scale of 1:27,777 are out of print although it may be possible to get second-hand copies; look for sheets OL33 covering the trail from St Bees to Keld and OL34 covering it from Keld to Robin Hood's Bay. If you find a set going cheap – apparently on Ebay they're selling for about £30 – get one though many can be quite tired looking.

In their place the Ordnance Survey now have a series of maps at a scale of 1:25,000 but in order to cover the whole trail you will need eight maps. The trouble here, of course, is one of weight and expense. The details are: Explorer series 303 (for St Bees); Outdoor Leisure (OL) 4 for the western Lake District; OL 5 for the eastern Lake District; OL 19 for the upper Eden Valley (Kirkby Stephen); OL 30 for Swaledale; Explorer series 304 for Richmond and the Vale of Mowbray; OL 26 for the western North York Moors; and OL 27 for the eastern half to Robin Hood's Bay. While it may be extravagant to buy all of these maps, members of the **Ramblers' Association** (see box p38) can borrow up to 10 maps for a period of six weeks at 30p per map from their library.

The alternative is to go for the strip maps produced by both Harvey Maps and Footprint, both of which cover the trail over two maps at a scale of

1:40,000. The problem here is that they only cover a narrow strip either side of the trail and consequently give little opportunity for exploring further afield. Of the two, most people seem to prefer Footprint, which has a mile count drawn on the maps that many trekkers appreciate, and is also cheaper at around £4.95.

❏ SOURCES OF FURTHER INFORMATION

Online trail information

🖳 **www.coast2coast.co.uk** Vying with the website immediately below for the title of best online guide, this one run by Sherpavan is crammed full of useful information and should be a compulsory stop for any net-head looking to do the trail. They also have an online shop for books and maps and an accommodation-booking/luggage-transfer service (see p21). Perhaps best of all, however, they have a bulletin board where trekkers can share their experiences and those who have yet to try the trail can post any questions they might have.

🖳 **www.coasttocoastguides.co.uk** Richmond-based organization and another excellent website with books and maps for sale and a thorough accommodation guide.

🖳 **www.walkingplaces.co.uk/c2c.htm** Another very extensive and useful website.

Tourist information organizations

● **Tourist information centres (TICs)** TICs are based in towns throughout Britain and provide all manner of locally specific information and an accommodation-booking service. There are four centres relevant to the Coast to Coast path: **Ullswater/ Glenridding** (near Patterdale, p118), **Kirkby Stephen** (p139), **Reeth** (p164) and **Richmond** (p175).

● **Yorkshire Tourist Board** (🖳 www.yorkshire.com) The tourist board oversees all the local tourist information centres in the county. It's a good place to find general information about the county as well as on outdoor activities and local events. They can also help with arranging holidays and accommodation.

● **Cumbria Tourist Board** (☎ 01539 82222, 🖳 www.cumbria-the-lake-district .co.uk) Performing much the same role as the Yorkshire board above but, of course, for the county encompassing the Lake District.

Organizations for walkers

● **The Backpackers' Club** (🖳 www.backpackersclub.co.uk) A club aimed at people who are involved or interested in lightweight camping through walking, cycling, skiing and canoeing. They produce a quarterly magazine, provide members with a comprehensive advisory and information service on all aspects of backpacking, organize weekend trips and also publish a farm-pitch directory. Membership is £12 a year.

● **The Long Distance Walkers' Association** (🖳 www.ldwa.org.uk) Membership includes a journal three times per year with details of challenge events and local group walks as well as articles on the subject. Information on over 500 long-distance paths is presented in the LDWA's *Long Distance Walkers' Handbook*. Membership is £13 a year.

● **The Ramblers' Association** (🖳 www.ramblers.org.uk) Looks after the interests of walkers throughout Britain. They publish a large amount of useful information including their *Yearbook* (£5.99 to non-members), a full directory of services for walkers. Membership is currently £24 a year for an individual, £32 a year for joint membership, and £14 for concessions.

RECOMMENDED READING

Most of the following books can be found in the tourist information centres; the centre at Richmond has a particularly good supply of books about the path and the places en route. As well as stocking many of the titles listed below, the tourist offices also have a number of books about the towns and villages en route, usually printed by small, local publishers.

General guidebooks

We have to mention here Wainwright's original *A Coast to Coast Walk (Wainwright Pictorial Guides)*, a veritable work of art and now reprinted by local publisher, Frances Lincoln. For those who have been bitten by the trekking bug there are plenty of other titles in the Wainwright oeuvre, including a number on the Lakeland fells and a *Pennine Way Companion*. As an alternative, *Wainwright's Coast to Coast Walk* (Mermaid Books) has the additional selling point of photos by Derry Brabbs. One for the coffee table is *Coast-to-Coasting* by John Gillham and Ronald Turnbull (a runner who completed the Coast to Coast in just four days!). Although not exclusively about Wainwright's trail – indeed, there are eight walks in this guide – the beauty of the photographs is reason enough to buy this tome. Returning with the Wainwright theme, for some late-night reading why not take Wainwright to bed with you? Hunter Davies's *Wainwright: The Biography* (Orion Press) is a wonderfully absorbing account of this most complex of men.

For general guidebooks, both Rough Guides and Lonely Planet publish guides to England; though neither, it must be said, covers the Coast to Coast trail in adequate detail. Better is Lonely Planet's *Walking in Britain* by David Else.

Other guidebooks

Other guides to the trail include Cicerone's *The Coast to Coast Trail: A Long-Distance Walking Guide* by Terry Marsh, and *Coast to Coast Walk (Walking Country Series)* by Paul Hannon (Hillside Publications). There are also a couple of accommodation guides, including Doreen Whitehead's long-running publication *Coast to Coast Bed & Breakfast Accommodation Guide*.

If you are a seasoned long-distance walker, or even new to the game and like what you see, check out the other titles in the Trailblazer series; see pp237-40.

Flora and fauna field guides

Collins *Bird Guide* with its beautiful illustrations of British and European birds continues to be the favourite field guide of both ornithologists and laymen alike. For a pocket-sized guide to the flora you'll encounter on the Coast to Coast path, *The Wild Flowers of Britain and Ireland: A New Guide to Our Wild Flowers* (Tandem) by Marjorie Blamey and Richard Fitter, with illustrations by Alastair Fitter, is comprehensive but, alas, not for the beginner, with the plants arranged by families. It's also too big to take with you. Another in the Collins Gem series, *Wild Flowers*, is thus more suitable for walkers and only costs a fiver.

Getting to and from the Coast to Coast path

Both St Bees and Robin Hood's Bay are quite difficult to reach. For this reason, many people are now opting to use Kirkby Stephen as their base. Not only is this town well connected by public transport (it lies on the Carlisle to Leeds line) but it is also the home of several baggage-carrying companies, some of whom offer taxi services to the start at St Bees and other destinations on the Coast to Coast path, and will also bring customers back to Kirkby Stephen at the end of their walk. See pp20-1 for details of a few of these companies.

❏ GETTING TO BRITAIN

● **By air** Manchester is the nearest major international airport to St Bees but for most foreign visitors one of the London airports is likely to be their entry point to the country. Nevertheless, if you've no business in London do check out flights to Manchester. From Manchester Airport to St Bees it's about 3½ hours by train (slightly less if you manage to catch the train via Barrow-in-Furness). Leeds Bradford (convenient for Kirkby Stephen) and Teeside (7 miles/11km outside Darlington and useful for Richmond; also the nearest airport to Robin Hood's Bay) are also worth investigating but are served mainly by domestic flights.

A number of **budget airlines**, namely ⌨ www.easyjet.com (though it doesn't serve Manchester), ⌨ www.bmibaby.com and ⌨ www.ryanair.com fly from many of Europe's major cities to Manchester and the London terminals of Stansted and Luton, with a few now flying to Gatwick and Heathrow too. From London it is around four hours to Carlisle by train, from where you can catch a second train back down the coast to St Bees; see opposite.

● **From Europe by train** Eurostar (⌨ www.eurostar.com) operates a high-speed passenger service via the Channel Tunnel between Paris, Brussels (and some other cities) and London. The new Eurostar terminal in London is at St Pancras station – convenient for both the trains for Carlisle (which leave from nearby Euston) and to the north-east coast (which leave from neighbouring King's Cross). For more information about rail services from Europe contact Rail Europe (⌨ www.raileu rope.com), or Railteam (⌨ www.railteam.eu).

● **From Europe by coach** Eurolines (⌨ www.eurolines.com) have a huge network of long-distance coach services connecting over 500 cities in 25 European countries to London. Check carefully, however: often, once such expenses as food for the journey are taken into consideration, it often does not work out that much cheaper than taking a flight, particularly when compared to the prices of some of the budget airlines.

● **From Europe by ferry (with or without a car)** Numerous ferry companies operate routes between the major North Sea and Channel ports of mainland Europe and the ports on Britain's eastern and southern coasts as well as from Ireland to ports in both Wales and England. For further information see ⌨ www.direct ferries.com.

● **From Europe by car** Eurotunnel (⌨ www.eurotunnel.com) operates the shuttle train service for vehicles via the Channel Tunnel between Calais and Folkestone taking one hour between the motorway in France and the motorway in Britain.

PLANNING YOUR WALK

If you want to make your own way to St Bees, it's best to catch a train from Carlisle or a bus/walk from Whitehaven. For Robin Hood's Bay, Arriva's No 93 Middlesbrough to Scarborough service operates daily (see box p45) and calls in at Whitby (at the top of the town); all of these towns well connected by rail.

NATIONAL TRANSPORT

All train **timetable and fare information** can be found at National Rail Enquiries (☎ 08457 484950, 24hrs; 🖳 www.nationalrail.co.uk). Alternatively, and to book tickets, you can look on the websites of the train companies concerned (🖳 www.virgintrains.co.uk, 🖳 www.nationalexpresseastcoast.com and 🖳 www.northernrail.org). Timetables and tickets are also available on 🖳 www.thetrainline.com and 🖳 www.qjump.co.uk.

Coach travel is generally cheaper (though with the excellent advance-purchase train fares that is not always true) but takes longer than travel by train. The principal coach (long-distance bus) operator in Britain is **National Express** (☎ 08705 808080, open 8am-8pm daily; 🖳 www.nationalexpress.com). **Megabus** (☎ 0900 160 0900, 🖳 www.megabus.com) has a more limited service though may be cheaper.

Getting to St Bees
● **Train** At the time of writing Virgin's services **from London** to Carlisle operated approximately hourly during the day, each taking between $3^1/2$ and 4 hours. Virgin also has services from the south coast, the south-west and Scotland to Carlisle. Between Carlisle and St Bees, there are 5-6 trains a day, Mon-Sat. (The service to Whitehaven, four miles up the road from St Bees, is more frequent with 15-16/day Monday to Saturday and 3/day on Sunday.)

Coming **from Manchester Piccadilly** there are plenty of trains Monday to Saturday to Barrow-in-Furness, though the Sunday service is limited to one train. From Barrow-in-Furness to St Bees there are 6/day Monday to Saturday.
● **Coach/bus** The nearest National Express coach service (NX570) runs to Whitehaven from London, four miles north of St Bees. Alternatively, National Express has services to Carlisle from several towns and cities in Britain; see box p44. From Carlisle Stagecoach operates two services (No 300/1 and No 600; see box p44) to Whitehaven. From there trekkers have the options of walking or taking a taxi, bus (Stagecoach No 20) or train (see above) to St Bees.
● **Car** You can of course drive to St Bees and leave your car (for a fee) at a B&B there. The nearest motorway is the M6 to Carlisle which joins the M1 just outside Coventry. From the south, leave the M1 at junction 36 (the Southern Lakes turn-off), then take the A590 till it meets the A5092; this then meets the A595 (to Whitehaven) and turn off just before Egremont.

Getting to Robin Hood's Bay
● **Train** Robin Hood's Bay is, if anything, even harder to get to than St Bees. The nearest rail station is at Whitby: trekkers coming up from London to Robin Hood's Bay need to change twice, at Darlington and Middlesbrough, in order to reach Whitby, from where they can catch a bus to the Bay (20 minutes). The

train journey takes about five hours. A better way, perhaps, involving only one change of train, is to catch one of the 14-16 services operated by National Express East Coast from London to Scarborough (changing at York) and then take a bus from there to the Bay. The bus journey is longer (approximately 40 minutes) but the train journey is only around three hours including changes.

● **Coach/bus** National Express operates one direct service (NX563) a day to Whitby (leaving London Victoria at 1pm, arriving in Whitby at 8.40pm). The NX561 London to Leeds service connects twice a day with Yorkshire Coastliner's YC840 Leeds to Whitby services (see box pp44-5). The last of Arriva's No 56/X56 services from Scarborough to Middlesborough which calls in at Whitby and Robin Hood's Bay (a journey time of about 20 minutes between the two) leaves at 10pm.

● **Car** It's not entirely straightforward to get to Robin Hood's Bay by car either, though compared to public transport it is at least the simplest. From London it's probably best to head up to Doncaster on the M1/A1(M), then the M18/A19 to York. From there you can head north-east to Scarborough on the A64, then the A171 heading towards Whitby, turning off on the B1447 for Robin Hood's Bay. Coming from Manchester take the M62 north-east to Leeds, then the A64 all the way to Scarborough, from where you pick up the A171 as outlined above.

Getting to Kirkby Stephen

● **Train** Kirkby Stephen is a stop on the Carlisle to Settle line. Coming from London (Kings Cross) take a train to Leeds (usually around 2 hours 20 minutes, operated by National Express East Coast), which also lies on the Carlisle to Settle line, and catch a train to Kirkby Stephen (Mon-Sat 5-6/day, Sun 2-3/day) from there. The journey takes just under two hours.

● **Coach/bus** The nearest National Express coach service runs to Kendal (a stop on the NX570 London to Whitehaven service); Stagecoach's No 564 service operates 4/day to Kirkby Stephen.

● **Car** The A685 runs through the town, though there are plans for a bypass to be constructed in the near future. The trans-Pennine A66 (which shadows the Coast to Coast path to the north) crosses the A685 just four miles north of the town. The nearest motorway, the M6, is 22 miles west of the A66 interchange.

LOCAL TRANSPORT

Public transport is limited along the Coast to Coast path. While most places do have some sort of bus service, these services are irregular and often just two or three times per day. Usually the choice of destination is limited too, with often the nearest big town being the only choice. If you have difficulty getting through to the transport companies in the box on pp44-5, you can contact **traveline** (☎ 0871 200 2233; 🖳 www.traveline.org.uk), which has public transport information for the whole of the UK. For information about transport in Cumbria contact Stagecoach North West or Cumbria County Council (see box p44) and ask for a copy of *The Lakesrider*, which gives details of buses, trains and ferries in the county and is published twice a year.

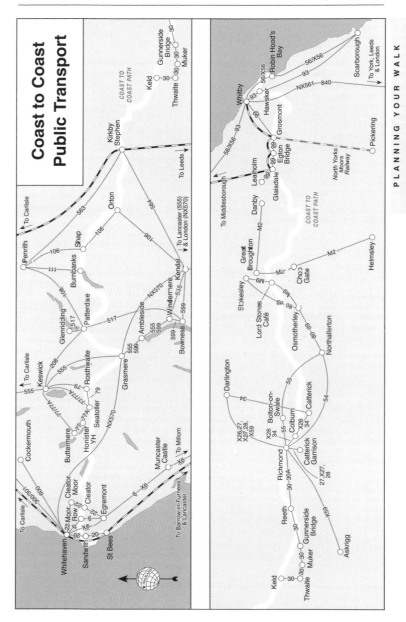

Coast to Coast Public Transport

PLANNING YOUR WALK

❏ PUBLIC TRANSPORT SERVICES

Notes
● Services on Bank Holiday Mondays are usually the same as Sunday services
● Services generally operate at the same frequency in both directions
● Frequencies given are between 9am and 6pm
● In rural areas where there are no fixed bus stops it is usually possible to 'hail and ride' a passing bus though it is important to stand where visibility is good and also somewhere where it would be safe for the driver to stop.

Services
Northern Rail Ltd (💻 www.northernrail.org, ☎ 0871 200 4950)
See pp41-2 for details of the services to Carlisle for St Bees, to Whitby for Robin Hood's Bay and to Kirkby Stephen
● Middlesbrough to Whitby via Glaisdale, Egton and Grosmont, Mon-Sat 4-5/day, Sun 5/day June to September

North York Moors Railway (enquiries ☎ 01751 472508, talking timetable ☎ 01751 -473535, 💻 www.nymr.co.uk
Grosmont to Pickering and vice versa, daily Mar-Oct plus in holiday periods such as Christmas/New Year and February half-term, weekends only at other times; 4-8/day depending on the time of year

National Express (☎ 08705 808080 8am-8pm daily, 💻 www.nationalexpress.com)
● **To Whitehaven** NX570 London to Whitehaven (stops en route include Grasmere, and Kendal for bus services to Kirkby Stephen) 1/day
● **To Carlisle** The services listed stop at least 1/day in Carlisle: NX590/592 London to Aberdeen; NX920 London to Stranraer; NX334 Coventry to Glasgow; NX536 Cardiff to Edinburgh; NX539 Bournemouth to Edinburgh; NX 533 Wrexham to Glasgow.
● **To Whitby** NX561 London to Whitby 1/day, London to Leeds 2/day (see YC840)

Yorkshire Coastliner (☎ 01653 692556, 💻 www.yorkshirecoastliner.co.uk)
840   Leeds to Whitby via York, Mon-Fri 4/day, Sat 1/day (the X40 also operates 1/day Mon-Fri and the 845 Leeds to Malton service connects 2/day with the 840 Whitby to York service).

Stagecoach North West (💻 www.stagecoachbus.com)/Cumbria County Council (☎ 01228 606705, 💻 www.cumbria.gov.uk/roads-transport)
20   Whitehaven to St Bees via Sandwith, Mon-Sat 5-6/day
6   Whitehaven to Muncaster via Moor Row & Egremont, Mon-Sat 3-4/day
X6   Whitehaven to Millom via Egremont and Muncaster, Sun 4/day
22   Whitehaven to Egremont via Cleator Moor and Cleator, Mon-Sat hourly
300/301 Whitehaven to Carlisle, Mon-Sat hourly, Sun 1/every two hours
600   Carlisle to Whitehaven via Cockermouth, Mon-Fri 3/day, Sat 5/day
77/77A   Keswick to Keswick (Honister Rambler) a circular route via Buttermere, Honister YH and Seatoller, Apr-Oct 4/day in each direction
79   Keswick to Seatoller (Borrowdale Rambler) via Rosthwaite, Apr-end July and Sep-Oct Mon-Sat 1/hr, end July-Aug Mon-Sat 2/hr, Sun hourly
555   Keswick to Lancaster via Grasmere, Ambleside, Windermere and Kendal, Apr-Aug daily 1/hr; Keswick to Carlisle connecting service, daily 3/day

Stagecoach North West *(cont'd from opposite)*

599   Grasmere to Bowness/Kendal (Open-top Lakeland Experience) via
         Ambleside and Windermere, Apr-Aug daily 3/hr; Aug-Oct daily 2/hr

517   Bowness to Glenridding (Kirkstone Rambler) via Patterdale Hotel, Easter to
         mid-Jul and Sep-Oct, Sat, Sun & Public Hols 3/day; mid-Jul to Aug daily 3/day

208   Patterdale Hotel to Keswick (Ullswater Connexion), May-July and Aug-Oct
         Sat, Sun and Public Holidays only 5/day; July-Aug daily 5/day

106   Penrith to Kendal via Shap & Orton (various operators), Mon-Sat 7/day

108   Penrith to Patterdale Hotel (Patterdale Bus), Mar-Oct Mon-Sat 5-7/day; Mar-
         early Sep Sun 4/day

111   Penrith to Burnbanks Village (Haweswater Rambler), Tue 2/day, Sat 3/day

563   Penrith (bus and rail stations) to Kirkby Stephen, Mon-Sat 5-6/day

564   Kirkby Stephen to Kendal, Mon-Sat 4/day

Harrogate District Little Red Bus (☎ 01423 526655, 🖳 www.littleredbus.co.uk)

30/30A Keld to Richmond via Thwaite, Muker (Farmer's Arms), Gunnerside Bridge
         and Reeth, Mon-Sat 2/day; and Reeth to Richmond Mon-Sat 6/day

Arriva North East (☎ 0870 102 1088, 🖳 www.arrivabus.co.uk/northeast)

34   Richmond to Darlington via Colburn Lanes and Catterick Village, Mon-Sat
         11/day

X59   Askrigg to Darlington via Richmond, Mon-Fri 1/day

X26   Catterick Village to Darlington via Colburn and Richmond, Mon-Sat 6/day

27   Catterick Garrison to Darlington via Richmond, daily 1/hr

X27   Catterick Garrison to Darlington via Richmond, Mon-Sat hourly, Sun 1/day

28   Catterick Garrison to Darlington via Richmond, daily, 2/hr

X56/56 Scarborough to Middlesbrough via Robin Hood's Bay and Whitby, Mon-Sat
         1/hr, Sun 5/day

93   Scarborough to Middlesbrough via Hawsker Village and Whitby, Mon-Sat
         10/day, Sun 7/day

Dales & District (☎ 01677 425203, 🖳 www.procterscoaches.co.uk)

54   Richmond to Northallerton via Catterick Bridge, Mon-Sat 3/day

55   Richmond to Northallerton via Bolton on Swale, Mon-Fri 5/day, Sat 4/day

Moorsbus Network (☎ 01845 597000, 🖳 www.moors.uk.net/moorsbus)

M2   Sutton Bank/Helmsley to Danby via Chop Gate & Great Broughton, late
         July-1st Sep 3/day; Jul & Sep Tue, Fri, Sun & bank hols; 1 Apr-June &
         Oct, Sun & bank hols only

M9   Osmotherley (The Cross) to Stokesley via Lord Stones Café, 3/day and via
         Clay Bank 1/day Sun & bank hols Easter-Oct plus daily late July-Aug

G Abbott & Sons (☎ 01677 422858)

80/89 Stokesley to Northallerton via Osmotherley, Mon-Sat 12/day

M&D Minicoaches (☎ 01947 895418)

99   Whitby to Lealholm via Grosmont, Egton, and Glaisdale, Mon-Sat 4-5/day.
         This is a hail-and-ride service.

Minimum impact walking

In this chaotic world in which people live their lives at an increasingly frenetic pace, many of us living in overcrowded cities and working in jobs that offer little free time, the great outdoors is becoming an essential means of escape. Walking in the countryside is a wonderful means of relaxation and gives people the time to think and rediscover themselves.

Of course, as the popularity of the countryside increases so do the problems that this pressure brings. It is important for visitors to remember that the countryside is the home and workplace of many others. Walkers in particular should be aware of their responsibilities. Indeed a walker who respects and understands the countryside will get far more enjoyment from their trip.

By following a few simple guidelines while walking the Coast to Coast path you can have a positive impact, not just on your own well-being but also on local communities and the environment, thereby becoming part of the solution.

ECONOMIC IMPACT

Rural businesses and communities in Britain have been hit hard in recent years by a seemingly endless series of crises. Most people are aware of the country code; not dropping litter and closing the gate behind you are still as pertinent as ever, but in light of the economic pressures that local countryside businesses are under there is something else you can do: buy local.

Support local businesses

Buy local
Look and ask for local produce to buy and eat. Not only does this cut down on the amount of pollution and congestion that the transportation of food creates, so-called 'food miles', but also ensures that you are supporting local farmers and producers – the very people who have moulded the countryside you have come to see and who are in the best position to protect it. If you can find local food which is also organic so much the better.

Support local businesses
It's a fact of life that money spent at local level – perhaps in a market, or at the greengrocer, or in an independent pub – has a far greater

impact for good on that community than the equivalent spent in a branch of a national chain store or restaurant. While no-one would advocate that walkers should boycott the larger supermarkets, which after all do provide local employment, it's worth remembering that businesses in rural communities rely heavily on visitors for their very existence. If we want to keep these shops and post offices, we need to use them. The more money that circulates locally and is spent on local labour and materials, the greater the impact on the local economy and the more power the community has to effect the change it wants to see.

Encourage local cultural traditions and skills

No part of the countryside looks the same. Buildings, food, skills, and language evolve out of the landscape and are moulded over hundreds of years to suit the locality. Discovering these cultural differences is part of the pleasure of walking in new places. Visitors' enthusiasm for local traditions and skills brings awareness and pride, nurturing a sense of place; an increasingly important role in a world where economic globalization continues to undermine the very things that provide security and a feeling of belonging.

ENVIRONMENTAL IMPACT

A walking holiday in itself is an environmentally friendly approach to tourism. The following are some ideas on how you can go a few steps further in helping to minimize your impact on the environment while walking the Coast to Coast path.

Use public transport whenever possible

Public transport along the Coast to Coast trail is not bad (though it can be a little infrequent at times), with just about everywhere served by at least one bus or train a day. Public transport is always preferable to using private cars as it benefits everyone: visitors, locals and the environment.

Never leave litter

'Pack it in, pack it out'. Leaving litter shows a total disrespect for the natural world and others coming after you. As well as being ugly, litter can be harmful to and even kill wildlife (small mammals often become trapped in discarded cans and bottles), pollutes the environment and can be dangerous to farm animals. **Please** carry a plastic bag so you can dispose of your rubbish in a bin in the next village. It would be very helpful if you could pick up litter left by other people too.

● **Is it OK if it's biodegradable?** Not really. Apple cores, banana skins, orange peel and the like are unsightly, encourage flies, ants and wasps and ruin a picnic spot for others. Even biodegradable foodstuffs attract common scavenging species such as crows and gulls to the detriment of less dominant species. Using the excuse that they are natural and biodegradable just doesn't cut any ice. When was the last time you saw a banana tree in the north of England?

● **The lasting impact of litter** A piece of orange peel left on the ground takes six months to decompose; silver foil 18 months; a plastic bag 10 years; clothes 15 years; and an aluminium can 85 years.

Erosion

● **Stay on the main trail** The effect of your footsteps may seem minuscule but when they are multiplied by several thousand walkers each year they become rather more significant. Avoid taking shortcuts, widening the trail or taking more than one path; your boots will be followed by many others. This is particularly true on the Coast to Coast path which has become a victim of its own success, with a number of sections of the trail now badly eroded. Indeed, over the Pennines the authorities have now established three trails, with each to be used for four months a year, thereby limiting the amount of erosion on any one trail.

● **Consider walking out of season** Maximum disturbance by walkers coincides with the time of year when nature wants to do most of its growth and repair. In high-use areas, like that along much of the Coast to Coast path, the trail is often prevented from recovering.

Walking at less busy times eases this pressure while also generating year-round income for the local economy. Not only that, but it may make the walk a more relaxing experience with fewer people on the path and less competition for accommodation.

Respect all wildlife

Care for all wildlife you come across along the path; it has as much right to be there as you. Tempting as it may be to pick wild flowers leave them so the next people who pass can enjoy them too. Don't break branches off or damage trees in any way.

If you come across wildlife keep your distance and don't watch for too long. Your presence can cause considerable stress, particularly if the adults are with young, or in winter when the weather is harsh and food is scarce.

Young animals are rarely abandoned. If you come across young birds keep away so that their mother can return.

The code of the outdoor loo

'Going' in the outdoors is a lost art worth reclaiming, for your sake and everyone else's. As more and more people discover the joys of the outdoors this is becoming an important issue. In some parts of the world where visitor pressure is higher than in Britain, walkers and climbers are required to pack out their excrement. This could soon be necessary here. Human excrement is not only offensive to our senses but, more importantly, can infect water sources.

● **Where to go** Wherever possible **use a toilet**. Public toilets are marked on the trail maps in this guide and you will also find facilities in pubs, cafés and campsites along the Coast to Coast path. If you do have to go outdoors choose a site that is not of historic or archaeological significance and is at least **30 metres away from running water**.

(Opposite) Approaching Greenup Edge (see p101) on the steep climb up from Borrowdale.

Use a stick or trowel to **dig a small hole** about 15cm (6") deep to bury your excrement in. It decomposes quicker when in contact with the top layer of soil or leaf mould. Then stir loose soil into your deposit as this speeds up decomposition. Do not squash it under rocks as this slows down the composting process. If you have to use rocks to cover it make sure they are not in contact with your faeces.

● **Toilet paper and tampons** Toilet paper takes a long time to decompose whether buried or not. It is easily dug up by animals and may then blow into water sources or onto the path.

The best method for dealing with it is to **pack it out**. Put the used paper inside a paper bag which you place inside a plastic bag (or two). Then simply empty the contents of the paper bag at the next toilet you come across and throw the bag away. You should also pack out **tampons** and **sanitary towels** in a similar way; they take years to decompose and may be dug up and scattered about by animals.

Wild camping
Unfortunately wild camping is not encouraged within the national parks which make up the majority of the walk. In any case there are few places where it is a viable option.

This is a shame since wild camping is an altogether more fulfilling experience than camping on a designated site. Living in the outdoors without any facilities provides a valuable lesson in simple, sustainable living where the results of all your actions, from going to the loo to washing your plates, can be seen.

If you do insist on wild camping always ask the landowner for permission. Follow these suggestions for minimizing your impact and encourage others to do likewise.

● **Be discreet** Camp alone or in small groups, spend only one night in each place and pitch your tent late and move off early.

● **Never light a fire** Accidental fire is a great fear for farmers and foresters. Never make a camp fire and take matches and cigarette butts out with you to dispose of safely. Aside from that, the deep burn caused by camp fires, no matter how small, damages the turf which can take years to recover. Cook on a camp stove instead.

● **Don't use soap or detergent** There is no need to use soap; even biodegradable soaps and detergents pollute streams. You won't be away from a shower for more than a day or so. Wash up without detergent; use a plastic or metal scourer, or failing that, a handful of fine pebbles or some bracken or grass.

● **Leave no trace** Learn the skill of moving on without leaving any sign of having been there: no moved boulders, ripped up vegetation or dug drainage ditches.

MINIMUM IMPACT & OUTDOOR SAFETY

(Opposite) Top: Bivvying at Applegarth Scar (see p170), Yorkshire Dales National Park. (Photo © Jim Manthorpe). **Bottom**: Don't disturb farm animals even if they appear as interested in you as you may be in them.

Make a final check of your campsite before departing; pick up any litter that you or anyone else has left, so leaving the place in the same state you found it in, or better.

ACCESS

Britain is a crowded island with few places where you can wander as you please. Most of the land is a patchwork of fields and agricultural land and the terrain through which the Coast to Coast path marches is no different. However, there are countless public rights of way, in addition to the Coast to Coast path, that criss-cross the land.

This is fine, but what happens if you feel a little more adventurous and want to explore the moorland, woodland and hills that can also be found near the walk.

Right to roam

The Countryside & Rights of Way Act 2000 (CRoW), or 'Right to Roam' as dubbed by walkers, came into effect in full on 31 October 2005 after a long campaign to allow greater public access to areas of countryside in England and Wales deemed to be uncultivated open country; this essentially means moorland, heathland, downland and upland areas.

Some land is covered by restrictions (ie high-impact activities such as driving a vehicle, cycling, horse-riding are not permitted) and some land is excluded (such as gardens, parks and cultivated land). Full details are given on 🖳 www.countrysideaccess.gov.uk.

With more freedom in the countryside comes a need for more responsibility from the walker. Remember that wild open country is still the workplace of farmers and home to all sorts of wildlife. Have respect for both and avoid disturbing domestic and wild animals.

The Countryside Code

The countryside is a fragile place which every visitor should respect. The Countryside Code seems like common sense but sadly some people still appear to have no understanding of how to treat the countryside they walk in.

Everyone visiting the countryside has a responsibility to minimize the impact of their visit so that other people can enjoy the same peaceful landscapes; it doesn't take much effort.

> ❏ **The Countryside Code**
> ● Be safe – plan ahead and follow any signs
> ● Leave gates and property as you find them
> ● Protect plants and animals, and take your litter home
> ● Keep dogs under close control
> ● Consider other people

The Countryside Code (see box opposite) has now been revised, in part because of the changes brought about by the CRoW Act (see above) and was relaunched in July 2004. The following is an expanded version of the new Countryside Code, launched under the logo 'Respect, Protect and Enjoy':

● **Be safe** The Coast to Coast path is pretty much hazard free but you're responsible for your own safety so follow the simple guidelines outlined on pp52-4.

● **Leave all gates as you found them** Normally a farmer leaves gates closed to keep livestock in but may sometimes leave them open to allow livestock access to food or water. Leave them as you find them and if there is a sign, follow the instructions.

● **Leave livestock, crops and machinery alone** Help farmers by not interfering with their means of livelihood.

● **Take your litter home** See p47.

● **Keep your dog under control** See p23. During lambing time they should not be taken with you at all (see box opposite).

● **Enjoy the countryside and respect its life and work** Access to the countryside depends on being sensitive to the needs and wishes of those who live and work there. Being courteous and friendly to those you meet will ensure a healthy future for all based on partnership and co-operation.

● **Keep to paths across farmland** Stick to the official path across arable or pasture land. Minimize erosion by not cutting corners or widening the path.

● **Use gates and stiles to cross fences, hedges and walls** The Coast to Coast path is well supplied with stiles where it crosses field boundaries. On some of the side trips you may find the paths less accommodating. If you have to climb over a gate because you can't open it always do so at the hinged end.

● **Guard against all risk of fire** See p49.

● **Help keep all water clean** Leaving litter and going to the toilet near a water source can pollute people's water supplies. See p48 for more advice.

● **Take special care on country roads** Drivers often go dangerously fast on narrow winding lanes. To be safe, walk facing the oncoming traffic and carry a torch or wear highly visible clothing when it's getting dark.

● **Protect wildlife, plants and trees** Care for and respect all wildlife you come across along the Coast to Coast path. Don't pick plants, break trees or scare wild animals. If you come across young birds that appear to have been abandoned leave them alone.

● **Make no unnecessary noise** Enjoy the peace and solitude of the outdoors by staying in small groups and acting unobtrusively.

> ❏ **Lambing**
> Lambing takes place from mid-March to mid-May when dogs should not be taken along the path. Even a dog secured on a lead can disturb a pregnant ewe.
>
> If you see a lamb or ewe that appears to be in distress contact the nearest farmer.

MINIMUM IMPACT & OUTDOOR SAFETY

Outdoor safety

AVOIDANCE OF HAZARDS

With good planning and preparation most hazards can be avoided. This information is just as important for those out on a day walk as for those walking the entire Coast to Coast path. Always make sure you have suitable **clothes** (see pp35-6) to keep you warm and dry, whatever the conditions, and a spare change of inner clothes. Carrying plenty of food and water is vital too.

A compass, whistle, torch, map and first-aid kit should be carried; this is discussed further on p36. The **emergency signal** is six blasts on the whistle or six flashes with a torch.

Safety on the Coast to Coast path

Sadly every year people are injured or killed walking the Coast to Coast path. The most dangerous section is in the Lake District, where the altitudes and the unpredictable weather combine to lead walkers to their doom. Mountain rescue teams are locally based and are staffed by volunteers who are ready 24 hours a day 365 days of the year.

In an emergency phone ☎ 999 as normal, and the police will activate the service. These rescue teams rely on donations (the Patterdale's running costs are estimated to be £30,000 per annum), and are called out on average about 60 times a year. There is another rescue team based at Kirkby Stephen.

All rescue teams should be treated as very much the last resort, however, and it's vital you take every precaution to ensure your own safety:

● Avoid walking on your own if possible, particularly on the Lakeland fells.
● Make sure that somebody knows your plans for every day that you are on the trail. This could be a friend or relative whom you have promised to call every night, or the place you plan to stay in at the end of each day's walk. That way, if you fail to turn up or call that evening, they can raise the alarm.
● If the weather closes in suddenly and fog or mist descends while you are on the trail, particularly on the moors or fells, and you become uncertain of the correct trail, do not be tempted to continue. Just wait where you are and you'll find that mist often clears, at least for long enough to allow you to get your bearings. If you are still uncertain, and the weather does not look like improving, return the way you came to the nearest point of civilization, and try again another time when conditions have improved.
● Always fill your water bottle/pouch at every opportunity and have some high-energy snacks.
● Always carry a torch, compass, map, first-aid kit, whistle and wet-weather gear with you.
● Wear strong sturdy boots with good ankle support and a good grip, not trainers.
● Be extra vigilant if walking with children.

Dealing with an accident

● Use basic first aid to treat the injury to the best of your ability.

● Work out exactly where you are. If possible leave someone with the casualty while others go to get help. If there are only two people, you have a dilemma. If you decide to get help leave all spare clothing and food with the casualty.

● In an emergency dial ☎ 999.

WEATHER FORECASTS

The Coast to Coast suffers from enormously unpredictable weather, so it's vital that you always try to find out what the weather is going to be like before you set off for the day.

Many hostels and tourist information centres will have pinned up somewhere a summary of the weather forecast. Or you can get a telephone forecast (**Weather Call** ☎ 09068 500419 for Cumbria/Lake District and 500417 for Yorkshire, ☎ 0901 471 0310 for next six hours in your local town; 🖳 www .weathercall.co.uk); these are frequently updated and generally reliable but calls are charged at the premium-rate (60p/min); if you have internet access you can look at the website. Pay close attention to the forecast and alter your plans for the day accordingly. That said, even if a fine sunny day is forecast, always assume the worst and pack some wet-weather gear.

BLISTERS

It is important to break in new boots before embarking on a long trek. Make sure the boots are comfortable and try to avoid getting them wet on the inside. Air your feet at lunchtime, keep them clean and change your socks regularly. If you feel any hot spots stop immediately and apply a few strips of zinc oxide tape and leave it on until it is pain free or the tape starts to come off.

If you have left it too late and a blister has developed you should surround it with 'moleskin' or any other blister kit to protect it from abrasion. Popping it can lead to infection. If the skin is broken keep the area clean with antiseptic and cover with a non-adhesive dressing material held in place with tape.

HYPOTHERMIA

Also known as exposure, hypothermia occurs when the body can't generate enough heat to maintain its normal temperature, usually as a result of being wet, cold, unprotected from the wind, tired and hungry. It is usually more of a problem in upland areas such as in the Lakes and on the moors.

Hypothermia is easily avoided by wearing suitable clothing, carrying and consuming enough food and drink, being aware of the weather conditions and checking the morale of your companions.

Early signs to watch for are feeling cold and tired with involuntary shivering. Find some shelter as soon as possible and warm the victim up with a hot drink and some chocolate or other high-energy food. If possible give them another warm layer of clothing and allow them to rest until feeling better.

MINIMUM IMPACT & OUTDOOR SAFETY

If allowed to worsen, strange behaviour, slurring of speech and poor co-ordination will become apparent and the victim can quickly progress into unconsciousness, followed by coma and death. Quickly get the victim out of wind and rain, improvising a shelter if necessary.

Rapid restoration of bodily warmth is essential and best achieved by bare-skin contact: someone should get into the same sleeping bag as the patient, both having stripped to the bare essentials, placing any spare clothing under or over them to build up heat. Send urgently for help.

HYPERTHERMIA

Not an ailment that you would normally associate with the north of England, hyperthermia (heat exhaustion and heatstroke) is a serious problem nonetheless.

Symptoms of **heat exhaustion** include thirst, fatigue, giddiness, a rapid pulse, raised body temperature, low urine output and, if not treated, delirium and finally a coma. The best cure is to drink plenty of water.

Heatstroke is another matter altogether, and even more serious. A high body temperature and an absence of sweating are early indications, followed by symptoms similar to hypothermia (see p53) such as a lack of co-ordination, convulsions and coma.

Death will follow if treatment is not given instantly. Sponge the victim down, wrap them in wet towels, fan them, and get help immediately.

SUNBURN

It can happen, even in northern England and even on overcast days. The only surefire way to avoid it is to stay wrapped up, but that's not really an option. What you must do, therefore, is to smother yourself in sunscreen (with a minimum factor of 15) and apply it regularly throughout the day. Don't forget your lips, nose, the back of your neck and even under your chin to protect against rays reflected up off the ground.

PART 3: ENVIRONMENT AND NATURE

Conserving the Coast to Coast path

Britain is an overcrowded island, and England is the most densely populated part of it. As such, the English countryside has suffered a great deal of pressure from both over-population and the activities of an ever more industrialized world. Thankfully, there is some enlightened legislation to protect the surviving pockets of forest and heathland.

Apart from these, it is interesting to note just how much man has altered the land that he lives on. Whilst the aesthetic costs of such intrusions are open to debate, what is certain is the loss of biodiversity that has resulted. The last wild boar was shot near the Coast to Coast trail a few centuries ago; add to that the extinction of bear and wolf as well as, far more recently, a number of other species lost or severely depleted over the decades and you get an idea of just how much of an influence man has over the land, and how that influence is all too often used negatively.

There is good news, however. In these enlightened times when environmental issues are quite rightly given more precedence, many endangered species, such as the otter, have increased in number thanks to the active work of voluntary conservation bodies. There are other reasons to be optimistic. The environment is no longer the least important issue in party politics and this reflects the opinions of everyday people who are concerned about issues such as conservation on both a global and local scale.

GOVERNMENT AGENCIES AND SCHEMES

Since 2006, the Countryside Agency, English Nature and the environment section of the Rural Development Service (RDS) have merged formally into a new agency, **Natural England**. A **Commission for Rural Communities** was also established; its role is to act as an independent adviser and watchdog for people living and working in rural areas of England, particularly for communities suffering economic disadvantage.

Natural England
Natural England is the single body responsible for identifying, establishing and managing: National Parks, Areas of Outstanding Natural Beauty (both previously managed by the Countryside Agency), National Nature Reserves, Sites of Special Scientific Interest, and Special Areas of Conservation (all previously managed by English Nature).

The highest level of landscape protection is the designation of land as a **National Park** which recognizes the national importance of an area in terms of landscape, biodiversity and as a recreational resource. At the time of writing there were eight national parks in England (plus the Norfolk and Suffolk Broads which enjoy comparable status and protection). Three of these are bisected by the Coast to Coast path (Lake District, Yorkshire Dales and North York Moors national parks). This designation does not signify national ownership and these are not uninhabited wildernesses, making conservation a knife-edged balance between protecting the environment and the rights and livelihoods of those living in the parks.

The second level of protection is **Area of Outstanding Natural Beauty** (AONB), of which there are 36 in England covering some 15% of the country. The only AONB passed on the Coast to Coast trail covers the North Pennines including Nine Standards Rigg. Their primary objective is conservation of the natural beauty of a landscape. As there is no statutory administrative framework for their management, this is the responsibility of the local authority within whose boundaries they fall.

Other levels of protection are National Nature Reserves and Sites of Special Scientific Interest. **National Nature Reserves** (NNRs), of which there are 218 (including Smardale in Cumbria), are places where the priority is protection of

---

❏ **Government agencies and other bodies**

● **Department for Environment, Food and Rural Affairs** (☎ 020 7238 6000, 🖳 www .defra.gov.uk; Nobel House, 17 Smith Sq, London SW1P 3JR) Government ministry responsible for sustainable development in the countryside.

● **Natural England** (☎ 0114 241 89201; 🖳 www.naturalengland.org.uk; East Parade, Sheffield, S1 2ET) See p55.

● **Commission for Rural Communities** (☎ 01242 521381, 🖳 www.ruralcommu nities.gov.uk, John Dower House, Crescent Place, Cheltenham GL50 3RA) See p55.

● **Council for Nature Conservation and the Countryside** (🖳 www.cncc.gov.uk) Advises the government on issues relating to nature conservation and protection of the countryside, particularly in relation to national parks, AONBs, nature reserves and SACs.

● **English Heritage** (☎ 0870 333 1181, 🖳 www.english-heritage.org.uk; PO Box 569, Swindon, SN2 2YP) Organization whose central aim is to make sure that the historic environment of England is properly maintained. It is officially known as the Historic Buildings and Monuments Commission for England.

● **Forestry Commission** (☎ 0131 334 0303, 🖳 www.forestry.gov.uk; 231 Corstophine Rd, Edinburgh EH12 7AT) Government department for establishing and managing forests for a variety of uses.

● **National Association of Areas of Outstanding Natural Beauty** (🖳 www.aonb .org.uk); for further information on the North Pennines AONB visit 🖳 www.north pennines.org.uk.

● **Lake District National Park Authority** (🖳 www.lake-district.gov.uk); **Yorkshire Dales National Park Authority** (🖳 www.yorkshiredales.org.uk); **North York Moors National Park Authority** (☎ 01439 770657; 🖳 www.moors.uk.net). The government authorities charged with managing the respective areas. None of the these has much in the way of specific Coast to Coast trail information on their websites, though they might be worth contacting to find out the latest developments to the path.

THE ENVIRONMENT & NATURE

the wildlife habitats and geological formations. They are either owned or managed by Natural England or by approved organizations such as wildlife trusts. **Local Nature Reserves** (LNRs) are places with wildlife or geological features that are of special interest to local inhabitants; there are nine in Cumbria and 18 in North Yorkshire.

Sites of Special Scientific Interest (SSSIs) range in size from little pockets protecting wild flower meadows, important nesting sites or special geological features, to vast swathes of upland, moorland and wetland. SSSIs, of which there are over 4000 in England, are a particularly important designation as they have some legal standing. They are managed in partnership with the owners and occupiers of the land who must give written notice before initiating any operations likely to damage the site and who cannot proceed without consent from Natural England. Many SSSIs are also either a NNR or a LNR.

Special Area of Conservation (SAC) is an international designation which came into being as a result of the 1992 Earth Summit in Rio de Janeiro, Brazil. This European-wide network of sites is designed to promote the conservation of habitats, wild animals and plants, both on land and at sea. At the time of writing 121 land sites in England had been designated as SACs. Every land SAC is also an SSSI.

Environmental Stewardship Scheme

In March 2005 the Environmental Stewardship Scheme (ESS) replaced the Environmentally Sensitive Area (ESA) scheme and the Countryside Stewardship Scheme (CSS). The ESS is a voluntary scheme that encourages farmers to adopt low-impact agricultural practices by being offered financial incentives. Farmers enter into a five-year management agreement with the **Department for Environment, Food and Rural Affairs** (DEFRA). The stricter the management controls are the higher the payments. This, in its own small way, was a step closer to seeing all land as worthy of protection so that it can be left in a decent state for future generations. The effect was that farmers were encouraged to set aside land ie not use it. However, the policy is now under review because the reality is that wheat and other prices are soaring and there is an increasing need to make the land as productive as possible.

CAMPAIGNING AND CONSERVATION ORGANIZATIONS

These voluntary organizations started the conservation movement in the mid-19th century and are still at the forefront of developments. Independent of government but reliant on public support, they can concentrate their resources either on acquiring land which can then be managed purely for conservation purposes, or on influencing political decision-makers by lobbying and campaigning.

Managers and owners of land include well-known bodies such as the RSPB, the NT and the CPRE. The **Royal Society for the Protection of Birds** (RSPB), has over 150 nature reserves and more than a million members. There are two reserves on the Coast to Coast path, both of great significance. St Bees Head, at the very start of the trail, is the largest seabird colony in north-west England,

---

❏ **Campaigning and conservation organizations – contact details**
● **Royal Society for the Protection of Birds** (RSPB; ☎ 01767 680551, 🖳 www.rs
pb.org.uk; The Lodge, Potton Rd, Sandy, Bedfordshire SG19 2DL) See p57.
● **National Trust** (NT; ☎ 0870 458 4000, 🖳 www.nationaltrust.org.uk; PO Box 39,
Warrington WA5 7WD) See below.
● **Campaign to Protect Rural England** (CPRE; ☎ 020 7981 2800, 🖳 www.cp
re.org.uk; 128 Southwark St, London SE1 0SW) See below.
● The umbrella organization for the 47 wildlife trusts in the UK is **The Wildlife
Trusts** (☎ 0870 036 7711, 🖳 www.wildlifetrusts.org), The Kiln, Waterside, Mather
Rd, Newark, Nottinghamshire, NG24 1WT. Two relevant to the Coast to Coast path
are **Cumbria Wildlife Trust** (☎ 01539 816300, 🖳 www.wildlifetrust.org.uk/cumbria)
and **Yorkshire Wildlife Trust** (🖳 www.yorkshire-wildlife-trust.org.uk).
● **Woodland Trust** (☎ 01476 581111, 🖳 www.woodland-trust.org.uk; Autumn Park,
Dysart Rd, Grantham, Lincs NG31 6LL) Restores woodland throughout Britain for
its amenity, wildlife and landscape value.
● **World Wide Fund for Nature** (WWF) (☎ 01483 426444, 🖳 www.wwf.org.uk;
Panda House, Weyside Park, Godalming, Surrey GU7 1XR) One of the world's
largest conservation organizations.

---

home in spring and summer to guillemots, kittiwakes, fulmars and razorbills;
while Haweswater, at the eastern end of the Lake District, is England's only
golden eagle territory.

The **National Trust** (NT) is a charity with 3.4 million members which aims
to protect, through ownership, threatened coastline, countryside, historic houses, castles and gardens, and archaeological remains for everybody to enjoy. On
the Coast to Coast trail, the NT's properties are concentrated in the Lakes where
they look after such beauty spots as Ennerdale, supposedly England's wildest
valley; parts of Ullswater; and 4925 hectares (12,170 acres) of Grasmere and
Great Langdale including, curiously, the bed of Grasmere Lake.

The **Campaign to Protect Rural England** (CPRE) exists to promote the
beauty and diversity of rural England by encouraging the sustainable use of land
and other natural resources in both town and country.

A huge increase in public interest and support of these and many other con-
servation/campaigning groups since the 1980s indicates that people are more
conscious of environmental issues and believe that it cannot be left to our political representatives to take care of them for us without our voice. We are becoming the most powerful lobbying group of all, an informed electorate.

BEYOND CONSERVATION

Pressures on the countryside grow year on year. Western society, whether directly or indirectly, makes constant demands for more oil, more roads, more houses, more cars. At the same time awareness of environmental issues increases and
the knowledge that our unsustainable approach to life cannot continue. Some
governments appear more willing to adopt sustainable ideals, others less so.

THE ENVIRONMENT & NATURE

Yet even the most environmentally positive of governments are some way off perfect. It's all very positive to classify parts of the countryside as national parks and Areas of Outstanding Natural Beauty but it will be of little use if we continue to pollute the wider environment, the seas and skies. For a brighter future we need to adopt that sustainable approach to life. It would not be difficult and the rewards would be great.

The individual can play his or her part. Walkers in particular appreciate the value of wild areas and should take this attitude back home with them. This is not just about recycling the odd green bottle or two and walking to the corner shop rather than driving, but about lobbying for more environmentally sensitive policies in local and national government.

The first step to a sustainable way of living is in appreciating and respecting this beautiful, complex world we live in and realizing that every one of us plays an important role within the great web. The natural world is not a separate entity. We are all part of it and should strive to safeguard it rather than work against it. So many of us live in a world that does seem far removed from the real world, cocooned in centrally heated houses and upholstered cars. Rediscovering our place within the natural world is both uplifting on a personal level and important regarding our outlook and approach to life.

Flora and fauna

The beauty of walking from one side of England to the other is that on the way you pass through just about every kind of habitat this country has to offer. From woodland and grassland to heathland, bog and beach, the variety of habitats is surpassed only by the number of species of flower, tree and animal that each supports.

The following is not in any way a comprehensive guide – if it were, you would not have room for anything else in your rucksack – but merely a brief guide to the more commonly seen flora and fauna of the trail, together with some of the rarer and more spectacular species.

MAMMALS

The Coast to Coast path is alive with all manner of native species and the wide variety of habitats encountered on the way means that the wildlife is varied too. Unfortunately, most of these creatures are shy and many are nocturnal, and walkers can consider themselves extremely lucky if during their trek they see more than three or four species.

One creature that you will see everywhere along the walk, from the cliffs at St Bees to the fields outside Robin Hood's Bay, is the **rabbit** (*Oryctolagus cuniculus*). Timid by nature, most of the time you'll have to make do with nothing more than a brief and distant glimpse of their white tails as they stampede for the nearest warren at the first sound of your footfall. Because they are so numerous, however, the laws of probability dictate that you will at some stage get close enough to observe them without being spotted; trying to take a decent photo of one of them, however, is a different matter.

If you're lucky you may also come across **hares**, often mistaken for rabbits but much larger, more elongated and with longer back legs and ears.

Rabbits used to form one of the main elements in the diet of the **fox** (*Vulpes vulpes*), one of the more adaptable of Britain's native species. Famous as the scourge of chicken coops, their reputation as indiscriminate killers is actually unjustified: though they will if left undisturbed kill all the chickens in a coop in what appears to be a mindless and frenzied attack, foxes will actually eat all their victims, carrying off and storing the carcasses in underground burrows for them and their families to eat at a later date. These days, however, you are far more likely to see foxes in towns, where they survive mostly on the scraps and leftovers of the human population, rather than in the country. While generally considered nocturnal, it's not unusual to encounter a fox during the day too, often lounging in the sun near its den.

One creature that is strictly nocturnal, however, is the **bat**, of which there are 14 species in Britain, all protected by law. Your best chance of spotting one is just after dusk while there's still enough light in the sky to make out their flitting forms as they fly along hedgerows, over rivers and streams and around street lamps in their quest for moths and insects. The most common species in Britain is the pipistrelle (*Pipistrellus pipistrellus*).

CAUTION
Red squirrels
crossing

The Lakes offer one of the few chances in England to see the rare **red squirrel** (*Sciurus vulgaris*). While elsewhere in the country these small, tufty-eared natives have been usurped by their larger cousins from North America, the **grey squirrel** (*Sciurus carolinensis*), in the Lakes the red squirrel maintains a precarious foothold. In Patterdale a count of the local red squirrel population is organized annually; contact the Youth Hostel (see p116) there for details. A number also hang around Ennerdale YH (see p84) in High Gillerthwaite.

Patterdale also offers walkers on the Coast to Coast their best chance of seeing the **badger** (*Meles meles*). Relatively common throughout the British Isles, these nocturnal mammals with their distinctive black-and-white-striped muzzle are sociable animals that live in large underground burrows called setts, appearing after sunset to root for worms and slugs.

One creature which you almost certainly won't encounter, though they are said to exist in the Lakes, is the **pine marten** (*martes martes*). Extremely rare in England since being virtually wiped out during the 19th century for their pelts and their reputation as vermin, there are said to be a few in the valley of Ennerdale.

In addition to the above, keep a look out for other fairly common but little-seen species such as the carnivorous **stoat** (*Mustela erminea*), its smaller cousin the **weasel** (*Mustela nivalis*), the **hedgehog** (*Erinaceus europaeus*) – these days, alas, most commonly seen as roadkill – and a number of species of **voles**, **mice** and **shrews**.

One of Britain's rarest creatures, the **otter** (*Lutra lutra*), is enjoying something of a renaissance thanks to concerted conservation efforts. Though more common in the south-west, otters are still present in the north of England. At home both in salt and freshwater, they are a good indicator of a healthy unpolluted environment. Don't come to the north expecting otter sightings every day. If you see one at all you should consider yourself *extremely* fortunate, for they remain rare and very elusive. There are said to be some in Swaledale.

A surprisingly large number of trekkers encounter deer on their walk. Mostly this will be the **roe deer** (*Capreolus capreolus*), a small native species that likes to inhabit woodland, though some can also be seen grazing in fields. As with most creatures, your best chance of seeing one is very early in the morning, with sightings particularly common in Ennerdale, the upper end of Swaledale and the Vale of Mowbray.

Britain's largest native land mammal, the **red deer** (*Cervus elaphus*), is rarely seen on the walk though it does exist in small pockets around the Lakes.

REPTILES

The **adder** is the only common snake in the north of England, and the only poisonous one of the three species in Britain. They pose very little risk to walkers – indeed, you should consider yourself extremely fortunate to see one, providing you're a safe distance away. They only bite when provoked, preferring to hide instead. The venom is designed to kill small mammals such as mice, voles and shrews, so deaths in humans are very rare, but a bite can be extremely unpleasant and occasionally dangerous to children or the elderly. You are most likely to encounter them in spring when they come out of hibernation and during the summer when pregnant females warm themselves in the sun. They are easily identified by the striking zigzag pattern on their back. Should you be lucky enough to encounter one, enjoy it but leave it undisturbed.

BIRDS

The Coast to Coast is without doubt an ornithologist's dream. The seaside cliffs, woods, moorland and hedgerows encountered on the path provide homes for a wealth of different species including the golden eagle, Britain's rarest and most majestic bird, and a flock of parrots.

The red sandstone cliffs above St Bees (see p73) have been owned by the RSPB since 1973 and dotted along the trail are viewpoints where you can gaze down at the nesting seabirds. This is in fact the only colony of cliff-nesting seabirds in north-west England to which birds return year after year to lay their eggs and hatch chicks.

THE ENVIRONMENT & NATURE

GUILLEMOT
L: 450MM/18"

The most common of the seabirds is the **guillemot** (*Uria aalge*), with an estimated minimum of 5000 crowding onto the cliff's open ledges, including the rare **black guillemot** (*Cepphus grylle*); indeed, the cliffs are believed to be the only place where this rare sub-species nests in England.

Razorbills (*Alca torda*), a close relative of the guillemot, are also present, as are **puffins** (*Fratercula arctica*), though their numbers seldom rise above two dozen or so.

Kittiwakes (*Rissa tridactyla*), **fulmars** (*Fulmarus glacialis*) and **gulls** (family *Larus*) are also present, while a little further inland **ravens** (*Corvus corax*) and **peregrine falcons** (*Falco peregrinus*) nest.

Away from the coast, the rarest species in England is the **golden eagle** *(Aquila chrysaetos)*, a pair of which had set up an eyrie near the Coast to Coast trail, on the way down to Haweswater Reservoir from Kidsty Pike (see p119). Enthusiastic twitchers could be seen peering up the valley most hours of the day, and there was also a 24hr guard keeping watch to protect it from the predations of the egg collectors. This was the only pair of breeding golden eagles in

BLACK GUILLEMOT
L: 350MM/13.5"

England. However, since the female has disappeared it is hoped another one can be attracted down from Scotland for the lone male.

The first wild **ospreys** (*Pandion haliaetus*) to breed in England for centuries are also present in the Lakes, though not near the trail.

Other birds of prey include **kestrel** (*Falco tinnunculus*), **buzzard** (*Buteo buteo*), **barn owl** (*Tyto alba*) and **short-eared owl** (*Asio flammeus*).

One of the most common birds seen on the path, particularly in the latter half of the walk, is the **pheasant** (*Phasianus colchicus*). Ubiquitous on the moors, the male is distinctive thanks to his beautiful long, barred

GOLDEN EAGLE
L: 910MM/36"

BLACK GROUSE
L: 580MM/23"

THE ENVIRONMENT & NATURE

tail feathers, brown body and glossy green-black head with red head-sides, while the female is a dull brown. Another way to distinguish them is by the distinctive strangulated hacking sound they make together with the loud flapping of wings as they fly off.

Another reasonably common sight on the moors of Yorkshire is the **lapwing** (*Vanellus vanellus*), also known as the peewit. Black and white with iridescent green upper parts and approximately the size of a pigeon or tern, the lapwing's most distinctive characteristic is the male's tumbling, diving swooping flight pattern when disturbed, believed to be either a display to attract a female or an attempt to distract predators from its nest, which is built on the ground.

LAPWING/PEEWIT
L: 320MM/12.5"

Less common but still seen by most walkers is the **curlew** (*Numenius arquata*), another bird that, like the lapwing, is associated with coastal and open fields, moors and bogs. With feathers uniformly streaked grey and brown, the easiest way to identify this bird is by its thin elongated, downward curling beak.

Both the lapwing and the curlew are actually wading birds that nest on the moors in the spring, but which winter by the coast.

Other birds that make their nest on open moorland and in fields include the **redshank** (*Tringa totanus*), **golden plover** (*Pluvialis apricaria*), **snipe** (*Gallinago gallinago*), **dunlin** (*Calidris alpina*) and **ring ouzel** (*Turdus torquatus*).

CURLEW
L: 600MM/24"

Somewhat ironically, these birds have benefited from the careful management of the moors which is mainly done to protect the populations of game birds such as **black grouse** (*Tetrao tetrix*).

In the deciduous woodland areas on the trail, look out for **treecreepers** (*Certhia familiaris*), **tits** (family *Paridae*, including blue, coal and great), **nuthatches** (*Sitta europaea*), **pied flycatchers** (*Ficedula hypoleuca*) and **redstarts** (*Phoenicurus phoenicurus*), while in the conifers watch out for **crossbills** (*Loxia curvirostra*) and **siskins** (*Carduelis spinus*).

Finally, for something completely different, in Kirkby Stephen there are ten or so '**homing parrots**': macaws let out by their owner to fly around the town during the day, before returning home each night.

THE ENVIRONMENT & NATURE

FLOWERS

Spring is the time to come and see the spectacular displays of colour on the Coast
to Coast path. Alternatively, arrive in August and you'll see the heathers carpet-
ing the moors in a blaze of purple flowers.

The coastal meadows

The coastline is a harsh environment subjected to strong, salt-laced winds. One
plant that does survive in such conditions, and which will probably be the first
you'll encounter on the path, is **gorse** (*Ulex europeous*) with its sharp-thorned
bright yellow, heavily perfumed flowers. Accompanying it are such cliff-top
specialists as the pink-flowering **thrift** (*Armeria maritima*) and white **sea campion** (*Silene maritima*) and **fennel** (*Foeniculum vulgare*), a member of the carrot family which grows to over a metre high.

Woodland and hedgerows

From March to May **bluebells** (*Hyacinthoides non-scripta*) proliferate in the
woods along the Coast to Coast, providing a wonderful spectacle. Littlebeck
(see p221) and Clain (see p198) woods are particularly notable for these displays. The white **wood anemone** (*Anemone nemorosa*) and the yellow **primrose** (*Primula vulgaris*) also flower early in spring. **Red campion** (*Silene
dioica*), which flowers from late April, can be found in hedgebanks along with
rosebay willowherb (*Epilobium augustifolium*) which also has the name fire-
weed due to its habit of colonizing burnt areas.

In scrubland and on woodland edges you'll find **bramble** (*Rubus fruticosus*),
a common vigorous shrub, responsible for many a ripped jacket thanks to its sharp
thorns and prickles. **Blackberry** fruits ripen from late summer into autumn. Fairly
common in scrubland and on woodland edges is the **dog rose** (*Rosa canina*)
which has a large pink flower, the fruits of which are used to make rose-hip syrup.

Other flowering plants common in wooded areas and in hedgerows include
the tall **foxglove** (*Digitalis purpurea*) with its trumpet-like flowers, **forget-me-
not** (*Myosotis arvensis*) with tiny, delicate blue flowers and **cow parsley**
(*Anthriscus sylvestris*), a tall member of the carrot family with a large globe of
white flowers which often covers roadside verges and hedgebanks.

Heathland and scrubland

There are three species of heather. The most dominant one is **ling** (*Calluna vulgaris*), with tiny flowers on delicate upright stems. The other two species are
bell heather (*Erica cinera*), with deep purple bell-shaped flowers, and **cross-
leaved heath** (*Erica tetralix*) with similarly shaped flowers of a lighter pink,
almost white colour. Cross-leaved heath prefers wet and boggy ground. As a
result, it usually grows away from bell heather which prefers well-drained soils.

Heather is an incredibly versatile plant which is put to many uses. It provides fodder for livestock, fuel for fires, an orange dye and material for bedding,
thatching, basketwork and brooms. It is still sometimes used in place of hops to
flavour beer, and the flower heads can be brewed to make good tea. It is also

THE ENVIRONMENT & NATURE

Spear Thistle
Cirsium vulgare

Common Knapweed
Centaurea nigra

Sea Campion
Silene maritima

Bell Heather
Erica cinerea

Heather (Ling)
Calluna vulgaris

Violet
Viola riviniana

Devil's-bit Scabious
Succisa pratensis

Harebell
Campanula rotundifolia

Bluebell
Endymion non-scriptus

Marsh Marigold (Kingcup)
Caltha palustris

Meadow Buttercup
Ranunculis acris

Cowslip
Primula veris

Tormentil
Potentilla erecta

Birdsfoot-trefoil
Lotus corniculatus

Ox-eye Daisy
Leucanthemum vulgare

Common Ragwort
Senecio jacobaea

Primrose
Primula vulgaris

Dandelion
Taraxacum officinale

Gorse
Ulex europaeus

Rowan tree
Sorbus aucuparia

Rosebay Willowherb
Epilobium angustifolium

Lousewort
Pedicularis sylvatica

Herb-Robert
Geranium robertianum

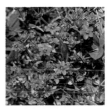

Scarlet Pimpernel
Anagallis arvensis

Hemp-nettle
Galeopsis speciosa

Ransoms (Wild Garlic)
Allium ursinum

Yarrow
Achillea millefolium

Foxglove
Digitalis purpurea

Meadow Cranesbill
Geranium pratense

Water Avens
Geum rivale

Common Vetch
Vicia sativa

Heartsease (Wild Pansy)
Viola tricolor

Germander Speedwell
Veronica chamaedrys

Early Purple Orchid
Orchis mascula

Thrift (Sea Pink)
Armeria maritima

Red Campion
Silene dioica

incredibly hardy and thrives on the denuded hills, preventing other species from flourishing. Indeed, at times, highland cattle are brought to certain areas of the moors to graze on the heather, allowing other species a chance to grow.

Not a flower but worthy of mention is the less attractive species, **bracken** (*Pteridium aquilinum*), a vigorous non-native fern that has invaded many heathland areas to the detriment of native species.

Grassland

There is much overlap between the hedge/woodland-edge habitat and that of pastures and meadows. You will come across **common birdsfoot-trefoil** (*Lotus corniculatus*), **Germander speedwell** (*Veronica chamaedrys*), **tufted** and **bush vetch** (*Vicia cracca* and *V. sepium*) and **meadow vetchling** (*Lathyrus pratensis*) in both.

Often the only species you will see in heavily grazed pastures are the most resilient. Of the thistles, the three most common species are **creeping thistle**, **spear thistle** and **marsh thistle** (*Cirsium arvense, C. vulgare* and *C. palustre*). Among them you may find **common ragwort** (*Senecio jacobaea*), **yarrow** (*Achillea millefolium*), **sheep's** and **common sorrel** (*Rumex acetosella* and *R. acetosa*), and **white** and **red clover** (*Trifolium repens* and *T. pratense*).

Other widespread grassland species include **harebell** (*Campanula rotundifolia*), delicate yellow **tormentil** (*Potentilla erecta*) which will often spread up onto the lower slopes of mountains along with **devil's-bit scablous** (*Succisa pratensis*). Also keep an eye out for orchids such as the **fragrant orchid** (*Gymnadenia conopsea*) and **early purple orchid** (*Orchis mascula*).

TREES

It seems incredible that, before man and his axe got to work, most of the bleak, empty moors and windswept Lakeland fells were actually covered by trees. These days, the biggest and most ubiquitous areas of tree cover are the ghastly pine plantations of Ennerdale and other places in the Lakes. But the overgrazing of land by sheep and, to a lesser extent, deer, which eat the young shoots of trees, has ensured that the ancient forests have never returned. Yet there are still small patches of indigenous woodland on the Coast to Coast path. Perhaps the most interesting are the Atlantic Oakwoods at Borrowdale, including Johnny's Wood (see p96) on the way to Longthwaite. The woods are owned and cared for by the National Trust and are actually correctly known as temperate rainforest, the moist Atlantic climate creating a landscape of boulders covered by liverworts and ferns, under **oaks** (*Quercus petraea*) dripping in moss and lichen.

There are other areas of woodland in the Lakes, including Easedale Woods on the way into Grasmere and Glenamara Park, just before Patterdale, which has some truly spectacular mature trees. One interesting thing about oak trees is that they support

OAK LEAVES SHOWING GALLS

THE ENVIRONMENT & NATURE

HAZEL (WITH FLOWERS)

ASH (WITH SEEDS)

more kinds of insects than any other tree in Britain and some of these insects affect the oak in interesting ways. The eggs of the gall-fly, for example, cause growths on the leaves, known, appropriately enough, as galls. Each of these contains a single insect. Other kinds of gall-flies lay eggs in stalks or flowers, leading to flower galls – growths the size of currants.

Oak woodland is a diverse habitat and not exclusively made up of oak. Other trees that flourish in oak woodland include **downy birch** (*Betula pubescens*), its relative the **silver birch** (*Betula pendula*), **holly** (*Ilex aquifolium*), and **hazel** (*Corylus avellana*) which has traditionally been used for coppicing (where small trees are grown for periodic cutting). Further east there are some examples of limestone woodland. **Ash** (*Fraxinus excelsior*) and oak dominate, along with **wych elm** (*Ulmus glabra*), **sycamore** (*Acer*) and **yew** (*Taxus*).

The **hawthorn** (*Crataegus monogyna*) also grows on the path, usually in isolated pockets on pasture. These species are known as pioneer species and play a vital role in the ecosystem by improving the soil. It is these pioneers, particularly the **rowan** (*Sorbus aucuparia*) and hawthorn, that you will see growing all alone on inaccessible crags and ravines. Without interference from man, these pioneers would eventually be succeeded by longer-living species such as the oak. In wet, marshy areas and along rivers and streams you are more likely to find **alder** (*Alnus glutinosa*).

ALDER (WITH FLOWERS)

Using the guide

The trail guide has been described from west to east and divided into 13 stages. Though each of these roughly corresponds to a day's walk, do not assume that this is the only way to structure the trek. There are so many places to stay en route that – except for a couple of stretches where there is no accommodation – you can pretty much divide up the walk whichever way you want. This is even more true if you have your own camping gear, in which case you can pitch your tent virtually anywhere, as long, of course, as you first have permission from the landowner.

On pp32-3 are tables to help you plan an itinerary. To provide further help, practical information is presented on the trail maps, including walking times, places to stay, camp and eat, as well as shops for supplies. Further service details are given in the text under the entry for each settlement.

TRAIL MAPS

Scale and walking times

The trail maps are to a scale of 1:20,000 (1cm = 200m; $3^1/_8$ inches = one mile). Walking times are given along the side of each map; the arrow shows the direction to which the time refers. Black triangles indicate the points between which the times have been taken. These times are merely a tool to help you plan and are not there to judge your walking ability.

Hopefully, after a couple of days you'll know how fast you walk compared with the time bars and can plan your days more accurately as a result. **See note on walking times in the box on p73**.

Up or down?

The trail is shown as a dashed line. An arrow across the trail indicates the slope; two arrows show that it is steep. Note that the arrow points towards the higher part of the trail. If, for example, you are walking from A (at 80m) to B (at 200m) and the trail between the two is short and steep, it would be shown thus: A- - - - >>- - - -B. Reversed arrow heads indicate a downward gradient.

Accommodation

Accommodation marked on the map is either on or within easy reach of the path. Many B&B proprietors whose accommodation is a mile or two off the trail will offer to collect walkers from the nearest point on the trail and deliver them back again next morning. This is particularly true of the B&Bs at Great Broughton and Urra, where walkers are collected at Clay Bank Top (see p204).

❏ Why do I keep getting lost?

The Coast to Coast path is widely considered to be the hardest of Britain's long-distance trails to follow. Much of the reason for this can be ascribed to the fact that it is not an official National Trail, and thus has not had the money spent on it for signage, track maintenance etc that other long-distance paths enjoy. But there are other reasons. For one thing, the trail passes through the Lake District where signposts are virtually non-existent anyway, supposedly, so it's said, because the park authorities prefer to keep the land as wild and 'untamed' as possible and don't want to plant signposts everywhere. Once you've successfully crossed the Lakes you then have to negotiate the section across the Pennines, another wilderness area that is rarely blemished by signposts and where people frequently lose the trail.

Of course it's not all bad news. After Richmond, somebody has scribbled 'Coast 2 Coast' in black marker pen on the North Yorkshire County Council's yellow waymark discs, while a little further east you join the Cleveland Way which is well signposted. The paths on the North Yorkshire Moors, too, are surprisingly easy to follow, with many paths paved with flagstones. Elsewhere on the trail there are wooden Coast to Coast signposts clearly pointing the way.

How to keep to the trail: a few tips

Taking a few precautions will help you to keep to the trail. You may, for example, like to invest in a few **OS maps** (see p37) at least for those parts, such as the Lake District, where people often lose the trail. Many people, however, have used just the book to find their way. A **compass** is, of course, also vital. You may wish to invest in a **GPS** too.

Finally, and we can't emphasize this enough, it is imperative that you follow the instructions on our maps closely. Whilst walking the trail for this latest edition, several people came up to me to complain that they had lost their way. Yet on all but one occasion, the reason they got lost was because they had been distracted by the views or their companions and didn't follow the instructions on the map closely enough. (On the other occasion, the walker had mistakenly bought the first edition of this book, rather than the second, and thus some of the instructions were a little dated. Do make sure, therefore, that the edition of this book you have is the latest one available.)

To try to counter this, in places where people frequently get lost – at the top of Greenup Gill or Loft Beck, for example, or crossing the Pennines – we have put special instructions on the maps (and highlighted them with the word 'Attention') to emphasize their importance in helping you find your way. Read these carefully. That's not to say that you won't get lost elsewhere, of course, but we think in most places it's relatively easy to rejoin the path again, and apart from a moment or two of uncertainty and panic when you realise you've taken the wrong route, you shouldn't suffer too much as a result of leaving the trail.

Of course it is still possible to lose your way: bad weather, a loss of concentration or changes to the route since this book was published can all lead you into taking the wrong path. Even though we try to describe the route as accurately as possible, sometimes there are a lack of landmarks or other details to help you find the way. And sometimes there's a path that's just more obvious and inviting than the correct one, leading many to stray from the trail. But pay close attention to the advice given in this book, use your OS map and compass or GPS as back up, and hopefully your walk will be relatively trouble-free. And you never know, one day the Wainwright Society (🖳 www .wainwright.org.uk) may get its way and the Coast to Coast will become a National Trail, with all the attendant signs and waymarks that this entails. We can but hope.

Details of each place are given in the accompanying text. The number of rooms of each type is given at the beginning of each entry, ie S=Single, T=Twin room, D=Double room, F=Family room (sleeps at least three people). The rates are also given; these are *per person* per night prices. As an example: £20/15 sgl/dbl means the rate is £20 for a single room, £15 per person in a double. Unless otherwise specified, the rates are for the summer high season. DB&B means dinner, bed and breakfast.

Other features

Features are marked on the map when they are pertinent to navigation. In order to avoid cluttering the maps and make them unusable, not all features have been marked each time they occur.

The route guide

ST BEES see Map p71

Nestling at the mouth of Pow Beck ('beck' is a local term meaning stream), St Bees is the perfect starting point for a long-distance walk: attractive, friendly and compact, with enough facilities to set you up for the trail yet nothing so captivating that you'll want to delay the start of your walk.

The village is definitely agricultural in character: many of the buildings along the main street were originally farm buildings dating back to the 17th century and there's even an ancient **pinfold** on Outrigg. This construction – a simple, circular, stone-walled enclosure – was used to house stray sheep and cattle that had been recovered

from the surrounding hills. The livestock would remain in the pinfold until the farmer could afford to pay a fine to retrieve them.

The town's main sight is its red sandstone **Priory Church**, once part of a thriving 12th-century Benedictine priory dedicated to the saints Bega and Mary. Original Norman features include the impressively elaborate Great West Door and, standing opposite, the curious carved Dragon Stone, a door lintel from the 12th century.

The church is believed to stand on a site that had been holy to Christians for centuries prior to the monastery's foundation and has seen over eight hundred years of unbroken worship since then. Not even

---

❏ **Who was St Bees?**

St Bees is actually a corruption of St Bega, an Irish princess who fled her native country sometime between the 6th and 9th centuries to avoid an arranged marriage with a Norwegian prince.

Landing on England's north-west coast, so the story goes, St Bega lived as a hermit and became renowned for the good deeds she carried out for the locals. And that's about it really, or at least it would be, if it wasn't for the legends that have grown up over the centuries. In the most famous of these, St Bega approaches the local landlord, Lord Egremont, for some land for a convent she wished to found.

Egremont, clearly not the most generous of men, promised St Bega all the land covered by snow the next day; which, seeing as the next day happened to be midsummer's day, was not as generous an offer as it first appeared. Miraculously, however, snow did fall that day and St Bega was able to build her convent, around which the village was built.

the dissolution of the monasteries ordered by Henry VIII in 1538, which led to the closure of this and every other priory you'll come across on the Coast to Coast path, could stop the site from being used by the villagers as their main centre of worship, even though Henry's commissioners had removed the lead from the roof, and the whole building, for much of the 16th century, was left open to the elements. Restoration began in the early 17th century, with a major overhaul of the building taking place in the 19th. Thankfully, however, the architects kept much of the church's sturdy Norman character and that is its most impressive feature today.

As with quite a few of the larger churches on the route, there's a table just inside the door with various pamphlets on the history of both the church and the village, each costing only about 20p. Don't miss the glass case in the southern aisle displaying a shroud and a lock of woman's hair unearthed in the excavation of a 14th-century grave; and the graveyard to the north of the church, where you'll find the shaft of a stone cross from the 10th century (in other words, older than every other part of the church), with its Celtic decorations still visible. Incidentally, the **grammar school** across the road from the church is one of the most venerable in Cumbria, having been founded on his deathbed in 1583 by a local man, **Edmund Grindal**, who had risen to become Archbishop of Canterbury during the reign of Elizabeth I. His birthplace, on the junction of Finkle St and Cross St, is the oldest surviving house in St Bees.

There's a statue of **St Bega** (see box p69) just to the west of the railway station on Station Rd.

Services

There's a well-stocked **post office** and **shop** (Mon-Fri 6.30am-9pm, Sat 9am-9pm, Sun 7.30am-8pm) with a decent selection of groceries – including hot pies and pasties – as well as a few Coast to Coast maps, T-shirts and souvenirs. It is also the home of the local Link **cash machine** (£1.50 fee); there's only one other (at Ennerdale Bridge)

before Grasmere. There is also a **tourist information point** by the train station but it has limited information; a better bet is the St Bees website (🖳 www.stbees.org.uk).

One thing the town lacks is a trekking or camping shop, so make sure you have everything you need until at least Seatoller (the first place with any sort of trekking outlet) or, preferably, Grasmere, where there are several trekking/camping shops.

Where to stay

On the front behind the RNLI lifeboat station is **Seacote Caravan Site** (Map 1, p74; ☎ 01946 822777, 🖳 www.seacote.com) where you can **camp** for an astronomical £8-13 (Feb-Nov), though a cheaper and more pleasant option (£3.50) is available in the back garden of **Stonehouse Farm** (☎ 01946 822224, 🖳 www.stonehousefarm .net, 133 Main St; 1S/4D/1T/3F), where you can fall asleep to the hooting of the barn owl that's taken up residence in the farm's derelict barn. A long-established and reliable B&B, Stonehouse is situated just 30 metres from the station and is one of only two working farms within St Bees (the other is **Town Head** at the top of the hill beyond Fairladies). Its en suite rooms with TV are located in its Georgian farmhouse, while the dairy next door has been converted into a spacious family suite. On the other side of the farmhouse is an even older cottage (dating back to 1660) where the character of the building with its impressive exposed beams more than compensates for the lack of en suite bathrooms for the double and twin room. Finally, long-term parking (£2 per day) is also available. Rates are £30/25 sgl/dbl; children are charged according to age, ie a three-year-old pays £3, a 15-year-old £15. They now take credit cards, too.

Unfortunately, one of the most charming accommodation options in town, the 17th-century **Queen's Hotel** (4S/8D/3T), Main St, was up for sale at the time of writing and its future was uncertain. However, there are a number of other places to stay:

Manor House Hotel (☎ 01946 822425, 🖳 manorhousemaz@aol.com, Main St; 1S/ 2D/2T/2F) is perhaps the most impressive-

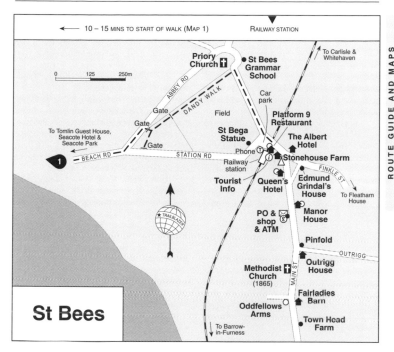

← 10 – 15 MINS TO START OF WALK (MAP 1)   RAILWAY STATION

To Carlisle & Whitehaven

Priory Church

St Bees Grammar School

Car park

ABBEY RD

DANDY WALK

Gate
Gate
Gate

Field

St Bega Statue

Platform 9 Restaurant

The Albert Hotel

To Tomlin Guest House, Seacote Hotel & Seacote Park

Phone

Stonehouse Farm

BEACH RD   STATION RD

Railway station

FINKLE ST

Tourist Info

Queen's Hotel

Edmund Grindal's House

To Fleatham House

TRAILBLAZER

PO & shop & ATM

Manor House

Pinfold

OUTRIGG

Methodist Church (1865)

Outrigg House

MAIN ST

Fairladies Barn

Oddfellows Arms

Town Head Farm

To Barrow-in-Furness

St Bees

0   125   250m

looking hotel in St Bees and one where they actively seek walkers' custom. Rates are from £35/56 sgl/dbl per person. *Outrigg House* (☎ 01946 822348, Main St; 1S/ 1T/1T or F; shared bathroom), open mid-April to end Sep, a lovely and very good-value place charging only £20 per person and £3 for a packed lunch; it's definitely worth trying.

Albert Hotel (☎ 01946 822345, 1 Finkle St; 7S/3D/3T/2F) isn't always open but, if it is, you'll find the rooms clean and comfortable with B&B from £25 per person.

Up at the top of the road, *Fairladies Barn Guest House* (☎ 01946 822718, 🖳 www.fairladiesbarn.co.uk, Main St; 5D/4T/ 1F) is a delight; a large, restored, 17th-century sandstone barn with charming rooms, each en suite with TV, and each different. As such, it's worth looking at a few before deciding which room you wish to stay in. Or you could simply go for the most popular

room, the unusually shaped studio flat under the roof at the end of the barn. Under new, friendly and enthusiastic ownership now, they've also just installed a small bar and received their licence. Single occupancy is possible in all the rooms. Rates are £35/50 sgl/dbl.

Away from the main road, *Fleatham House* (☎ 01946 822341, 🖳 www.fleatham house.com, High House Rd; 3S/3D, all en suite) is where Tony Blair, former UK Prime Minister, stayed in an attempt to show solidarity with the north-west's tourist industry following the 2001 foot and mouth crisis. Predictably grand, it lies at the end of a steep driveway at the top of the village and charges an equally steep £55/40 sgl/dbl (midweek rates), or £65 for single occupancy of a double room.

Tomlin Guest House (Map 1, p74; ☎ 01946 822284, 🖳 id.whitehead@which .net, 1 Tomlin House, Beach Rd; 4D or T) is the closest B&B to the sea, a friendly little place just opposite the large Seacote Hotel. The only disadvantage is that it's a little way from any restaurants that are open in the evening (the Seacote excluded). Rates sgl/dbl £25/20. Off-road parking costs £1 per night, or you can hire a lock-up garage for the duration of your walk for £2.50 per night.

Seacote Hotel (Map 1 p74; ☎ 01946 822300, 🖳 www.seacotehotel.co.uk, Beach Rd; 72 rooms all en suite) is the rather imposing building by the beach car park. Rooms here are £25 per person, £35 for a single. At the time of writing it was undergoing extensive refurbishment and they were not certain when they would reopen.

Platform 9 (☎ 01946 822600, 🖳 www .platform9.co.uk; 1S/2D) has long been known as St Bees's smartest restaurant and is now also winning plaudits for its accommodation, boasting three well-equipped rooms, each named after a famous train (*Flying Scotsman* etc), plus use of the hotel computer. The single costs £47.50 and a double £65. Note prices rise at the weekends.

Where to eat
Queen's Hotel (see p71) was the most popular place in town, with decent-sized platefuls of warming food and the bar was known for its real ales (such as the Jennings Bitter) and malt whiskies. However, since it was up for sale at the time of writing things may change.

The *Oddfellows Arms* at the top of the hill is similar to what the Queen's Hotel used to be like but cheaper; the atmosphere is also more subdued, and the standard of food lower.

Providing healthy competition, *Manor House* (Tue-Sun noon-4pm, daily 6-9pm) has a huge menu including Indian and Thai takeaway. Their three-course Sunday lunch for £8.95 has been recommended, not least because children eat for free if accompanied by two paying adults. They also have the Coast to Coast bar – so how can you not have at least a quick drink here.

Elsewhere, *Platform 9 Restaurant* (see column opposite; daily noon-4.30pm, 6-11pm) is, unsurprisingly, located at the station. The high prices will probably put off most walkers who want to save their extravagant slap-up meal for the end of the trek. If you do decide to indulge early, you'll find the chef uses local ingredients where possible (including herbs and vegetables from their garden and eggs from their chickens); the stuffed loin of Cumbrian lamb will set you back £14.95.

Finally, for cream teas and sea views, call in at *Hartley's Tea Rooms* (Map 1 p74).

Transport (see also pp43-5)
For **trains** to St Bees, see p41. From St Bees to Carlisle there are 7-8/day Mon-Sat.

Stagecoach's **Bus** No 20 runs to Whitehaven (Mon-Fri, hourly 9.15am-2.15pm except 12.15pm, Sat hourly 9.15am-3.15pm).

STAGE 1: ST BEES TO ENNERDALE BRIDGE   MAPS 1-7

Introduction

There is a lot of variety in this **14-mile (22.5km, 6¼hr)** stage, beginning with a cliff-top walk along the Irish Sea and ending with a high-level view across to the Lake District fells.

Some who are lacking fitness may find this first day a bit of a struggle, particularly the final haul over Dent and into Ennerdale Bridge. If you think this may be you, and you have the time, consider stopping in Cleator or, a mile or so off the path, Egremont for the first night, before possibly continuing on the second day either to the youth hostel at High Gillerthwaite, the eccentric Black Sail, or the youth hostel at Honister Hause.

The route

The Coast to Coast path officially begins from the sea wall in St Bees which protects the village from the Irish Sea. The best way to the shore from 'downtown' St Bees is along **Dandy Walk** (see map p71), so called because the 'dandy' students from the grammar school would walk along this path in their caps and gowns.

Follow Beach Rd to the coast and wet your boots in the Irish Sea. Having done so, turn north-west, leaving the sea wall of St Bees to climb up the cliff-top path, steep at first. You are now on the Coast to Coast path, with a fence on one side and a 300-foot (90m) drop on the other.

The cliffs themselves are made of red sandstone, used in the construction of many of the buildings around here. There are some features along the way to help you judge your progress, the first being the **Pattering Holes**, fissures of uncertain origin in the ground beyond the fence by the ruined coastguard's hut.

Progressing further north the small **Fleswick Bay** (Map 2) is reached, a secluded pebble beach surrounded by red sandstone cliffs with some interestingly weathered boulders lying on the shore. It is also your last chance on the trail to dip your feet in the Irish Sea.

This bay marks the dividing line between the constituent parts of St Bees Head: South Head, which you have been walking on up to now, and **North Head** (Map 2), which you now climb up to from the bay. Two features distinguish this latter part of St Bees Head: the three **RSPB observation points**, to the left of the path, which allow you to safely peer over the cliffs and observe the seabirds nesting there (including puffins, terns and England's only colony of black guillemots); and **St Bees Lighthouse**, a little way inland from the path but clearly visible since South Head. *(cont'd on p76)*

❏ **Important note – walking times**
Unless otherwise specified, **all times in this book refer only to the time spent walking**. You will need to add 20-30% to allow for rests, photography, checking the map, drinking water etc. When planning the day's hike count on 5-7 hours' actual walking.

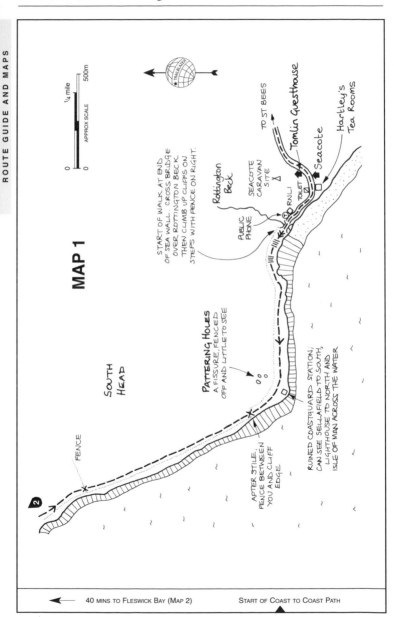

MAP 1

SOUTH HEAD

FENCE

PATTERING HOLES
A FISSURE, FENCED OFF AND LITTLE TO SEE

AFTER STILE, FENCE BETWEEN YOU AND CLIFF EDGE

RUINED COASTGUARD STATION; CAN SEE SELLAFIELD TO SOUTH, LIGHTHOUSE TO NORTH AND ISLE OF MAN ACROSS THE WATER

START OF WALK AT END OF SEA WALL. CROSS BRIDGE OVER ROTTINGTON BECK THEN CLIMB UP CLIFFS ON STEPS WITH FENCE ON RIGHT.

Rottington Beck

SEACOTE CARAVAN SITE

PUBLIC PHONE

RNLI

TOILET

Tomlin Guesthouse

Seacote

Hartley's Tea Rooms

TO ST BEES

¼ mile

500m

APPROX SCALE

★ TRAILBLAZER

40 MINS TO FLESWICK BAY (MAP 2)

START OF COAST TO COAST PATH

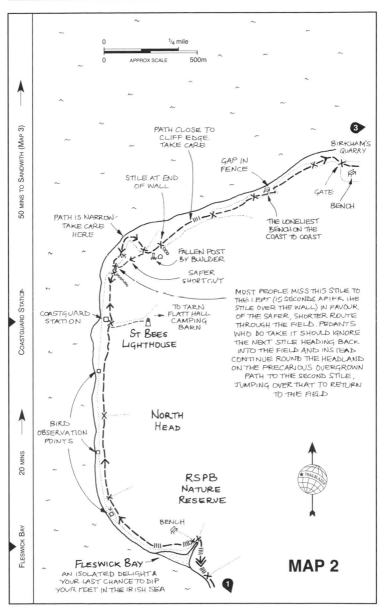

1/4 mile

APPROX SCALE   500m

PATH CLOSE TO
CLIFF EDGE.
TAKE CARE

BIRKHAM'S
QUARRY

GAP IN
FENCE

STILE AT END
OF WALL

GATE

BENCH

PATH IS NARROW—
TAKE CARE
HERE

THE LONELIEST
BENCH ON THE
COAST TO COAST

FALLEN POST
BY BOULDER

SAFER
SHORTCUT

50 MINS TO SANDWITH (MAP 3)

TO TARN
FLATT HALL
CAMPING
BARN

MOST PEOPLE MISS THIS STILE TO
THE LEFT (15 SECONDS AFTER THE
STILE OVER THE WALL) IN FAVOUR
OF THE SAFER, SHORTER ROUTE
THROUGH THE FIELD. PEDANTS
WHO DO TAKE IT SHOULD IGNORE
THE NEXT STILE HEADING BACK
INTO THE FIELD AND INSTEAD
CONTINUE ROUND THE HEADLAND
ON THE PRECARIOUS OVERGROWN
PATH TO THE SECOND STILE,
JUMPING OVER THAT TO RETURN
TO THE FIELD

COASTGUARD
STATION

St Bees
Lighthouse

COASTGUARD STATION

North
Head

BIRD
OBSERVATION
POINTS

RSPB
Nature
Reserve

20 MINS

TRAILBLAZER

FLESWICK BAY

BENCH

MAP 2

Fleswick Bay
AN ISOLATED DELIGHT &
YOUR LAST CHANCE TO DIP
YOUR FEET IN THE IRISH SEA

1

(cont'd from p73) **Tarn Flatt Hall** (bookings ☎ 01946 758198), a **camping barn**, is best reached by turning off the path here towards the lighthouse and continuing east for ¼ mile/400m. It sleeps around eight and costs just £6 per person. The barn comes with an electric light, cooking slab and an open fire, with wood available from the farm.

After the lighthouse the path continues up to the tip of **North Head** before heading east along the coast, eventually turning inland at **Birkham's Quarry**. Fifteen minutes later you arrive at Sandwith.

SANDWITH   MAP 3, opposite

Sandwith (pronounced *Sanith*) is the first settlement of note that you come to on the trail, almost five miles/8km along the path from St Bees (though, dishearteningly, only two miles/3km as the crow flies!).

Other than the bus stop and phone box, and unless the pub (the Dog and Partridge) is open, there's little to warrant much of a stay, particularly as you'll probably be wanting to crack on to the Lakes.

The nearest **accommodation** is *Tarn Flatt Hall* (see above).

Stagecoach's **bus** No 20 passes through 5-6/day, Mon-Sat, on its route between St Bees and Whitehaven. See pp43-5 for further details.

Taking the road alongside the Dog and Partridge, with the chemical works an eyesore to your left, the path crosses the Byerstead Road and, just over half a mile (0.8km) later, the B5345 linking Whitehaven to St Bees.

From the small underpass beneath the railway line (Map 3) at the foot of the hill the trail crosses fields and a small stream (**Scalegill Beck**; Map 4), before passing underneath a disused railway. If you were to continue straight on and look behind you, you would see St Bees nestling in the valley of Pow Beck. We, however, advise you to take the steps on your right that climb up the side of the tunnel to the disused railway track; take a left here and follow the 'track' to Moor Row.

MOOR ROW   MAP 4, p79

Moor Row has little to delay you save, perhaps, for the **post office and store** (Mon, Tue, Thur & Fri 6.30am-12.30pm, 1.30-5.30pm, Wed 6am-12.30pm, 1.30-6pm Sat 9am-3.30pm, Sun 9am-noon) which sells snacks, chocolate etc. Nearby, *Jasmine House* (☎ 01946 815795, 🖳 www.jasminehousebandb.com; 1S/2D/2F) is home to a small **teashop** and charges from £30 single, £58 for a double room. A packed lunch costs from £5; for an evening meal they'll run you down to the Manor House Hotel in St Bees (which they also own) and back. However, at the time of writing, they were closed due to flooding so check they have been able to re-open.

Stagecoach's No 6 **bus** passes through 3-4 times a day each way, Mon-Sat, between Whitehaven and Seascale/ Muncaster Castle. See pp43-5 for further details.

Taking the road south out of Moor Row (signposted to Egremont), leave it via a kissing gate leading into a field. A whole series of kissing gates follows as you cross the dismantled railway once more on your way down into Cleator, arriving by St Leonard's Church.

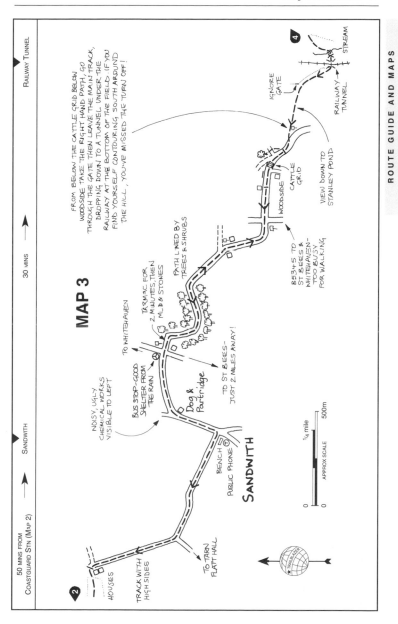

MAP 3

50 MINS FROM COASTGUARD STN (MAP 2) — SANDWITH — 30 MINS — RAILWAY TUNNEL

TO WHITEHAVEN

NOISY, UGLY CHEMICAL WORKS VISIBLE TO LEFT

HOUSES

TRACK WITH HIGH SIDES

TO TARN FLATT HALL

SANDWITH

BENCH
PUBLIC PHONE

Dog & Partridge

TO ST BEES - JUST 2 MILES AWAY!

BUS STOP-GOOD SHELTER FROM THE RAIN

TARMAC FOR 2 MINUTES, THEN MUD & STONES

PATH LINED BY TREES & SHRUBS

B5345 TO ST BEES & WHITEHAVEN- TOO BUSY FOR WALKING

WOODSIDE

CATTLE GRID

VIEW DOWN TO STANLEY POND

FROM BELOW THE CATTLE GRID BELOW WOODSIDE TAKE THE RIGHT HAND PATH, GO THROUGH THE GATE THEN LEAVE THE MAIN TRACK, DROPPING DOWN TO A TUNNEL UNDER THE RAILWAY AT THE BOTTOM OF THE FIELD. (IF YOU FIND YOURSELF CONTOURING SOUTH AROUND THE HILL, YOU'VE MISSED THE TURN OFF!

IGNORE GATE

RAILWAY TUNNEL

STREAM

¼ mile
500m
APPROX SCALE
0

TRAILBLAZER

ROUTE GUIDE AND MAPS

CLEATOR   MAP 4, opposite

Remnants of some 12th-century masonry in Cleator's church give some indication of just how old this village is, though you'll struggle in vain to find much else of antiquity in the plain, identical terraced houses that make up much of the rest of the place. These houses were built for the miners who worked in the nearby iron-ore pits. As the industry collapsed in the latter half of the 20th century, so the town suffered, and continues to do so today. It's a sad but familiar story repeated time and again throughout west Cumbria.

However, don't let the village's troubles put you off Cleator. True, the village is not one of the prettiest en route and it's true, too, that for many years the facilities for walkers were minimal. But it does provide an antidote to the somewhat twee nature of many Lake District hamlets further east and with a great B&B, the walker-friendly **Farren's Family Store** (Mon-Fri 6am-6.45pm, Sat 8am-5.30pm, Sun 8.30am-1.30pm) and a **pub** (*The Three Tuns*; food is not served) with a colourful landlord, there's enough in Cleator to warrant an overnight stay, should you already be feeling the effects of this first day.

Stagecoach's **Bus** No 22 calls in at Cleator on its way (almost hourly Mon-Sat) between Whitehaven and Egremont. Cleator Moor, a bigger town and separate place one mile to the north, has more services.

Where to stay

Those on expenses might want to consider the Grade 1 listed ***Ennerdale Country House Hotel*** (☎ 01946 813907, 🖳 www .oxfordhotelsandinns.com/OurHotels/Enne rdale; 3S / 24D or T / 3F, all en suite), set in ten acres of landscaped gardens at the top end of town, where each of the rooms comes with an entertainment system with satellite TV, Sony Playstation, videos and a CD player. It all sounds lovely – though it's hardly a typical Coast to Coast place, and at about £89 per person for B&B, or £109 for dinner as well, it ain't cheap! (That said, do check to see if they have one of their periodic offers on, which see those rates tumbling dramatically.)

A place that is more in keeping with the walk is the extremely pleasant and good-value ***Chapel Nook*** (☎ 01946 810366 or 07801 862234, 🖳 keithrhodes@supanet .com; 2D, one en suite) on Kiln Brow. Rates start at £22.50 and they are generally open March to October.

As an alternative to Cleator, **Egremont** is only 1½ miles/2.5km away, with more B&Bs such as ***Bookwell Garth Guest House*** (☎ 01946 820271, 16 Bookwell; 5S/6T/1F). Rates start from £23 (there are no en suite rooms).

From Cleator it is possible to take the road route north around Dent to Ennerdale Bridge, though unless the weather is positively treacherous, or you've had enough climbing for the day, take the high route. It would be a shame to miss the view from the summit of **Dent Hill** (Map 5) and the tranquillity of Nannycatch Beck that lies hidden away at its foot. Long and fairly arduous, the climb up Dent takes about 50 minutes from Cleator. At the top there are views to the Lakeland fells ahead and the sea behind, with the gigantic plant of Sellafield to the south-west, the largish town of Egremont before it and, on a good day, the silhouette of the Isle of Man.

After passing over the top of the hill look out for the signpost by the complicated track junction on the descent. The signpost urges you to turn right which is indeed the original trek suggested by Wainwright. We strongly urge you, however, to ignore this sign and take a *left* onto the steep track down to Nannycatch Beck, as indicated on the maps in this book. One novice trekker has complained vociferously about the steepness of this path – but trust us, it is a lot quicker and more scenic and has become the *de facto* official path now.

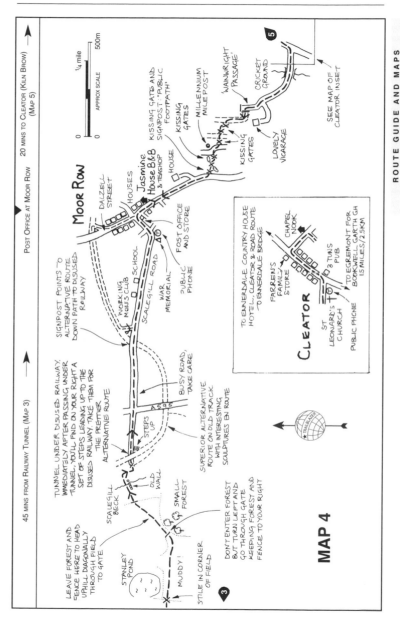

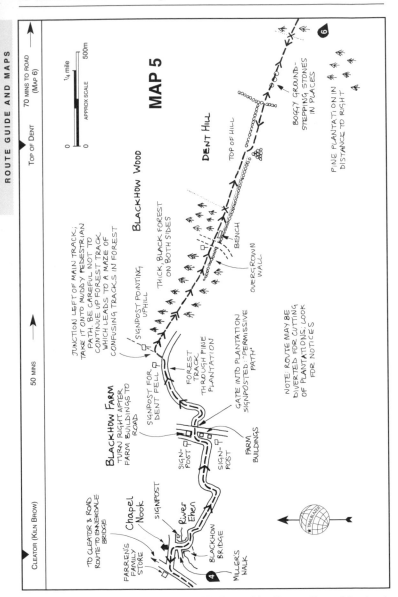

CLEATOR (KILN BROW) 50 MINS TOP OF DENT 70 MINS TO ROAD (MAP 6)

MAP 5

APPROX SCALE

0 — ¼ mile
0 — 500m

TO CLEATOR & ROAD
ROUTE TO ENNERDALE
BRIDGE

FARREN'S FAMILY STORE

Chapel Nook

SIGNPOST

River Ehen

BLACKHOW BRIDGE

MILLER'S WALK

BLACKHOW FARM
TURN RIGHT AFTER
FARM BUILDINGS TO
ROAD

SIGNPOST FOR
DENT FELL

SIGN-POST

SIGN-POST

FARM BUILDINGS

GATE INTO PLANTATION
SIGNPOSTED "PERMISSIVE
PATH"

FOREST TRACK
THROUGH PINE
PLANTATION

NOTE: ROUTE MAY BE
DIVERTED FOR CUTTING
OF PLANTATIONS, LOOK
FOR NOTICES

JUNCTION LEFT OF MAIN TRACK;
TAKE IT ONTO MUDDY PEDESTRIAN
PATH. BE CAREFUL NOT TO
CONTINUE UP FOREST TRACK
WHICH LEADS TO A MAZE OF
CONFUSING TRACKS IN FOREST

SIGNPOST POINTING
UPHILL

BLACKHOW WOOD

THICK, BLACK FOREST
ON BOTH SIDES

BENCH

OVERGROWN
WALL

DENT HILL

TOP OF HILL

BOGGY GROUND-
STEPPING STONES
IN PLACES

PINE PLANTATION IN
DISTANCE TO RIGHT

(Opposite) Top: Stonethwaite Beck (see p97), Borrowdale. **Bottom**: Parts of the church at St Bees (see p69), including the Great West Door, date back to Norman times.

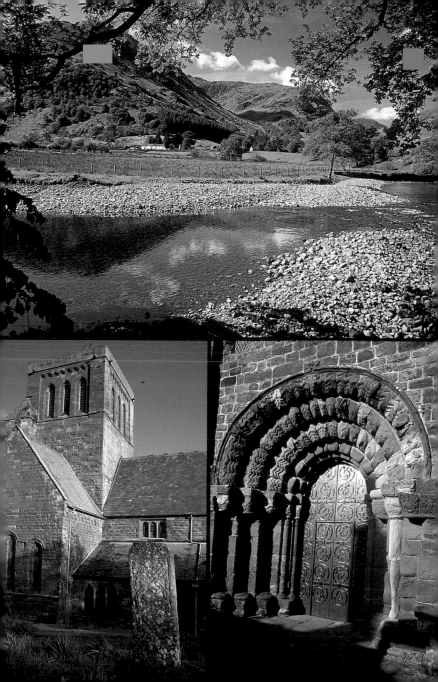

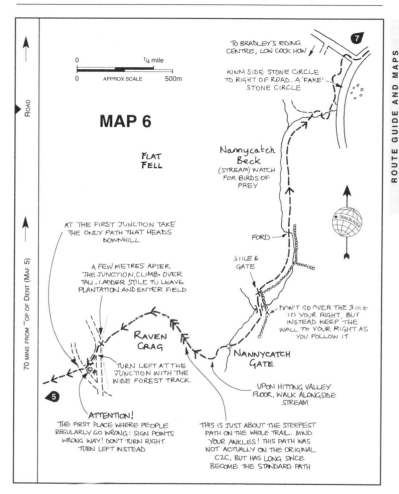

TO BRADLEY'S RIDING CENTRE, LOW COCK HOW

KINNISIDE STONE CIRCLE TO RIGHT OF ROAD. A 'FAKE' STONE CIRCLE

MAP 6

FLAT FELL

Nannycatch Beck (STREAM) WATCH FOR BIRDS OF PREY

0 ¼ mile
0 APPROX SCALE 500m

ROAD

70 MINS FROM TOP OF DENT (MAP 5)

★ TRAILBLAZER

AT THE FIRST JUNCTION TAKE THE ONLY PATH THAT HEADS DOWNHILL

A FEW METRES AFTER THE JUNCTION, CLIMB OVER TALL LADDER STILE TO LEAVE PLANTATION AND ENTER FIELD

FORD

STILE & GATE

DON'T GO OVER THE STILE TO YOUR RIGHT, BUT INSTEAD KEEP THE WALL TO YOUR RIGHT AS YOU FOLLOW IT

RAVEN CRAG

TURN LEFT AT THE JUNCTION WITH THE WIDE FOREST TRACK

NANNYCATCH GATE

UPON HITTING VALLEY FLOOR, WALK ALONGSIDE STREAM

ATTENTION! THE FIRST PLACE WHERE PEOPLE REGULARLY GO WRONG: SIGN POINTS WRONG WAY! DON'T TURN RIGHT. TURN LEFT INSTEAD

THIS IS JUST ABOUT THE STEEPEST PATH ON THE WHOLE TRAIL. MIND YOUR ANKLES! THIS PATH WAS NOT ACTUALLY ON THE ORIGINAL C2C, BUT HAS LONG SINCE BECOME THE STANDARD PATH

From Nannycatch, head due north along the beck before veering to the right, still following the course of the water, to the road leading into Ennerdale Bridge. Joining the road, before continuing north to Ennerdale Bridge take a few steps south along the road to check out the 'false' **stone circle of Kinniside**

(Opposite) Top: It's easy to lose the path at the top of Loft Beck. Follow the directions on Map 12 (see p92) closely. **Bottom**: The most remote accommodation on the route: the Black Sail Youth Hostel (p92) at the head of Ennerdale.

Circle. False, not because it isn't made of stone (it is), nor because it isn't a circle (it is that, too) but because it isn't, as it at first appears, a prehistoric circle (of which we'll be seeing a number of examples on the walk) but a 20th-century one built by a local academic. From the circle, the trail hugs the roadside down to Ennerdale Bridge, with paths constructed firstly to the left and then to the right of the road so walkers do not have to share the tarmac with the traffic.

A mile or so before Ennerdale Bridge is the turn-off to *Bradley's Riding Centre* (off Map 6, p81; ☎ 01946 861354, 🖳 www.walk-rest-ride.co.uk; 3D or T/ 1F), Low Cock How Farm. B&B costs from £26. There's also a well-equipped **bunkhouse** (with room for up to 12 people) from £13 or £18 with breakfast, and **camping** from £5. Not surprisingly they offer riding holidays.

ENNERDALE BRIDGE
MAP 7, opposite

Ennerdale Bridge is a postcard-pretty little place occupying a wonderful location spanning the River Ehen in one of Britain's least developed valleys. Unfortunately the **post office/shop** has very limited opening hours (it's supposed to open for a couple of hours on Tuesday and Wednesday mornings, though it struggles to even keep to those minimal hours) now. However, the reception desk at the Shepherd's Arms (see below) sells postcards and various C2C items.

The village has also been let down somewhat by its lack of accommodation, leading many to look elsewhere for somewhere to sleep, and taking taxis to and from St Bees or Ennerdale Bridge, especially as at the time of writing the only bus service had stopped. Any of the pubs or hotels will be able to advise on a taxi company; expect to pay £10 to St Bees.

Of the **accommodation** that does exist, the *Fox and Hounds* (☎ 01946 861373, 🖳 www.foxandhoundscumbria.co .uk; 2D or T/1F, all en suite) is a tastefully restored inn that retains many original features including exposed beams. And a ghost. B&B is £35 per person or £45 for a single room. They also allow **camping** (£5) outside, a useful addition given the demise of the village campsite in the centre of town. (In truth, that campsite is still taking in campers, though the reports we've received from people who've stayed there are uniformly negative, with no running water, scruffy grounds and sinks filled with bird shit. All this for £4. Our advice: avoid.)

In the centre of the village, the reliable if slightly officious *Shepherd's Arms Hotel* (☎ 01946 861249, 🖳 www.shepherdsarms hotel.co.uk; 3T/3D/1T or D; 6 en suite) is more expensive than any other at £47.50/ £38.50 sgl/dbl, though that reflects the extra features available in this hotel, including wi-fi **internet access** (for guests only; £2 per day if you have your own computer, £2.50 per hour otherwise). They're also the keepers of the village **ATM** (£1.75 charge).

The last choice in the village, *Cloggers* (☎ 01946 862487; 1D/1T), has received mixed reviews from trekkers; it's not the friendliest of places, though at £22.50 per person for two sharing, £25-30 single occupancy, it's certainly reasonable value.

If all of these are full, another top choice is *The Stork* (☎ 01946 861213, 🖳 www.storkhotel.co.uk; 1S/1D/1T/2F) in **Rowrah** which, although a fair distance away, offers free lifts to and from Ennerdale Bridge for Coast to Coasters. Rates start at £30 in the single, £55 for the double room.

Food-wise, the best place is probably the *Shepherd's Arms* (daily noon-3pm and 6-9pm), which not only has a tearoom (daily in summer and on winter weekends, 11am-5pm), with good homemade food using local produce and a decent vegetarian selection, though stiff competition is provided by the *Fox and Hounds* (daily, noon-9pm) with friendly staff, homemade dishes and a good selection of local ales. Main dishes are around £6.50-9. They are also open for breakfast (7am-2pm) for £5.

Packed lunches are available from both the Fox and Hounds (£5) and Shepherd's Arms Hotel.

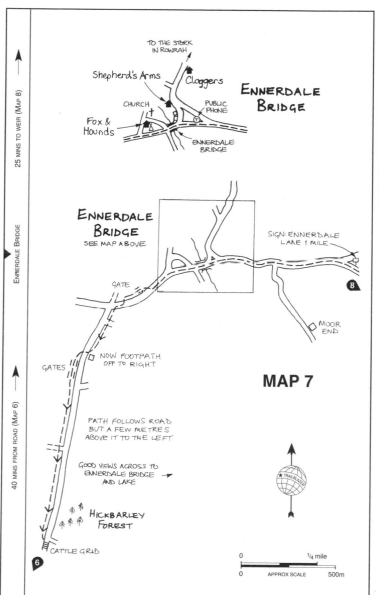

TO THE STORK
IN ROWRAH

Shepherd's Arms   Claggers

**ENNERDALE
BRIDGE**

CHURCH   PUBLIC
PHONE

Fox &
Hounds

ENNERDALE
BRIDGE

25 MINS TO WEIR (MAP 8)

ENNERDALE BRIDGE

**ENNERDALE
BRIDGE**
SEE MAP ABOVE

SIGN: ENNERDALE
LAKE 1 MILE

8

GATE

MOOR
END

NOW FOOTPATH
OFF TO RIGHT

GATES

MAP 7

40 MINS FROM ROAD (MAP 6)

PATH FOLLOWS ROAD
BUT A FEW METRES
ABOVE IT TO THE LEFT

GOOD VIEWS ACROSS TO
ENNERDALE BRIDGE
AND LAKE

HICKBARLEY
FOREST

★ TRAILBLAZER

CATTLE GRID

6

| 0 | | ¼ mile |
| 0 | APPROX SCALE | 500m |

STAGE 2: ENNERDALE BRIDGE TO BORROWDALE   MAPS 7-14

Introduction

As with any day, the enjoyment level of this **14½-mile (23.5km, 6¾hr, low route)** stage depends to a large degree on the weather. Indeed, perhaps more so here than elsewhere: without the sun you cannot fully appreciate the stunted, dappled, mossy forest growing along the southern edge of Ennerdale Water. Without clear conditions you won't have the opportunity to take in the extensive views down to Lake Buttermere from the top of Loft Beck. And if the weather looks like closing in, you'd be foolhardy to attempt the fell-top alternative via Red Pike, as detailed on p88. It's a fairly long walk today, though hostellers are particularly well served on this stage with four hostels spaced out along the route.

The route

The stage's first half involves a stroll along the southern side of **Ennerdale Water**, the path hugging the lakeshore round **Robin Hood's Chair** – an appropriate name given your final destination, although, as with Robin Hood's Bay, it probably has no real association with the legendary hero – to the very eastern extremity of the lake. It's a lovely walk and flat for the most part, at the end of which you turn north around some sheep enclosures and across the river to join a rather shadeless forest track passing through acre after acre of dull pine plantations.

If you're not stopping at Ennerdale Youth Hostel nor wish to take the Red Pike Alternative route, we strongly recommend the path along the southern banks of the **River Liza**, as shown on Maps 9-11. It's not the official route, but it is a more interesting, wilder one; it's also a fairly straightforward path to follow, though if you find yourself drifting up the slope too far, you may wish to retrace your steps to find the correct lower route. However, the three accommodation possibilities are all on the dull, official path on the other side of the river.

Low Gillerthwaite Field Centre (☎ 01946 861229, 🖳 www.lgfc.org.uk) has camping for the very reasonable price of £3.50. Note, however, that if they have a school group in residence (which is not unusual) you won't be allowed to stay; for this reason, it's essential you call ahead to find out whether you can stop there.

Ennerdale Youth Hostel (Map 10; ☎ 0870 770 5820, 🖳 ennerdale@yha .org.uk; 24 beds; £12), at **High Gillerthwaite**, lies between the river and the road and has recently undergone a major renovation. It is open to individuals from the week before Easter to the end of October; meals are available and it has a licence to sell alcohol.

High Gillerthwaite Camping Barn (☎ 0870 770 8868, 🖳 campingbarns @yha.org.uk; 14 beds) is further up the track and is now managed by the YHA. Beds here are only £6; there is a cooking area though no cooking facilities. The hostel is closed during the day so don't rely on filling your water bottle here. Just beyond the camping barn is the start of the alternative trail up to Red Pike, High Stile and Hay Stacks (see p88 and Maps 10a, p89, and 10b, p90). See p92 if staying on the main trail.

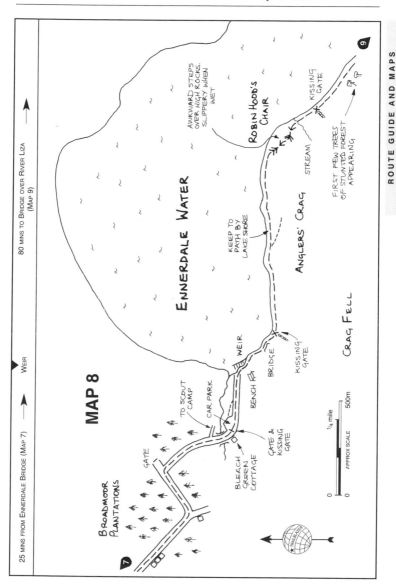

25 MINS FROM ENNERDALE BRIDGE (MAP 7) → WEIR → 80 MINS TO BRIDGE OVER RIVER LIZA (MAP 9)

MAP 8

BROADMOOR PLANTATIONS

GATE

TO SCOUT CAMP

CAR PARK

BLEACH GREEN COTTAGE

GATE & KISSING GATE

BENCH

WEIR

ENNERDALE WATER

KEEP TO PATH BY LAKE SHORE

AWKWARD STEPS OVER HIGH ROCKS. SLIPPERY WHEN WET

ROBIN HOOD'S CHAIR

KISSING GATE

FIRST FEW TREES OF STUNTED FOREST APPEARING

ANGLERS' CRAG

STREAM

CRAG FELL

BRIDGE

KISSING GATE

APPROX SCALE
¼ mile
500m

ROUTE GUIDE AND MAPS

BRIDGE OVER RIVER LIZA →

80 MINS FROM WEIR (MAP 8) →

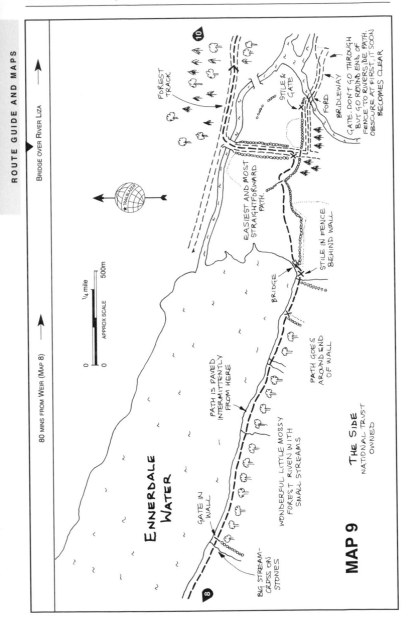

MAP 9

ENNERDALE WATER

THE SIDE
NATIONAL TRUST OWNED

BIG STREAM-CROSS ON STONES

GATE IN WALL

WONDERFUL LITTLE MOSSY FOREST RIVER WITH SMALL STREAMS

PATH IS PAVED INTERMITTENTLY FROM HERE

PATH GOES AROUND END OF WALL

BRIDGE

STILE IN FENCE BEHIND WALL

EASIEST AND MOST STRAIGHTFORWARD PATH.

APPROX SCALE
0 — ¼ mile
0 — 500m

FOREST TRACK

STILE & GATE

FORD

BRIDLEWAY

GATE...DON'T GO THROUGH BUT GO ROUND END OF FENCE TO RIVER. BE PATH. OBSCURE AT FIRST, IT SOON BECOMES CLEAR.

TRAILBLAZER

25 MINS FROM ERIDGE OVER RIVER LIZA (MAP 9) ◄ ► TURN-OFF TO RED PIKE ► ◄ 75 MINS TO YH (MAP 11) VIA TWO LOW ROUTES ►

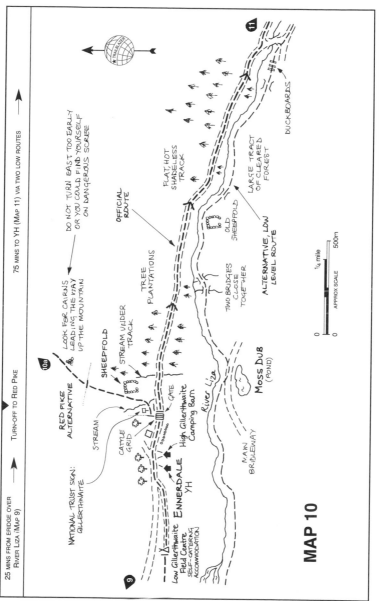

★ TRAILBLAZER

DO NOT TURN EAST TOO EARLY OR YOU COULD FIND YOURSELF ON DANGEROUS SCREE

LOOK FOR CAIRNS LEADING THE WAY UP THE MOUNTAIN

NATIONAL TRUST SIGN: GILLERTHWAITE

RED PIKE ALTERNATIVE

STREAM

CATTLE GRID

SHEEPFOLD

STREAM UNDER TRACK

TREE PLANTATIONS

OFFICIAL ROUTE

FLAT, HOT SHADELESS TRACK

LARGE TRACT OF CLEARED FOREST

DUCKBOARDS

11

GATE

High Gillerthwaite Camping Barn

River Liza

OLD SHEEPFOLD

ALTERNATIVE, LOW LEVEL ROUTE

TWO BRIDGES CLOSE TOGETHER

10a

ENNERDALE YH

Low Gillerthwaite Field Centre SELF-CATERING ACCOMMODATION

MAIN BRIDLEWAY

MOSS DUB (POND)

9

MAP 10

0 ¼ mile
0 500m
APPROX SCALE

The Red Pike, High Stile & Hay Stacks route;
Maps 10, 10a, 10b & 12

'All I ask for, at the end, is a last, long resting place by the side of Innominate Tarn, on Haystacks where the water gently laps the gravelly shore and the heather blooms and Pillar and Gable keep unfailing watch. A quiet place, a lonely place. I shall go to it, for the last time, and be carried: someone who knew me in life will take me there and empty me out of a little box and leave me there alone. And if you, dear reader, should get a bit of grit in your boot as you are crossing Haystacks in the years to come, please treat it with respect. It might be me.   **Alfred Wainwright** *Memoirs of an Ex-Fellwanderer*

In his Coast to Coast guide Wainwright describes this route as suitable only for 'very strong and experienced fellwalkers' in clear weather. While we don't think the group of people who can do this walk is quite as exclusive as Wainwright suggests, we certainly agree that the weather needs to be clear, if only because the views possible at the top – in particular across Buttermere to the north and to Gable and Pillar in the south – demand it. (If the weather takes a significant turn for the worse whilst you are up there, you can drop down from Scarth Gap on steps to the Black Sail hostel; see map 10b.) There are no technically difficult parts, though there are some steep ascents and descents which jolt the joints, and route finding on the way up to Red Pike can be tricky. All being well, this alternative route should add about **1¹/₂ miles (2.5km, 1³/₄hr)** to this stage.

This high-level route takes in a number of summits, including Red Pike (755m), High Stile (807m), High Crag (744m) and Hay Stacks (597m), the smallest in height but the most interesting. The place where many trekkers get a little lost is on the climb up to Red Pike, where it's tempting to branch off eastwards too early: make sure that, having crossed the stream, continue north-east (following cairns) until you are firmly on the grassy upper reaches of Red Pike (Map 10a). There are *just* enough cairns to show the way, though if in doubt, your motto should be: head up the slope rather than along it.

Having gained the ridge the path becomes clear and you'll find yourself ticking off one peak after another as you make your way to **Innominate Tarn**. From there, Wainwright recommends ignoring the obvious path that continues in an eastern direction to **Blackbeck Tarn**, continuing in a south-easterly direction to a reunion with the 'regular' route at **Loft Beck**, and this trail, though you'll struggle to see any clear path in the ground, is marked on Map 12 on p92. In my experience, however, few trekkers actually manage to successfully rejoin the regular trail, and instead forge their own path to **Honister Quarry**. (If you wish to try, the best tactic from the tarn is to aim towards **Brandreth Fence**, and continue along it until you come to a reunion with the regular route.) But the easiest solution is to continue on the clear trail to **Blackbeck**, from where you can follow the clear wide track to Honister (see p95). Just make sure you don't start to descend to Buttermere.

❏ **Important note – walking times**
Unless otherwise specified, **all times in this book refer only to the time spent walking**. You will need to add 20-30% to allow for rests, photography, checking the map, drinking water etc. When planning the day's hike count on 5-7 hours' actual walking.

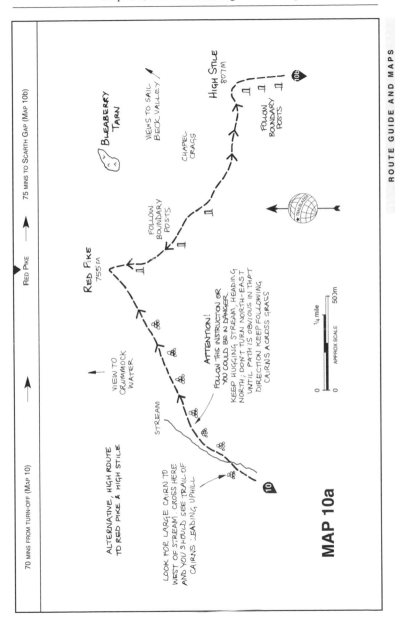

70 MINS FROM TURN-OFF (MAP 10) → RED PIKE → 75 MINS TO SCARTH GAP (MAP 10b)

ALTERNATIVE, HIGH ROUTE
TO RED PIKE & HIGH STILE

VIEW TO CRUMMOCK
WATER

LOOK FOR LARGE CAIRN TO
WEST OF STREAM. CROSS HERE
AND YOU SHOULD SEE TRAIL OF
CAIRNS LEADING UPHILL

STREAM

ATTENTION!
FOLLOW THIS INSTRUCTION OR
YOU COULD BE IN DANGER.
KEEP HUGGING STREAM, HEADING
NORTH; DON'T TURN NORTH-EAST
UNTIL PATH IS OBVIOUS IN THAT
DIRECTION. KEEP FOLLOWING
CAIRNS ACROSS GRASS

RED PIKE
755M

FOLLOW
BOUNDARY
POSTS

BLEABERRY
TARN

VIEWS TO SAIL
BECK VALLEY

CHAPEL
CRAGS

HIGH STILE
807M

FOLLOW
BOUNDARY POSTS

TRAILBLAZER

1/4 mile

APPROX SCALE

50m

0

10a

0

MAP 10a

ROUTE GUIDE AND MAPS

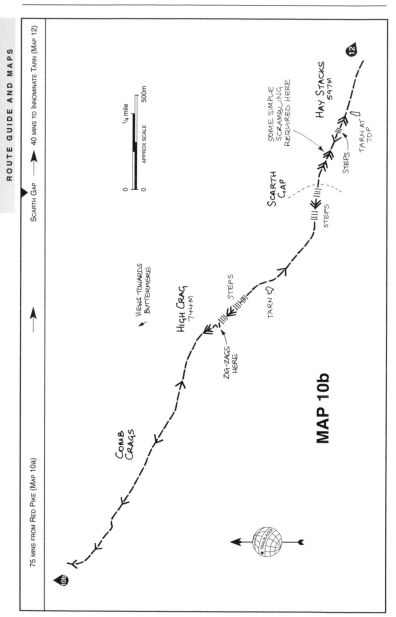

75 MINS FROM RED PIKE (MAP 10a)

SCARTH GAP — 40 MINS TO INNOMINATE TARN (MAP 12)

COMB CRAGS

HIGH CRAG
744M

VIEWS TOWARDS
BUTTERMERE

ZIG-ZAGS
HERE

STEPS

TARN

SCARTH
GAP

STEPS

SOME SIMPLE
SCRAMBLING
REQUIRED HERE

HAY STACKS
597M

STEPS

TARN AT
TOP

MAP 10b

¼ mile

0   500m

0
APPROX SCALE

10b

12

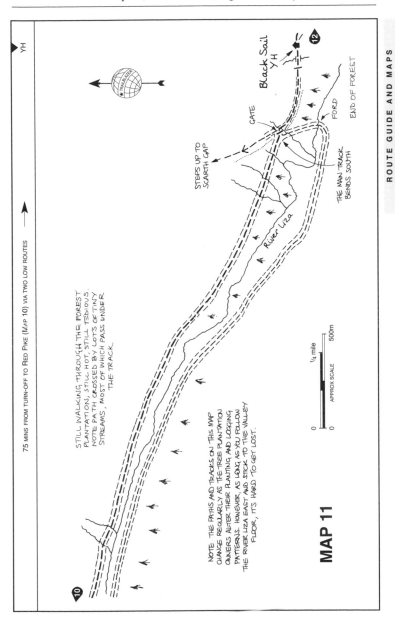

75 MINS FROM TURN-OFF TO RED PIKE (MAP 10) VIA TWO LOW ROUTES

STILL WALKING THROUGH THE FOREST PLANTATION, STILL HOT, STILL TEDIOUS. NOTE PATH CROSSED BY LOTS OF TINY STREAMS, MOST OF WHICH PASS UNDER THE TRACK

NOTE THE PATHS AND TRACKS ON THIS MAP CHANGE REGULARLY AS THE TREE PLANTATION OWNERS ALTER THEIR PLANTING AND LOGGING PATTERNS. HOWEVER, AS LONG AS YOU FOLLOW THE RIVER LIZA EAST AND STICK TO THE VALLEY FLOOR, IT'S HARD TO GET LOST.

MAP 11

¼ mile
500m
APPROX SCALE
0 — 0

YH

TRAIL BLAZER

Black Sail YH

GATE

STEPS UP TO SCARTH GAP

FORD

END OF FOREST

THE MAIN TRACK BENDS SOUTH

River Liza

ROUTE GUIDE AND MAPS

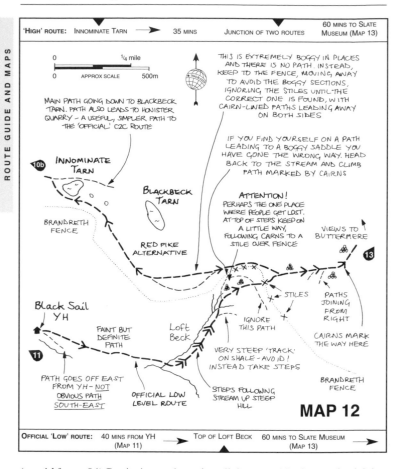

'HIGH' ROUTE: INNOMINATE TARN ⟶ 35 MINS   JUNCTION OF TWO ROUTES   60 MINS TO SLATE MUSEUM (MAP 13)

0 — ¼ mile
0 — APPROX SCALE — 500m

MAIN PATH GOING DOWN TO BLACKBECK TARN. PATH ALSO LEADS TO HONISTER QUARRY – A USEFUL, SIMPLER PATH TO THE 'OFFICIAL' C2C ROUTE

THIS IS EXTREMELY BOGGY IN PLACES AND THERE IS NO PATH. INSTEAD, KEEP TO THE FENCE, MOVING AWAY TO AVOID THE BOGGY SECTIONS, IGNORING THE STILES UNTIL THE CORRECT ONE IS FOUND, WITH CAIRN-LINED PATHS LEADING AWAY ON BOTH SIDES

IF YOU FIND YOURSELF ON A PATH LEADING TO A BOGGY SADDLE YOU HAVE GONE THE WRONG WAY. HEAD BACK TO THE STREAM AND CLIMB PATH MARKED BY CAIRNS

10b INNOMINATE TARN

BLACKBECK TARN

ATTENTION! PERHAPS THE ONE PLACE WHERE PEOPLE GET LOST. AT TOP OF STEPS KEEP ON A LITTLE WAY, FOLLOWING CAIRNS TO A STILE OVER FENCE

BRANDRETH FENCE

RED PIKE ALTERNATIVE

VIEWS TO BUTTERMERE

13

Black Sail YH

FAINT BUT DEFINITE PATH

Loft Beck

IGNORE THIS PATH

STILES

PATHS JOINING FROM RIGHT

CAIRNS MARK THE WAY HERE

11

PATH GOES OFF EAST FROM YH – NOT OBVIOUS PATH SOUTH-EAST

OFFICIAL LOW LEVEL ROUTE

VERY STEEP 'TRACK' ON SHALE – AVOID! INSTEAD TAKE STEPS

STEPS FOLLOWING STREAM UP STEEP HILL

BRANDRETH FENCE

MAP 12

OFFICIAL 'LOW' ROUTE: 40 MINS FROM YH ⟶ TOP OF LOFT BECK ⟶ 60 MINS TO SLATE MUSEUM
(MAP 11)   (MAP 13)

(cont'd from p84) Continuing on the main trail, just over 90 minutes after joining the forest track you emerge above the trees at the head of Ennerdale and ***Black Sail Youth Hostel*** (Map 11/12; ☎ 0870 770 8868 or 07711 108450; 16 beds, £12). The remotest and smallest of the youth hostels on our route, this former shepherd's bothy is now also the hostel with the biggest reputation. One look at the extensive wine list – far more than one would expect in any youth hostel, let alone one in such an isolated spot as this – provides the first indication that this isn't your typical hostel. The hostel is often left open during the day, providing very welcome shelter when it's raining, with tea and cake on sale in the kitchen. Breakfast and evening meals are served. Note, however, that Sherpa and a number of other baggage carriers do not deliver to Black Sail; and the hostel is only

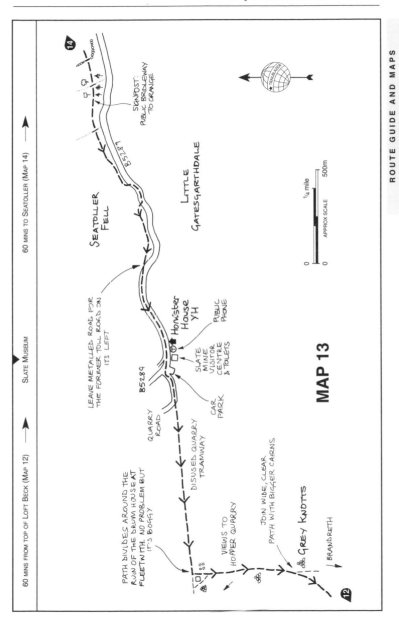

60 MINS FROM TOP OF LOFT BECK (MAP 12) → SLATE MUSEUM 60 MINS TO SEATOLLER (MAP 14) →

MAP 13

14

SIGNPOST: PUBLIC BRIDLEWAY TO GRANGE

B5289

SEATOLLER FELL

LITTLE GATESGARTHDALE

LEAVE METALLED ROAD FOR THE FORMER TOLL ROAD ON ITS LEFT

Honister House YH

PUBLIC PHONE

SLATE MINE VISITOR CENTRE & TOILETS

B5289

CAR PARK

QUARRY ROAD

DISUSED QUARRY TRAMWAY

PATH DIVIDES AROUND THE RUIN OF THE DRUM HOUSE AT FLEETWITH. NO PROBLEM BUT IT'S BOGGY

VIEWS TO HOPPER QUARRY

JOIN WIDE, CLEAR PATH WITH BIGGER CAIRNS

GREY KNOTTS

BRANDRETH

12

APPROX SCALE
0 ¼ mile
0 500m

open to individuals from the week before Easter to October. Incidentally, just before the hostel are some steps leading all the way up to Scarth Gap (Map 10a) on the High Level Alternative (see p88).

From the hostel things get a little tricky, with a sharp climb up **Loft Beck** followed by a long descent to Honister Hause (Maps 12-13). In fine weather this section is reasonably straightforward, if a little sweaty. Unfortunately, fine weather can never be guaranteed around these parts, particularly in the afternoon when most people attempt the climb.

The ascent up Loft Beck is hard but it's at the top, when you're trying to locate the correct path to Honister Hause, that real problems can occur: follow Map 12 carefully to negotiate this section.

❑ Honister Slate Mine

The story of mining at Honister begins 400 million years ago when volcanic ash, combined with water and compressed, formed the strong, fine-grained slate that is so popular today. When the glaciers of the last Ice Age retreated across Gatesgarthdale they exposed three parallel veins of this slate in the steep sides of the valley.

The mine (along with the nearby quarry) that tourists are allowed to visit today was reopened in 1997 after an 11-year break in production. When slate was first extracted from Gatesgarthdale, however, is a matter of debate. Certainly by the 1750s slate was being quarried on an industrial scale here, and from 1833, when entrepreneur Sam Wright took over, it was also being mined. As well as the disused tramway that you walk down, there were roads and aerial ropeways to take the slate to the road. The workers who split and finished the slate would live in barracks at Honister during the week; the youth hostel is in fact a converted quarry workers' building.

The slate produced at the Honister mine is green in both senses of the word, being a dull shade of green in colour and, because this is the only slate mine in England (as opposed to an open quarry that scars the land), more environmentally friendly too. The slate from this mine has been used to roof some of Britain's most famous buildings, including both the Ritz Hotel and St James's Palace in London.

The **Visitors' Centre** (☎ 01768 777230, 🖳 www.honister.com; Mon-Fri 9am-5.30pm, Sat 10am-5pm) is well worth visiting. There are guided tours into the mine daily at 10.30am, 12.30pm and 3.30pm for £8.50 which includes a free cup of tea in the adjacent tearoom. They've also set up a *via ferrata*. Common in some of the mountain regions of Europe, particularly the Dolomites of northern Italy, a via ferrata, or 'iron way', is essentially a series of fixed iron ropes, ladders and other climbing aids to help non-climbers reach places that would otherwise be inaccessible. The one at Honister, for which a guide is compulsory, takes climbers through the quarry up to Fleetwith Pike on what they claim is the old miners' route to work. The cost is £19.50, including equipment hire, with climbs conducted twice a day, at 11am and 1pm. Book via the website.

The **shop** is full of slate souvenirs, from great slabs of the stuff that have been fashioned into coffee tables, to smaller chippings carved into chess pieces, and even smaller flakes that are sold by the bagful. Some of the stuff is lovely – but think twice before purchasing: this walk is hard enough without carrying a full-size slate coffee table on your back for the next fortnight. Thankfully, the website has an online shopping service and they'll deliver the stuff to your home, or you could buy something small such as a Coast to Coast coaster (£.4.90). They also sell cheap waterproof ponchos, which could prove invaluable.

From **Brandreth Fence**, a fairly clear path – though indistinct at first – contours around the western face of Brandreth and **Grey Knotts** (Map 13), with several cairns along the way to aid navigation in misty conditions. Ahead, the working Hopper Quarry can be seen in the distance on your left.

Your path drops gently to Fleetwith and unravels into a number of paths at the **Drum House**. Walking round the Drum House – now little more than a massive pile of stones and slate – you come upon a much more definite path heading off east down the hill. The path's arrow-straight course betrays its previous incarnation as a quarry tramway, now dismantled, and the Drum House's original purpose was to house the cable that operated the tramway that ran to the cutting sheds.

At the bottom of the tramway is **Honister Hause**, one of the highest road passes in the Lake District at 332m. *Honister Youth Hostel* (☎ 0870 770 5870, 🖥 honister@yha.org.uk; 26 beds; £13) is here and serves meals and is licensed. The pass also plays host to a car park, and the **Honister Slate Mine Visitor Centre** (see box opposite) with its own tearoom and toilets.

Stagecoach's No 77 **bus** runs from here to Seatoller (eight minutes) and to Keswick (40 minutes) four times daily and the 77A goes via Buttermere to Keswick (60 mins, 4/day); both services operate from Easter to the end of Oct (see pp43-5 for details).

From Honister the Coast to Coast path follows the B5289 down Little Gatesgarthdale on an old toll road, with both road and path following much the same course. The path loops round to join up with the road again at **Seatoller**.

SEATOLLER   MAP 14, p97

The National Trust village of Seatoller has a tearoom and restaurant and a very fine **information barn** (☎ 017687 77714; Mar-Oct daily 10am-5pm, Oct-Mar weekends only) packed full of souvenirs and books as well as useful advice and a few simple bits of trekking equipment such as socks, torches etc. It also has a car park, a public phone and toilet, a post-box and a couple of B&Bs – not bad for a hamlet that can't contain, in this author's opinion, more than 20 houses.

Seatoller also has rain, and lots of it: indeed, at 3500mm per year, the rainfall in Seatoller is one of the highest in the UK, and is considerably greater than that of Keswick just 8 miles/13km further down the valley, which gets less than 1500mm annually.

Above it is a **camping barn** (phone the information barn for bookings), where for £6 you get to sleep in comfy if basic accommodation (up to 30 people can sleep on the mattresses provided), and for £2.45 extra you get a breakfast too (£4.45 for the full English), with a packed lunch a further £4.25.

As for **B&Bs**, Seatoller Farm and Seatoller House sit virtually opposite one another on the main road. *Seatoller House* (☎ 01768 777218, 🖥 www.seatollerhouse .co.uk; 1D/3T/6F; Mar-Nov only) is a 300-year-old building that's been a guesthouse for over a century (previous guests have included the artist John Constable). They have ten rooms each with their own bathroom (though only four are en suite) and charge from £42 per person for B&B, or £52 including a four-course dinner with coffee and homemade truffles (light supper only on Tuesdays). Single occupancy is subject to a £5 supplement.

Seatoller Farm (☎ 01768 777232, 🖥 www.seatollerfarm.co.uk; 2D/1T, all en suite) is a working National Trust hill farm that charges £30 per person; they close mid-Dec to mid-Jan. Their farmhouse breakfasts are said to be the perfect start to the day. Note that pets are not allowed here, though **camping** is allowed (£5 per person with showers).

The *Yew Tree* (☎ 01768 777634, 🖥 yew tree@seatoller.wanadoo.co.uk) is a curious place, a traditional English tearoom by day and an African restaurant at night, with all the ingredients locally sourced but given an African twist in the cooking. It's open Tuesdays to Sundays and Bank holidays 11am-late and is generally open March to October. The building itself dates back to 1628.

Finally, for a sneak preview of Seatoller visit their **webcam**, 🖥 www.bbc.co.uk/cumbria/webcams/seatoller.shtml.

From Seatoller the trail wends its way through **Johnny's Wood** into Borrowdale (Map 14).

BORROWDALE   MAP 14, opposite

These three charming settlements (Longthwaite, Rosthwaite and Stonethwaite) in Borrowdale are quintessential Lake District hamlets: small, picturesque, friendly and composed largely of slate-roofed, white-washed-stone farm cottages.

Longthwaite

The first building you come to in Borrowdale is ***Borrowdale Youth Hostel*** (☎ 0870 770 5706, borrowdale@yha.org.uk; £15.50; 88 beds), a comfortable-enough place that allows non-guests to join them for dinner (from £8.40); the hostel has an alcohol licence. Breakfasts for guests are £4.20, packed lunch £3.80. The hostel has a TV, games room, BBQ and internet access.

Longthwaite also plays host to the best **campsite** (£5) in the valley and a fine B&B, *Gillercombe* (☎ 017687 77602; 1S/4D or T). The owner of both, Rachel Dunckley, is a mine of useful local information and gossip, and her B&B remains a very comfortable and convenient place to stay right in the heart of Borrowdale. Rates are around £26 per person.

Rosthwaite

The biggest settlement of the three is Rosthwaite to the north, with a pub, a hotel, a couple of B&Bs, a camping barn and a shop. This last, the **General Store** (summer Mon-Sat 9am-5pm, Sun 9am-4pm, Nov-Mar 9am-1pm), is decidedly walker-friendly, with maps, books and small items such as compasses for sale; they also sell sandwiches. Twenty metres up the road, *The*

Royal Oak (☎ 017687 77214, 🖥 www.roy aloakhotel.co.uk; 15 rooms, most en suite) is a fine-looking place with a long history. Once an 18th-century farmhouse, the hotel played host to the poet William Wordsworth (see p101 and box p118) in 1812 and is said to be where he shared a bed (innocently, it should be added) with 'a Scotch pedlar'. Rates start at £46/42 sgl/dbl (plus £4 if it's a weekend) for DB&B in rooms with shared facilities, up to £52 per person for an en suite room in the nearby converted barn annexe, Merrybreeches, with views over the river. Dinner is for residents only unless it's unusually quiet.

Next door is the *Scafell Hotel and Riverside Bar* (☎ 017687 77208, 🖥 www .scafell.co.uk; 24 rooms all en suite), a large place which has served as a coaching inn since 1850. Some of the rooms have been decorated with antique furniture; rates start at £49.95 per person. The menu here is large and the **food** (daily noon-2pm, 6-9pm, high summer noon-9pm), while not of the supremely high quality of the Langstrath (see p98), is still fine.

There are two National Trust farms that are worth checking out: *Nook Farm* (☎ 017687 77677, 🖥 nookfarm1@aol.com; 1D/1F) is a 16th-century farmhouse with lovely open fires – the perfect treat after a rainy day's walk. Rates start at £26, £28 en suite. Dogs are not allowed. Behind it, *Yew Tree Farm* (☎ 017687 77675, 🖥 www.bor rowdaleflockin.co.uk; 2D/1T; closed Dec & Jan), which dates from 1720, charges £35 for B&B in an en suite room (falling to £30 for stays of more than one night). They

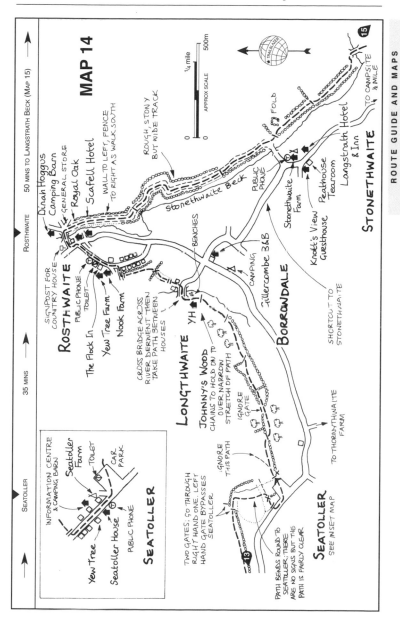

SEATOLLER | 35 MINS | ROSTHWAITE | 50 MINS TO LANGSTRATH BECK (MAP 15)

MAP 14

Dinah Hoggus
Camping Barn
GENERAL STORE
Royal Oak
Scafell Hotel

WALL TO LEFT, FENCE
TO RIGHT AS WALK SOUTH

ROUGH, STONY
BUT WIDE TRACK

Stonethwaite Beck

SIGNPOST FOR
COUNTRY HOUSE
PUBLIC PHONE
TOILET

ROSTHWAITE

The Flock In
Yew Tree Farm
Nook Farm

CROSS BRIDGE ACROSS
RIVER DERWENT THEN
TAKE PATH BETWEEN
HOUSES

BENCHES

PUBLIC PHONE

Stonethwaite
Farm

FOLD

Knott's View
Guesthouse

Peathouse
Tearoom

Langstrath Hotel
& Inn

TO CAMPSITE
½ MILE

STONETHWAITE

SHORTCUT TO
STONETHWAITE

BORROWDALE

Gillercombe B&B

CAMPING

LONGTHWAITE
YH

JOHNNY'S WOOD
CHAINS TO HOLD ON TO
OVER NARROW
STRETCH OF PATH

IGNORE
GATE

IGNORE
THIS PATH

TO THORNYTHWAITE
FARM

0   ¼ mile
0   500m
APPROX SCALE

TRUE BLACK

15

SEATOLLER
SEE INSET MAP

TWO GATES; GO THROUGH
RIGHT HAND ONE, LEFT
HAND GATE BYPASSES
SEATOLLER

13

PATH BENDS ROUND TO
SEATOLLER; THERE
ARE NO SIGNS BUT THIS
PATH IS FAIRLY CLEAR

INFORMATION CENTRE
& CAMPING BARN

Seatoller
Farm
TOILET

CAR
PARK

Yew Tree

Seatoller House
PUBLIC PHONE

SEATOLLER

❏ **Borrowdale public transport (see also pp43-5)**
Stagecoach's No 79 bus, known as the **Borrowdale Rambler**, runs between Seatoller and Keswick (from where buses run to other destinations in Cumbria) via Rosthwaite. From April to October there are 1-2 buses an hour Mon-Sat and in late July-Aug Sun 1/hr. From October to Easter there are 1/hr (Mon-Sat). The buses take two minutes to reach the junction with the road to Stonethwaite, five minutes to reach Rosthwaite (opposite the general store), and half an hour to reach Keswick. In addition, between April and late October, bus Nos 77/77A (the **Honister Rambler**) runs in a loop (4/day) between Keswick, Seatoller, Buttermere, and Honister youth hostel, taking 30 minutes from Keswick to Seatoller on the 77A and just over an hour on the 77.

also run the nearby self-styled 'walkers' tearoom', *The Flock In* (Feb-Oct Thur-Tue 10am-5pm, Nov Fri-Tue, closed Dec & Jan), a rather idiosyncratic little place where everything, from the tea to the soup, is served in pints (and half pints). Many of their dishes are made with produce from the farm, such as 'Herdie-burgers', and the terrace out back is covered by a roof, allowing trekkers to enjoy the outside space even when it's throwing it down.

On the path leading out of the village is the *Dinah Hoggus Camping Barn* (bookings ☎ 01946 758198, 🖳 www.lakeland campingbarns.co.uk), a very simple but attractively rustic place sleeping 12 people; £6 per person (bring your own sleeping bag and camping stove; mattresses provided). Booking in advance is essential.

Stonethwaite

Just under a mile (about 1.5km) to the south, Stonethwaite is little more than a dead-end road running parallel to the beck that shares its name. But boy! What a dead end, a gorgeous string of farmhouses with views south to the menacing presence of Eagle Crag and Greenup Gill, which you'll be passing on the next stage.

The hamlet is capped at the end by a small hotel and inn, *The Langstrath* (☎ 017687 77239, 🖳 www.thelangstrath.com; 1S/2D/4D or T/1F), whose reputation for fine **food** (Tue-Sat 12.30pm-2.30pm and 6-8.45pm) extends well beyond Borrowdale; indeed, one trekker of my acquaintance was still raving about the roast lamb he had here

over one week later! What's more, other than the Riverside Restaurant at Scafell Hotel in Rosthwaite and the Borrowdale YH, this is the only place for food in the evening in the 'thwaites'. Here you can sample some local produce, including slow-roasted Rosthwaite Herdwick lamb (£13.50). The rooms are just as worthy of praise, all en suite and with radio/CD player. Room rates are £37.50-42.50 per person low season (from £27.50 in the family room), £39.50-45 high season (from £30 in family room); prices rise £2-3 at weekends. All in all, a fantastic place. However, note that in 2008 they are only planning to open Tuesday to Saturday.

Besides the inn, Stonethwaite boasts a couple of other B&Bs including the former drovers' alehouse, *Knotts View* (☎ 017687 77604; 3D/2T), which charges £27. According to the owner the building is said to be 450 years old and, with its low ceilings, it feels like it. The place is full of character but there are no en suite rooms. They also own the *Peathouse tearoom* (flexible opening hours) next door; it will be open for the 2008 season but after that will be closed.

Yet another National Trust place, *Stonethwaite Farm* (☎ 017687 77234; 1S/2D/1T) comes highly recommended. It sits adjacent to the phonebox by the path to the bridge across the beck. It's a pretty place and also offers **camping** (£4) in a field a short way up the valley (see map 15). B&B rates start at £20 per person for two sharing (£25 en suite), £25 single occupancy.

STAGE 3: BORROWDALE TO GRASMERE   MAPS 14-18

Introduction

In good weather this 9¹/₂-mile (15km, 4¹/₂-5hr low/high routes) stage is one of
the loveliest, a reasonably straightforward climb up to Lining Crag and Greenup
Edge followed by either a high-level ridge walk (see p100) or a simple stroll
down the valley to Grasmere. A few people get lost on this section, usually just
after Greenup Edge, but providing you're careful there's no reason why you
should be one of them.

Wainwright combines this stage with the next one to Patterdale, and a few
walkers do just that, completing the trek from Borrowdale to Patterdale in one
long day. But we strongly recommend you don't: not only would that mean
rushing through one of the prettiest and wildest parts of the whole walk, but it
would also mean that you probably won't have time to attempt the wonderful
high-level routes described on p100 and pp112-14 and will have to keep to the
valleys. Furthermore, to bypass Grasmere without stopping for at least one
night is little short of criminal.

So, unless you're really pushed for time, keep the stages separate, take at
least one of the high-level paths if conditions allow, and tackle these walks at a
pace that will allow you to fully savour the beauty of the lakes and fells. You
won't regret it.

The route

The stage begins with a slightly strenuous amble through the fields alongside
Stonethwaite Beck (Maps 14 and 15), with **Eagle Crag** a permanent, looming,
malevolent presence across the water.

Climbing steadily higher alongside one of Stonethwaite Beck's tributaries,
Greenup Gill (Map 15), with views back down to Borrowdale growing ever
more impressive, the path bends slowly right and south round Eagle Crag to
arrive, via various obstacles such as a basin of drumlins and a rock wall, at
Lining Crag (Map 16) and, weather permitting, views towards Scafell Pike,
England's highest summit at 3210ft (963m).

Look to the south and you'll also make out the beginning of the path to
Greenup Edge. This next section is where most people get lost, the boggy
ground and the occasional rocky surface helping to obscure the correct direction. The important things to look out for are the fence support posts, the
remains of a fence that demarcated Greenup Edge and which clearly once
stretched up and over the Low White Stones, the rocky outcrop up to your right
as you look south.

If you've followed the right path and come to the right post, a few metres
further on you'll see a **cairn** marking the correct way east and down into the
head of **Wythburn Valley**. However, it's not Wythburn that we want, but its
neighbour, **Far Easedale**, so you'll have to maintain your easterly direction
for the next ten minutes and aim for the ridge opposite, the other side of the
valley head.

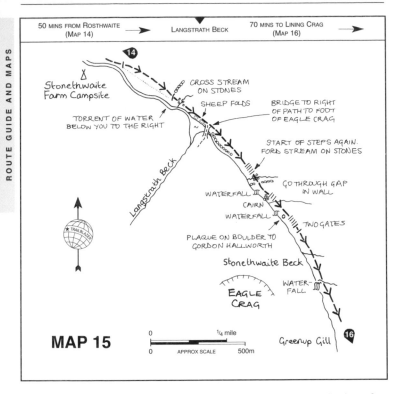

50 MINS FROM ROSTHWAITE (MAP 14) → LANGSTRATH BECK 70 MINS TO LINING CRAG (MAP 16) →

Stonethwaite Farm Campsite

CROSS STREAM ON STONES

SHEEP FOLDS

BRIDGE TO RIGHT OF PATH TO FOOT OF EAGLE CRAG

TORRENT OF WATER BELOW YOU TO THE RIGHT

START OF STEPS AGAIN. FORD STREAM ON STONES

Langstrath Beck

GO THROUGH GAP IN WALL

WATERFALL

CAIRN

WATERFALL

TWO GATES

PLAQUE ON BOULDER TO GORDON HALLWORTH

Stonethwaite Beck

EAGLE CRAG

WATER-FALL

MAP 15

0   ¼ mile
0   APPROX SCALE   500m

Greenup Gill

The easier path down the valley of Far Easedale to Grasmere now begins a few metres to the right of the 'gateposts' on Map 17. This **low-level route** is simplicity itself, the most gentle of ambles down the valley alongside **Easedale Beck**.

It's a peaceful walk, too, as most hikers take the high route these days, attracted by the fact that it's the easiest of the high-level alternatives on the Coast to Coast. Indeed, sheep are likely to be your only company. At the bottom there are some pleasant riverside grassy patches which positively cry out for picnickers, before the first few farms on the outskirts of Grasmere are passed.

The ridge-walk alternative to Grasmere via Helm Crag
Map 17 p102 & Map 18 p103

For the more rewarding high-level route to **Calf Crag**, **Gibson Knott** and **Helm Crag** amongst other, lesser heights, having crossed the head of the Wythburn follow the path that contours round the hill ahead. The walking is not difficult, and though the ground is often saturated the climbs up to the various peaks from the ridge take little more than three or four minutes each time. It is a long walk, however, and despite the awesome views, with Castle, Land and Silver Hows behind you to the south-west on one side and Helvellyn and Great Rigg to the north-east on the other, by the time you've conquered Helm Crag you'll be glad to see the path dropping sharply to the western outskirts of Grasmere.

From the foot, it's just a few minutes or so along the road to the heart of one of the Lake District's – and England's – prettiest villages, or you can take the even prettier route via Lancrigg Wood and the grounds of the Lancrigg Hotel – which is the route you should take if you're keen on reaching Patterdale the same day and have no interest in visiting Grasmere.

GRASMERE see map p105

Wordsworth called this valley 'the fairest place on earth' and it is his association with Grasmere that has done so much to popularize the place over the years. Though

Wordsworth lived here for only nine years, the period was a productive one and he wrote many of his best-known works here. His grave is in the grounds of St Oswald's Church, one of the more peaceful spots in

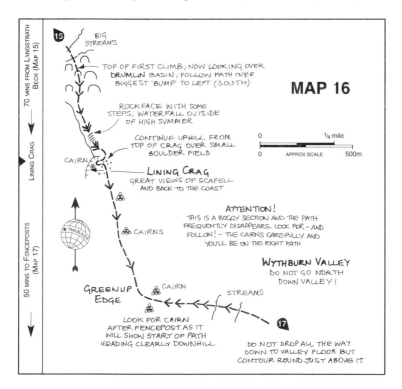

15 BIG STREAMS

TOP OF FIRST CLIMB; NOW LOOKING OVER DRUMLIN BASIN; FOLLOW PATH OVER BIGGEST 'BUMP' TO LEFT (SOUTH)

MAP 16

ROCK FACE WITH SOME STEPS; WATERFALL OUTSIDE OF HIGH SUMMER

CONTINUE UPHILL FROM TOP OF CRAG OVER SMALL BOULDER FIELD

CAIRN

LINING CRAG
GREAT VIEWS OF SCAFELL AND BACK TO THE COAST

0   ¼ mile
0   APPROX SCALE   500m

ATTENTION!
THIS IS A BOGGY SECTION AND THE PATH FREQUENTLY DISAPPEARS. LOOK FOR – AND FOLLOW! – THE CAIRNS CAREFULLY AND YOU'LL BE ON THE RIGHT PATH

CAIRNS

WYTHBURN VALLEY
DO NOT GO NORTH DOWN VALLEY!

GREENUP EDGE
CAIRN
STREAMS

LOOK FOR CAIRN AFTER FENCEPOST AS IT WILL SHOW START OF PATH HEADING CLEARLY DOWNHILL.

17

DO NOT DROP ALL THE WAY DOWN TO VALLEY FLOOR BUT CONTOUR ROUND JUST ABOVE IT

70 MINS FROM LANGSTRATH BECK (MAP 15)

LINING CRAG

50 MINS TO FENCEPOSTS (MAP 17)

★ TRAILBLAZER

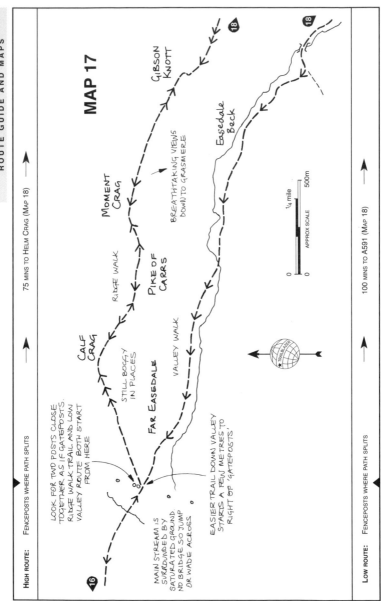

HIGH ROUTE: FENCEPOSTS WHERE PATH SPLITS → 75 MINS TO HELM CRAG (MAP 18) →

MAP 17

GIBSON KNOTT

Easedale Beck

MOMENT CRAG

BREATHTAKING VIEWS DOWN TO GRASMERE

RIDGE WALK

CALF CRAG

PIKE OF CARRS

STILL BOGGY IN PLACES

FAR EASEDALE

VALLEY WALK

LOOK FOR TWO POSTS CLOSE TOGETHER AS IF GATEPOSTS. RIDGE WALK TRAIL AND LOW VALLEY ROUTE BOTH START FROM HERE

MAIN STREAM IS SURROUNDED BY SATURATED GROUND NO BRIDGE SO JUMP OR WADE ACROSS

EASIER TRAIL DOWN VALLEY STARTS A FEW METRES TO RIGHT OF 'GATEPOSTS'

0   ¼ mile
0   500m
APPROX SCALE

LOW ROUTE: FENCEPOSTS WHERE PATH SPLITS → 100 MINS TO A591 (MAP 18) →

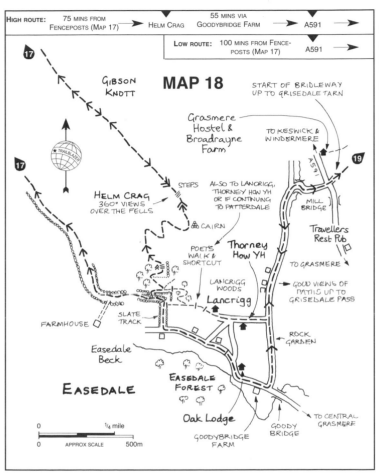

HIGH ROUTE: 75 MINS FROM FENCEPOSTS (MAP 17) ➔ HELM CRAG 55 MINS VIA GOODYBRIDGE FARM ➔ A591 ➔

LOW ROUTE: 100 MINS FROM FENCEPOSTS (MAP 17) A591 ➔

17

GIBSON KNOTT

MAP 18

START OF BRIDLEWAY UP TO GRISEDALE TARN

Grasmere Hostel & Broadrayne Farm

TO KESWICK & WINDERMERE

17

★ TRAILBLAZER

19

HELM CRAG 360° VIEWS OVER THE FELLS

STEPS

ALSO TO LANCRIGG, THORNEY HOW YH OR IF CONTINUING TO PATTERDALE

MILL BRIDGE

CAIRN

Travellers Rest Pub

POETS WALK & SHORTCUT

Thorney How YH

TO GRASMERE

LANCRIGG WOODS

GOOD VIEWS OF PATHS UP TO GRISEDALE PASS

FARMHOUSE

SLATE TRACK

Lancrigg

ROCK GARDEN

Easedale Beck

EASEDALE

EASEDALE FOREST

EASEDALE

Oak Lodge

GOODYBRIDGE FARM

GOODY BRIDGE

TO CENTRAL GRASMERE

0 ¼ mile

0 APPROX SCALE 500m

Grasmere's busy centre. The village hasn't lost any of its charm since Wordsworth's day. It is the harmony of the natural and the man-made that makes Grasmere so enchanting.

To the west of the village the large farmhouses and stately homes share the smooth, undulating land with forests of mature deciduous trees and flocks of dozy sheep; through the busy jumble of buildings

in the centre flows the gentle River Rothay, a tranquil haven for ducks and other waterfowl; while to the south lies brooding Grasmere Lake, flanked by steep, forested hills and almost entirely undeveloped.

Sure, more than a few Coast-to-Coasters of my acquaintance complain that they find it all a bit twee, with its cream-tea shops and folksy olde-worlde charm. But it's a hard-hearted trekker who doesn't appreciate the picture-postcard perfection of the place while even its critics will be pleased with the facilities on offer here, from hiking shops to a cash machine and even an internet connection.

If you're under no time constraints, consider stopping over for more than one night: there's enough here – from Wordsworth's Dove Cottage to a host of small private galleries and some lovely little walks around the surrounding countryside – to keep you contented for a couple of days.

Services

Grasmere's tourist information office closed in 2005; the nearest office is at Glenridding, see box p118, though there is a **Visitor information point** (daily 10am-4pm) in Dale Lodge Hotel.

The **post office** (Mon-Wed & Fri 9am-5pm, Thu & Sat 9am-12.30pm) is small but central and plays host to Grasmere's only **cash machine** (£1.75, or free to Alliance & Leicester customers). Alternatively, if you have an account with certain banks and building societies (see p20) you can withdraw cash from the counter.

If the post office is closed, the **Co-op** (Mon-Sat 8.30am-8pm; Sun 10am-6pm) provides a cashback service and is the best place to stock up on trekking provisions. Next to the Co-op is a **pharmacy** (Mon-Fri 9am-5.30pm, Sat 9am-1pm).

There are three or four **trekking shops** dotted around the town centre, including the recommended Rock Bottom by Harwood Hotel. If you can't find what you need in one of these, a bus leaves from the Green every 20 minutes for Ambleside, where there are loads of trekking outlets.

Internet access is provided by Butharlyp Youth Hostel for the usual eye-wateringly expensive rates, or you can use the terminal (Mon-Sat 9.30am-6pm, Sun 11am-5pm; for customers only) by the café inside the Garden Centre opposite the church. Unfortunately, they limit your time to ten minutes during busy periods; turn up at 9.30am when the place opens if you want more time, as it's quieter then.

Where to stay

Hostels There are two YHA hostels (☎ 0870 770 5836, 🖳 grasmere@yha.org.uk) in Grasmere: *Thorney How* (Map 18, p103; 49 beds; £13) and *Butharlyp Howe* (80 beds; £15.50). The former is right on the route, though a 15-minute walk from central Grasmere, however the latter is perhaps the pick of the two as it is larger and enjoys the advantages of a more central location, an internet connection, a licence to sell alcohol, a smarter self-catering kitchen and more attractive grounds. The food is superior here too. Be warned, however, that because it is the larger it tends to attract more marauding school groups, making Thorney How by far the more preferable on these days. The two share the same booking system, so if you fail to get into one they'll look for space at the other. Thorney How is closed to individuals Nov to mid-Feb and Butharlyp is closed mid-Dec to Feb.

There's also the independent and rather plush *Grasmere Hostel* (Map 18, p103; ☎ 015394 35055, 🖳 www.grasmere hostel.co.uk; 24 beds), Broadrayne Farm, with features including fully equipped kitchens, a drying room, a really pleasant residents' lounge and even a Nordic sauna (!). Bedrooms contain no more than six beds charging £17.50 per bed. Please note that bookings cannot be accepted more than six weeks in advance unless for large groups taking the whole hostel.

B&Bs Most B&Bs will be very reluctant to accept a one-night-only booking on summer weekends. Either stay for two nights or try to avoid the high-season weekends.

Oak Lodge (☎ 015394 35527, 🖳 www .oaklodge-grasmere.co.uk; 2D/1T, all en suite) is the first place you see as you enter Grasmere on the Easedale Road. It's a very smart little establishment in a wonderful location next to tranquil Easedale Forest and charges from £28 per person.

Silver Lea (☎ 015394 35657, 🖳 www .silverlea.com; 2T or D/2D all en suite) on Easedale Rd is a charming ivy-clad slate cottage, surprisingly bright inside, where

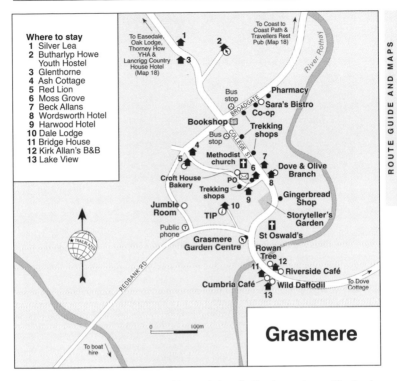

Where to stay
1 Silver Lea
2 Butharlyp Howe Youth Hostel
3 Glenthorne
4 Ash Cottage
5 Red Lion
6 Moss Grove
7 Beck Allans
8 Wordsworth Hotel
9 Harwood Hotel
10 Dale Lodge
11 Bridge House
12 Kirk Allan's B&B
13 Lake View

To Easedale, Oak Lodge, Thorney How YHA & Lancrigg Country House Hotel (Map 18)

To Coast to Coast Path & Travellers Rest Pub (Map 18)

River Rothay

Bus stop

Pharmacy

Sara's Bistro

Co-op

Bookshop

Trekking shops

Bus stop

Methodist church

Dove & Olive Branch

Croft House Bakery

PO

Trekking shops

Gingerbread Shop

Jumble Room

Storyteller's Garden

TIP

St Oswald's

Public phone

Grasmere Garden Centre

Rowan Tree

Riverside Café

Cumbria Café

Wild Daffodil

To Dove Cottage

TRAILBLAZER

REDBANK RD

0   100m

Grasmere

To boat hire

each room has a TV and tea-/coffee-making facilities. Rates are from £41 per person for a twin or double, or £45 for a suite (with lounge). An evening meal costs £15.50 though it is only provided when enough people request it.

Back towards the centre, the large *Glenthorne Guest House* (☎ 015394 35389, 🖳 www.glenthorne.org; 7S/12T/ 4D) is a Victorian, Quaker country house (though folk of any creed can stay) next to another of Wordsworth's old houses, Allan Bank. Though the place feels like a hostel when you first walk in – thanks in part to the wonderfully informal, convivial atmosphere to the place – the rooms are fine. Overriding everything, however, is this place's hospitality, with plates of sandwiches laid out for guests to take with them on

their walk. Evening meals are offered and a minute's silence is held before eating and there is a voluntary 15-minute (30 mins on Sundays) prayer meeting in the mornings. Rates are £32/39 standard/en suite.

Beck Allans (☎ 015394 35563, 🖳 www.beckallans.com; 5D) is a guesthouse with some self-catering apartments overlooking the Rothay. It lies in the heart of the village next to the Wordsworth Hotel (see p106), whose pool and gym facilities residents at Beck Allans are allowed to use. All rooms (£29-40 per person) are en suite with bath and shower, and come with TV, tea- and coffee-making facilities, hair dryer – and room No 2 has a four-poster bed (£37-40 per person for two sharing). Note that no pets are allowed, and there's a single supplement of 50 per cent.

By the bridge is **Kirk Allan's B&B** (☎ 015394 35745; 2D) with rooms for £27.50 per person (there is a £12.50 single occupancy supplement). It's centrally located and convenient for exploring the nearby teashops and the lake shore.

Lake View (☎ 015394 35384, 🖳 www .lakeview-grasmere.com; 3D/1T) is, as its name suggests, one of the few places to stay from where you can actually see the lake (though with every passing year the growing vegetation ensures the view diminishes). It's a lovely place near the centre of Grasmere, quietly tucked away at the end of a lane. Rates vary from £51 to £72.50.

Hotels

Moss Grove Organic Hotel (☎ 015394 35251, 🖳 www.mossgrove.com; 11D) is a smashing place whose strict green ethos extends beyond the kitchen to their accommodation, with beds made from reclaimed timber sitting atop oak floors from sustainable forests. All this, and yet the building still retains its original Victorian charm. The prices, however, do reflect the quality, with rooms from £125 (Sun-Thur in the cheaper executive rooms) up to £195.

Ash Cottage (☎ 015394 35224, 🖳 www.ashcottage.com; 1T/5D) sits in the absolute heart of Grasmere, fronted by a pleasant terrace that's usually buzzing with walkers when the weather allows. Room prices vary from £80 up to £140 for the honeymoon suite.

Opposite, **Red Lion Hotel** (☎ 015394 35456, 🖳 www.hotelslakedistrict.com; 47 en suite rooms) *is* the centre of town, a pleasant-enough place though one that lacks a little of the charm of some of the others around here. Nevertheless, it's a bit cheaper too, and all rooms are en suite, many with Jacuzzi baths. Rates are £51-72.50. Dogs are welcome for a fee of £20, regardless of length of stay.

Wordsworth Hotel (☎ 015394 35592, 🖳 www.grasmere-hotels.com; 4S/33D or T – two with four-poster beds – and two suites; all en suite) was formerly the smartest address in the centre of town (but Moss Grove provides stiff competition now). It's a large but attractive hotel with

facilities including gym, pool, sauna, Jacuzzi and cocktail bar. They also offer fishing on the nearby Rothay. Rooms come with satellite flat-screen TV, radio, wi-fi access, phone and computer points. Rates in summer are £70/70-90 for sgl/dbl and £110 for a suite.

Bridge House Hotel (☎ 015394 35425, 🖳 www.bridgehousegrasmere.co.uk; 11D/ 8D or T) is another large place and is also near the river; this one has no single rooms but all 19 rooms are en suite with a TV, telephone and tea-/coffee-making facilities. Unfortunately, they accept one-night bookings only if it's quiet which, in summer, it is unlikely to be. They also do not allow pets. Nevertheless, the hotel has two acres of gorgeous grounds. Rates, for one night with breakfast and dinner, are £59/66.50 standard/superior (ie larger) rooms in summer, falling to £36/41 in winter.

Dale Lodge Hotel (☎ 015394 35300, 🖳 www.dalelodgehotel.co.uk; 2T/10D en suite) is a strange old place. A tired-looking old pile on the outside, inside it is all polished floorboards and original tilework and really rather chic. The three acres of sprawling gardens are another attraction, as is its location in the heart of town. Each bedroom, individually furnished and decorated has colour TV, tea- and coffee-making facilities and direct dial telephone. The attached bar, *Tweedies*, is also recommended. Dogs are allowed. Rates start at £60 per person, £70 at weekends. Single occupancy (not allowed on summer weekends) is £20 extra.

Very nearby, *Harwood Hotel* (☎ 015394 35248, 🖳 www.harwoodhotel.co .uk; 3D en suite/2S/1D/1T private bath) has rooms from £29.50 per person (less out of season).

Our favourite hotel in Grasmere, however, is the **Lancrigg Vegetarian Country House Hotel** (Map 18, p103; ☎ 015394 35317, 🖳 www.lancrigg.co.uk; 10D/2T and a room in the annex). It's certainly the most beautiful and, given its position next to the magical Lancrigg Wood, the location can't be beat either – which, bearing in mind the competition, is really saying something. Lancrigg is a large country house, with parts dating back to the 17th century, a little way to the north-west of the village, very near Thorney How Youth Hostel. One of the previous occupants was Elizabeth Fletcher, a friend of Wordsworth (he found and helped her buy the house in 1839), and the house and adjoining woods became something of a meeting place for the Lakeland poets.

All the rooms are individually furnished with many affording a magnificent view across Easedale Forest and the neighbouring fields. Some also have four-poster beds and whirlpool baths.

If you don't eat meat and have got the money, this is the place to spend it. Rates are £75-105. Discounts are available at certain times of the year. I can't think of a more splendid hotel on the walk – and I'm not even vegetarian.

Where to eat

For takeaway sandwiches you can't really beat *Croft House Bakery* (Mon-Sat 9am-4pm, Sun 9.30am-4pm), next to the post office, which does a nice line in spuds, baguettes and butties.

As you'd expect for a major tourist centre like Grasmere, tearooms are plentiful throughout the village. Best of all is *Jumble Room* (☎ 015394 35188; Wed-Sun noon-3pm, 6pm 'till food runs out'). Aptly named, this is a quirky little place that resembles, from the outside, a cross between an art gallery and a toy shop. Don't be put off, however, for the food is some of the most imaginative in town, the menu changes daily and includes dishes from all four corners of the globe, including the locally inspired haddock in beer batter for £10.95.

Another place that's open for teas during the day is the *Rowan Tree* (☎ 015394 35528; daily 10am-5pm, weekends only Dec & Jan), overlooking the river. However, our advice is to save a visit until the evening (from 6pm, closed Tue), when they do a fine selection of pizzas from £7.25 and other Italian or English dishes.

A number of other tea shops and cafés vie for position near the bridge including the contemporary *Riverside Café*, aka

Williams of Grasmere, which does delicious hot chocolate dip ice cream, and the *Cumbria Café* (daily 9am-5pm, Tue-Sun 6pm-late) which does an excellent-value Yorkshire pudding for £3.95.

The *Wild Daffodil* (☎ 015394 35770; Fri-Tue 10am-9pm, Wed 10am-4pm, Thur closed) also does evening meals such as lamb Henry for £10.95 and sandwiches from £2.50.

The *Dove and Olive Branch* (☎ 015394 35592), part of the Wordsworth Hotel, is a typically upmarket place with an interesting menu, including slow-roasted belly of Gloucester Old Spot pork for £10.95). The Red Lion (see opposite) offers limited menus of good food in either its *Garden Room* or *Courtyard* restaurants.

Moving north, *Sara's Bistro* (☎ 015394 35266; Tue-Sun 10.30am-4pm, 6-9pm) has been recommended for its exquisite food (poached fillet of salmon for £11.50 is particularly delicious).

Finally, at least a 20-minute walk north from town, the *Traveller's Rest Pub* (see Map 18, p103) serves hearty portions of mainly local dishes.

What to see

Dove Cottage William Wordsworth lived for less than ten years in beautiful Dove Cottage (☎ 015394 35544, 🖳 www.words worthtrust.org.uk; daily 9.30am-5.30pm closed 24-26 Dec and early Jan to early Feb; £6.50, children £4.10; student tickets available), yet its importance in both his development as a poet and his life is enormous. Many of his best loved and most powerful works were penned here (altogether now: 'I wandered lonely as a cloud...'), and this is where he first lived with his wife Mary Hutchinson and where his first three children were born.

Today all but the first room is furnished entirely with items owned, at one time or another, by the poet, though it should be added not all the pieces of furniture were originally part of Dove Cottage, but have come from other Wordsworth properties.

Guides show visitors around the cottage every hour on the half-hour, pointing out such items of interest as Wordsworth's **suitcase** (where he's sewn his name inside but didn't leave enough room and ended up embroidering 'Wordswort' on one line, with the final 'h' tucked up in the corner); a letter of introduction – a precursor to the modern-day passport – penned by the French authorities, and which has been stamped on the back by the border guards of a whole host of European countries that Wordsworth visited; and the **Royal Warrant** of 1843 in which he was bestowed with the honour of being Queen Victoria's poet laureate. It was an honour he accepted grudgingly, having already turned down the position twice, and one that he never truly fulfilled; indeed, from his acceptance of the post to his death in 1850, Wordsworth wrote precisely no official poems as poet laureate, the first (and so far only) poet laureate to do so.

The cottage is, by the standards of the Lake District, relatively large, containing eight rooms rather than the more typical three or four, thus betraying its origins as a 17th-century pub. It might interest you to know that one of Wordsworth's visitors at the cottage was that other well-known literary figure (and opium fiend) Thomas de Quincey. At the time of his visit de Quincey declared the house to be a fortuitous one for writers, and when the Wordsworths vacated the house in 1808 the de Quinceys moved in, thus extending the literary connections of the place still further.

The **museum** next door contains original manuscripts by both Wordsworth and de Quincey, as well as a whole host of other poetic paraphernalia.

Other sights Before you leave Grasmere, pay a visit to **Wordsworth's family grave** around the back of **St Oswald's**, a 13th-century church named after the 7th-century king of Northumbria who preached on this site. Wordsworth's prayer-book is on display in the church.

Standing by the side entrance to the church grounds is the 150-year-old **Gingerbread Shop** (☎ 015394 35428, 🖳 www.grasmeregingerbread.co.uk; Mon-Sat 9.15am-5.30pm, Sun 12.30-5.30pm), a tiny 'factory' that, incredibly, used to be the local school. It is said that Wordsworth taught here occasionally.

Opposite is the **Storyteller's Garden** which plays host to several events throughout the year – ask at the tourist office for a schedule.

Around the village centre are a number of **galleries** displaying works by local artists.

Make sure, too, that you check out **Lancrigg Woods** and the **Poet's Walk** (Map 18, p103), the start of which you walked past on your way into Grasmere. It's a tranquil delight and it comes as no surprise to find that the Lakeland poets enjoyed it too. Indeed, they planted many of the trees that grow in the woods. Along the way is an inscription, in Latin, describing how Wordsworth's sister Dorothy would sit at this spot while her brother walked up and down composing verses. The path finishes up going round the front of the very smart Lancrigg Hotel, where it joins the road to the youth hostel.

Transport (see also pp43-5)

From Easter to October Stagecoach's open-top No 599 **bus** service travels 2-3/day via Ambleside (15 mins) and the train station and Bowness Pier at Windermere, from where in the evening a few buses go on to Kendal. The No 555 goes from Keswick to Lancaster (hourly, daily) via Ambleside, Windermere and Kendal (Grasmere to Lancaster takes 1hr 50min).

For other destinations, Grasmere **Taxis** can be reached on ☎ 015394 35506.

STAGE 4: GRASMERE TO PATTERDALE   MAPS 18-25

Introduction

Ignoring the alternative routes on this stage for the moment, this is one of the shortest and easiest stages. Short, but no less sweet, for during this stage walkers can enjoy some great views both over the shoulder to Grasmere and, once over the pass, down Grisedale to Patterdale, another gorgeous valley with the lake of Ullswater hiding away to the north.

The most direct route is a mere **10 miles (16km, 3¹/₂hr)** and is a simple up and down, involving a crossing of **Grisedale Pass**. The stage can, however, be lengthened by attempting a conquest of one of the nearby peaks, Helvellyn or St Sunday. Both of these are described on pp112-14. You can delay your choice on which path to take until Grisedale Tarn, where the three paths go their separate ways.

The route

First of all you need to reach Grisedale Tarn, which involves a longish climb up a bridleway running off the A591 (Map 18, p103) reached by walking up the A591 to the bridleway from Grasmere or, more enjoyably, on the 'official' Coast to Coast path near Thorney How Youth Hostel.

The bridleway divides at the foot of **Great Tongue** (Map 19) and a choice must be made. The steeper route alongside **Little Tongue Gill** is harder on the calves but easy on the eye: this is the route to take for views back down to Grasmere. The 'easier path' to the east of Great Tongue along Tongue Gill is paved for much of its length; the gradients are slightly less on this trail, though, of course, at the end of the day you're still climbing to the same height and from the same starting point as the other trail.

At the top of the climb there's a wall and a great view of the entire **Grisedale Tarn** (Map 20). You will also note, behind it, the path up **Dollywaggon Pike** to Helvellyn etched into the grass. Keeping to the easier path down Grisedale, the descent is as uncomplicated as the ascent, a reasonably straight scamper down the valley.

Just below the tarn is the **Brothers' Parting Stone** (so-called because it is said that in 1800 Wordsworth last saw his brother John here, who died at sea in 1805) and, just under a mile further on by rushing Ruthwaite Beck, **Ruthwaite Lodge**, a climbers' hut.

The path continues fairly straight down the valley and joins a tarmac road before leaving it to the right to bend left through the National Trust's **Glenamara Park** (Map 24), with some wonderful views over Patterdale and beyond to Ullswater (Norse for 'Water with a Bend'). All being well, you'll drop onto the road just below the post office and pub just over two hours (plus breaks) after leaving Grisedale Tarn.

ROUTE GUIDE AND MAPS

ROUTE GUIDE AND MAPS

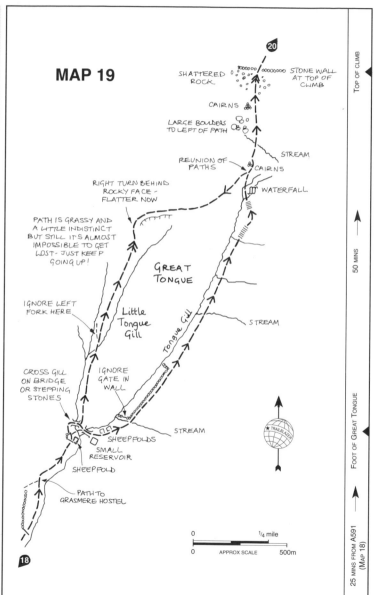

MAP 19

SHATTERED ROCK

STONE WALL AT TOP OF CLIMB

CAIRNS

LARGE BOULDERS TO LEFT OF PATH

REUNION OF PATHS

STREAM

CAIRNS

RIGHT TURN BEHIND ROCKY FACE - FLATTER NOW

WATERFALL

PATH IS GRASSY AND A LITTLE INDISTINCT BUT STILL IT'S ALMOST IMPOSSIBLE TO GET LOST- JUST KEEP GOING UP!

GREAT TONGUE

Tongue Gill

IGNORE LEFT FORK HERE

Little Tongue Gill

STREAM

CROSS GILL ON BRIDGE OR STEPPING STONES

IGNORE GATE IN WALL

STREAM

SHEEPFOLDS

SMALL RESERVOIR

SHEEPFOLD

PATH TO GRASMERE HOSTEL

TRAILBLAZER

0   1/4 mile
0   APPROX SCALE   500m

TOP OF CLIMB

50 MINS

FOOT OF GREAT TONGUE

25 MINS FROM A591 (MAP 18)

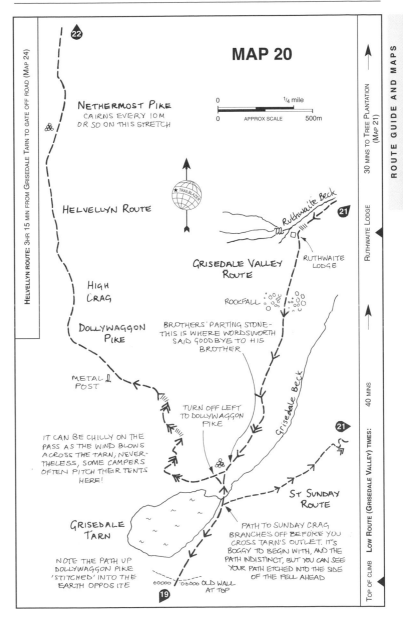

MAP 20

22

NETHERMOST PIKE
CAIRNS EVERY 10M
OR SO ON THIS STRETCH

0 ____ ¼ mile

0 ____ APPROX SCALE ____ 500m

HELVELLYN ROUTE

★ TRAILBLAZER

HELVELLYN ROUTE: 3HR 15 MIN FROM GRISEDALE TARN TO GATE OFF ROAD (MAP 24)

Ruthwaite Beck

21

GRISEDALE VALLEY
ROUTE

RUTHWAITE
LODGE

HIGH
CRAG

ROCKFALL

DOLLYWAGGON
PIKE

BROTHERS' PARTING STONE –
THIS IS WHERE WORDSWORTH
SAID GOODBYE TO HIS
BROTHER

METAL
POST

Grisedale Beck

TURN OFF LEFT
TO DOLLYWAGGON
PIKE

IT CAN BE CHILLY ON THE
PASS AS THE WIND BLOWS
ACROSS THE TARN, NEVER-
THELESS, SOME CAMPERS
OFTEN PITCH THEIR TENTS
HERE!

21

ST SUNDAY
ROUTE

GRISEDALE
TARN

PATH TO SUNDAY CRAG
BRANCHES OFF BEFORE YOU
CROSS TARN'S OUTLET. IT'S
BOGGY TO BEGIN WITH, AND THE
PATH INDISTINCT, BUT YOU CAN SEE
YOUR PATH ETCHED INTO THE SIDE
OF THE FELL AHEAD

NOTE THE PATH UP
DOLLYWAGGON PIKE
'STITCHED' INTO THE
EARTH OPPOSITE

ooooo ooooo OLD WALL
AT TOP

19

30 MINS TO TREE PLANTATION (MAP 21)

RUTHWAITE LODGE

40 MINS

LOW ROUTE (GRISEDALE VALLEY) TIMES:

TOP OF CLIMB

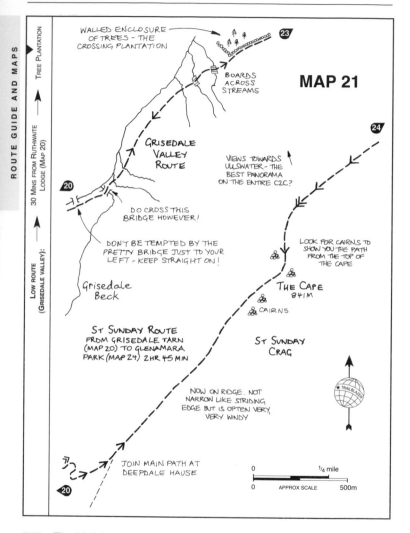

ROUTE GUIDE AND MAPS

TREE PLANTATION

30 MINS FROM RUTHWAITE LODGE (MAP 20)

LOW ROUTE (GRISEDALE VALLEY):

WALLED ENCLOSURE OF TREES - THE CROSSING PLANTATION

BOARDS ACROSS STREAMS

MAP 21

23

GRISEDALE VALLEY ROUTE

20

DO CROSS THIS BRIDGE HOWEVER!

DON'T BE TEMPTED BY THE PRETTY BRIDGE JUST TO YOUR LEFT - KEEP STRAIGHT ON!

Grisedale Beck

VIEWS TOWARDS ULLSWATER - THE BEST PANORAMA ON THE ENTIRE C2C?

24

LOOK FOR CAIRNS TO SHOW YOU THE PATH FROM THE TOP OF THE CAPE

THE CAPE 841M

CAIRNS

ST SUNDAY ROUTE FROM GRISEDALE TARN (MAP 20) TO GLENAMARA PARK (MAP 24) 2HR 45 MIN

ST SUNDAY CRAG

NOW ON RIDGE. NOT NARROW LIKE STRIDING EDGE BUT IS OFTEN VERY, VERY WINDY

TRAILBLAZER

JOIN MAIN PATH AT DEEPDALE HAUSE

20

0   ¼ mile

0   APPROX SCALE   500m

The high-level alternatives: Helvellyn & Striding Edge; St Sunday Crag

If weather conditions allow, one of these two high-level options should be seriously considered instead of the simple trail down Grisedale. After all, it would be a shame on this, the penultimate stage in the Lake District, if you didn't try to climb as many peaks as possible.

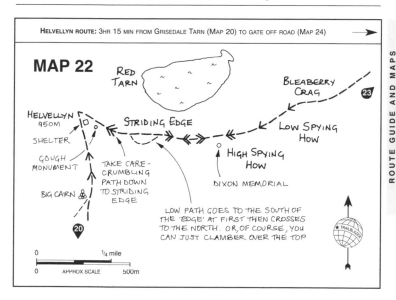

MAP 22

RED TARN

BLEABERRY CRAG

23

HELVELLYN 950M

STRIDING EDGE

SHELTER

LOW SPYING HOW

GOUGH MONUMENT

TAKE CARE - CRUMBLING PATH DOWN TO STRIDING EDGE

HIGH SPYING HOW

BIG CAIRN

DIXON MEMORIAL

20

LOW PATH GOES TO THE SOUTH OF THE 'EDGE' AT FIRST THEN CROSSES TO THE NORTH. OR, OF COURSE, YOU CAN JUST CLAMBER OVER THE TOP

0   ¹/₄ mile

0   APPROX SCALE   500m

TRAILBLAZER

ROUTE GUIDE AND MAPS

Helvellyn & Striding Edge   Map 20, p111, Maps 22-24, pp113-15

Of the two high-level alternatives, **Helvellyn** (950m), the third highest peak in England after Scafell Pike and Scafell, is perhaps the more popular. The climb is arduous and, having reached the top, you then face a nerve-tingling drop on a crumbling slope followed by a tightrope walk along Striding Edge to reach the onward trail to Patterdale; the memorial plaque to Robert Dixon who was killed here in 1858 whilst following his fox hounds during a hunt does little to calm the nerves. Still, the views and sense of achievement are ample reward for your efforts.

Wainwright himself waxes lyrical about this side trip, describing the famous/notorious Striding Edge as the 'best quarter mile between St Bees and Robin Hood's Bay'. You may feel less enamoured as you slide down on your backside to the start of Striding Edge, the scree tumbling down the sheer slope below you.

The route takes about 3hr 15 mins from Grisedale Tarn, though that assumes you will take the lower route just below the summit of Striding Edge which could be completed in as little as 20 minutes. However, with the inevitable trips up to the summit and with all the waiting that needs to be done to let people coming the other way go by (at least at weekends), expect it to take nearer an hour. You won't regret the extra time – it is truly exhilarating.

Wainwright visited Helvellyn on his first trip to the Lakes in 1930, and although the weather was such that the 'rain still sluiced down, making rivulets on our bellies', it was this first trip that inspired his passion for the Lakes. He approached the peak from the opposite direction to that described here, *from* Striding Edge, which he described edging along 'in agonies of apprehension'.

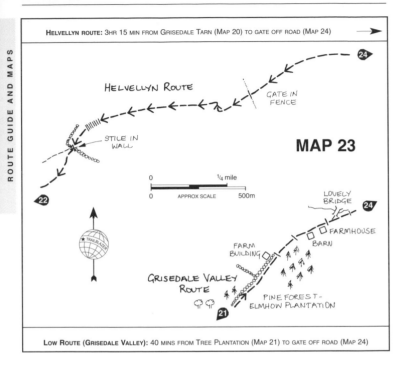

HELVELLYN ROUTE: 3HR 15 MIN FROM GRISEDALE TARN (MAP 20) TO GATE OFF ROAD (MAP 24) →

HELVELLYN ROUTE

GATE IN FENCE

STILE IN WALL

MAP 23

0   ¼ mile
0   APPROX SCALE   500m

LOVELY BRIDGE

FARMHOUSE

BARN

FARM BUILDING

GRISEDALE VALLEY ROUTE

PINE FOREST - ELMHOW PLANTATION

LOW ROUTE (GRISEDALE VALLEY): 40 MINS FROM TREE PLANTATION (MAP 21) TO GATE OFF ROAD (MAP 24)

St Sunday Crag
Map 20 p111, Map 21 p112, Map23 above, Map 24 p115

Better for views, if not excitement, than Helvellyn is the scramble up St Sunday Crag, to the south of Grisedale. Indeed, for many people these are the best views on the entire route. What's more, the effort required to climb up to St Sunday is, by the standards of the lakes, fairly negligible, a steady ascent followed – at least until the drop into Glenamara Park – by a reasonably steady descent.

Initially, the path from Grisedale Tarn is rather unclear as it passes through terrain that's usually pretty saturated, though you should be able to see the trail for Deepdale Hause etched into the side of the slope ahead between the peaks of Fairfield and St Sunday. Once the ridge is gained, path finding up to St Sunday (841m) and its summit, known as The Cape, shouldn't be a problem.

After that the path starts off bending more to the north (left), before skirting below the ridge and dropping down to Glenamara Park, where you meet up with the low-level route to Patterdale.

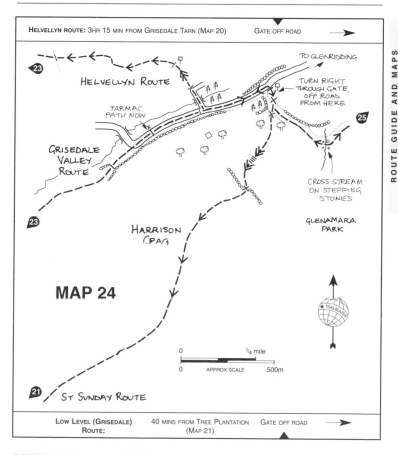

PATTERDALE   MAP 25, p117

Patterdale is little more than a meandering collection of houses strung along the A592. Nevertheless, it's a cracking place. Normally valleys this beautiful would be full of souvenir shops and tearooms. But Patterdale, while not exactly undiscovered if the huge volume of hikers walking through the village on a summer weekend is anything to go by, *is* mercifully free of the worst excesses of tourism.

It also has some cute touches. The **fountain of St Patrick** (Patterdale is a corruption of St Patrick's Dale) is an ornate Victorian construction set in a bank by the side of the road just outside Glenridding, and is said to mark the spot where the saint baptized the locals. The valley is also something of a wildlife haven, including a population of red squirrels – some of the last remaining in England – and badgers. And finally there's **Crookabeck Herdwicks** (ring first for an appointment on ☎ 017684 82742, 🖳 www.herdwickwool.com), a farm selling clothes and hats made from wool sheared from the local Herdwick flocks.

The only official tourist office (see box p118) is in Glenridding; internet access (see p119) is also available there. If you can't be bothered to traipse down there, you could try the **post office** (daily 9.30am-6pm) in Patterdale, whose owners seem reasonably well versed in the latest happenings on the Coast-to-Coast path. They also have a small selection of sandwiches (£1.50-2.50), including bacon butties (£1.95) and Cumberland baguettes (£2.95), as well as fresh fruit and a small selection of trekking supplies.

Where to stay and eat

There's a range of **accommodation** in Patterdale, though booking ahead is, as elsewhere, vital, else you could end up having to stay in Glenridding. Not that there's anything wrong with Glenridding, of course, and indeed its location by Ullswater is a delight – it's just a fair distance from the start of the next stage, which is one of the more wearying stretches and not one you'd want to extend if you can help it.

For **campers**, across the Goldrill Beck is *Side Farm* (☎ 017684 82337; £5 per person; open Easter to the end of October). The campsite actually lies a little way from the farm on the edge of the lake. They insist that you check in at the farm first, however, and considering they have a **tearoom** (Easter to end Oct daily 10.30am-5pm) that serves some delicious home-made cakes, it's a good place to recuperate from the day's trek before pitching your tent. Believe it or not, Wordsworth was a regular visitor to Side Farm.

At the other end of the village, *Patterdale Youth Hostel* (☎ 0870 770 5986, 🖳 patterdale@yha.org.uk; 82 beds; £14) is on the main road. The hostel looks a bit like a comprehensive school, but inside it's comfortable and, unusually, is open all day. Facilities include TV, a games room, internet access and the current chef is said to be one of the best in the association. Though the building itself is only 30-or-so years old, it stands on the site of a previous hostel from the 1930s, making it one of the oldest in Britain.

Just before the hostel, *Old Water View* (☎ 01768 482175, 🖳 www.oldwaterview .co.uk; 4D/2T) is a wonderful place, a favourite of Wainwright's. The current owner is a mine of information regarding the walk, having guided trekkers over parts of it before; he's also a local ranger and the guy to speak to about short-cuts along High Street to Shap. The accommodation itself is great too, with some nice touches including, ahem, teddy bears bearing chocolates. Rates are £39.50 for single occupancy (Sun-Thur only), £27.50-32.50 for double occupancy. Apparently, he also knows the whereabouts of a nearby otter holt. Nearer the centre of the village the no-nonsense *Glebe House* (☎ 017684 82339; 1D/1F) lies set back from the road and charges from £25. Kids under ten and pets are not welcome.

Very close to the path and the focus of the village is the local pub, the 19th-century *White Lion* (☎ 017684 82214; 1S/1S or D/2D/3T, all en suite or with private facilities). B&B starts at £31 and they do bar meals too. The extensive menu includes steaks, curry and fish & chips (noon-9pm); whatever dish you choose, it will be big! They also do **breakfasts** for non-residents.

There are other B&Bs further south along the road beyond the youth hostel. Less than a mile from the path, *Noran Bank Farm* (☎ 017684 82201; 1S/2D/1T/1F) is a whitewashed 16th-century farmhouse about half a mile from the centre of Patterdale. Rates are £23/20 sgl/dbl. Another 16th-century farmhouse, *Greenbank Farm* (☎ 017684 82292; 1D/1T/1F) is nearby, a working sheep farm charging from £20.

The smartest and most expensive address in the village is *Patterdale Hotel* (☎ 017684 82500, 🖳 www.patterdalehotel .co.uk; 4S/50D or F), an enormous establishment by Patterdale's standards. Part of a chain, it's pleasant enough though not really memorable and their reluctance to allow one-night stays will deter most trekkers. The tariff is complex, but expect to pay around £70 for B&B, with small discounts if booked early or if you're staying for two

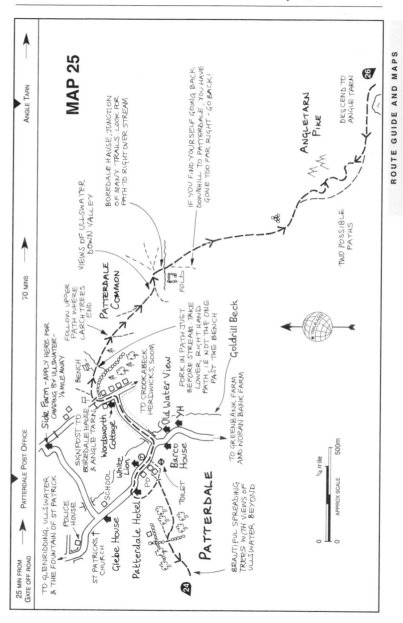

MAP 25

25 MIN FROM GATE OFF ROAD

PATTERDALE POST OFFICE

70 MINS

ANGLE TARN

TO GLENRIDDING, ULLSWATER & THE FOUNTAIN OF ST PATRICK

POLICE HOUSE

ST PATRICK'S CHURCH

SCHOOL

GLEBE HOUSE

WHITE LION

Patterdale Hotel

PATTERDALE

BEAUTIFUL SPREADING TREES WITH VIEWS OF ULLSWATER BEYOND

Side Farm - APPLY HERE FOR CAMPING BY ULLSWATER - ¼ MILE AWAY

SIGNPOST TO BOREDALE HOUSE & ANGLE TARN

Wordsworth Cottage

PO

Barco House

TOILET

TO GREENBANK FARM AND NORAN BANK FARM

TO CROOKABECK HERDWICKS, 500M

Old Water View

YH

Bench

FOLLOW UPPER PATH WHERE LARCH TREES END

VIEWS OF ULLSWATER DOWN VALLEY

PATTERDALE COMMON

BOREDALE HOUSE, JUNCTION OF MANY TRAILS. LOOK FOR PATH TO RIGHT OVER STREAM

FORK IN PATH JUST BEFORE STREAM. TAKE LOWER, RIGHT HAND PATH, i.e. NOT THE ONE PAST THE BENCH

Goldrill Beck

FOLDS

IF YOU FIND YOURSELF GOING BACK DOWNHILL TO PATTERDALE, YOU HAVE GONE TOO FAR RIGHT - GO BACK!

ANGLETARN PIKE

TWO POSSIBLE PATHS

DESCEND TO ANGLE TARN

26

24

¼ mile

0

APPROX SCALE

0

500m

TRAILBLAZER

nights or more. Food is served daily noon-5pm, 6-8pm (6.30-8.30pm at weekends).

Wordsworth Cottage (☎ 017684 82084, 💻 www.wordsworthcottage.co.uk; 2D en suite or with private bathroom; £30 per person), at the end of the village just before the climb up to Angle Tarn, is a delightful, secluded little place dating back to 1670 (the year is carved into a beam in the living room) whose use of the name of the Lakes' most famous son is not opportunistic, for the poet actually owned the cottage – though he never actually lived here. Later, in the first half of the twentieth century, Ann Macbeth, who embroidered the wall hangings at St Patrick's Church, also lived here. Both double rooms have views over the garden or across to the fells. Recommended.

Grisedale Lodge (☎ 017684 82155, 💻 www.grisedalelodge.co.uk; 3D or T) is set halfway between Patterdale and Glenridding

villages, close to the shores of Ullswater. It's a lovely location and by all accounts a lovely B&B too, with swish en suite rooms and large breakfasts. Rates from £30 per person, £40 single occupancy (Sun-Thurs only).

Transport (see also pp43-5)

Stagecoach's **Bus** No 517 (Kirkstone Rambler; 3/day) travels daily between Windermere's Bowness Pier and Glenridding via Patterdale Hotel from mid-July to late August; between Easter and mid-July on Saturdays, Sundays and Bank Holidays only; and from Easter to mid-July and September to late October on Saturdays and Sundays only.

The No 208 (Ullswater Connexion; 5/day) travels between Patterdale and Keswick on a similar basis. The No 108 (Patterdale Bus; Mon-Sat, 5-7/day; Sunday only, 4/day, between late March and late

---

❏ Ullswater and Glenridding

I wandered lonely as a cloud,
That floats on high o'er vales and hills,
When all at once I saw a crowd,
A host of golden daffodils,
Beside the lake, beneath the trees,
Fluttering and dancing in the breeze.
William Wordsworth, *Daffodils*

It is said that Wordsworth was inspired to write these words after a trip to Ullswater. Certainly it's a beautiful lake and unlike neighbouring Grasmere and Haweswater there's plenty to do *on* the water too.

There is a **tourist information centre** (☎ 017684 82414) in the main car park in Glenridding; it is open daily 9.30am-5.30pm March until the end of October and at weekends (roughly 9.30am-3.30pm, though phone first to check) only the rest of the year. On the board outside they put up a list of B&Bs with vacancies that evening, which could prove invaluable. Behind it, across the stream, is Catstycam **trekking shop**. **Boats** can be hired from the café at the lake's southern corner. A motorboat costs £12 for 30 mins or £18 per hour for up to two people, or it's £13/20 for 30 mins/1hr for up to four people. These boats are fine, though don't try to emulate Donald Campbell, who broke the 200mph water speed record on Ullswater in 1955. For something more sedate, a rowing boat costs £6/8 for 30 mins/1hr for up to two people, £7/9.50 for three people, and £8/11 for four. Or you can take a cruise on a **steamer** (☎ 017684 82229; 💻 www.ullswatersteamers.co.uk). There have been steamers on the lake since 1859 and two of the boats currently in service, *Lady of the Lake* and *Raven*, have been operating since the late 19th century. There are up to ten services daily to Howton, Pooley Bridge and back. Some Coast to Coasters have even recommended taking the trip to Pooley Bridge (£6.50 single) and continuing on from there as an alternative to the exhausting next stage to Shap – though how this is supposed to save time or effort I have yet to work out!

October, Sundays to early September only) travels to/from Penrith railway station.

GLENRIDDING

There is a **tourist information centre** (see box opposite) here and **internet access** is available at Kilner's Coffee House & Cybercafé (Mon-Fri 10am-5pm, Sat & Sun 10am-6pm; £1 for 30 mins). If that's closed, Ratcher's Tavern next door has two terminals. See column opposite for details of bus services.

If everywhere is full in Patterdale, or you are determined to stay by Ullswater, Glenridding has a couple of places. Almost the first house you come to on the road from Patterdale is *Beech House* (☎ 017684 82037, ☐ www.beechhouse.com; 2S/3D/ 3T, some en suite), charging from £28 per

person for a standard room and £33 for en suite.

Just a few yards away is *Glenridding Hotel* (☎ 017684 82228, ☐ www.glenriddinghotel.co.uk; 36D or T), part of the Best Western chain and the only hotel with a swimming pool in Patterdale. Rates are from £65 Sun-Thurs, £85 Fri & Sat.

Finally, *Mosscrag GH* (☎ 017684 82500, ☐ www.mosscrag.co.uk; 1T/5D) lies behind the tourist office across the river and has a variety of double and twin rooms, including one with a four-poster bed and all but one is en suite. Rates are £28 in the non en suite room, rising to £32 in the en suites and £35 in the four-poster. Single occupancy (not available at weekends) is £40, £45 in an en suite.

STAGE 5: PATTERDALE TO SHAP

MAPS 25-34

Introduction

Be prepared to feel very, very tired at the end of this **16-mile (26km, 6¹/₂hr)** stage from Patterdale to Shap. It's not the climb up to Angletarn and Kidsty pikes that makes most walkers feel weary, nor the long haul around the ups and downs of the western rim of the giant Haweswater Reservoir (see box pp122-3) that has them begging for an end to the punishment. Rather, it's the gentle stretch over field and farmland at the very end of the day that, coming on top of all that has gone before, causes hikers to curse the name 'Wainwright' and regret the day they first donned a pair of walking boots.

Unfortunately, with no accommodation directly on the route nor, indeed, any shops, tearooms or pubs, you have little choice but to grit your teeth, shoulder your backpack and knuckle down to some serious long-haul trekking. To shorten the day, a few walkers now take a one-mile detour to Bampton (see p120).

The route

In spite of the difficulties, there are plenty of positives about this stage too: today is the day you leave the Lake District behind, and **Kidsty Pike** (Map 27) – at 780m the highest point, alternative routes excepted, on the Coast to Coast path – is the perfect summit from which to take a last, long look at the crags, knotts, pikes, fells and raises that have been your high-level companions for much of the past few days.

From the top, looking west, you can see the Pillar, Scafell Pike, Helvellyn and St Sunday; to the south, the deep valley of Riggindale, while to the east, below, is Haweswater and, in the far distance, the grey, fuzzy form of the Pennines. Just near Kidsty, too, in the crags above Riggindale, is said to be the

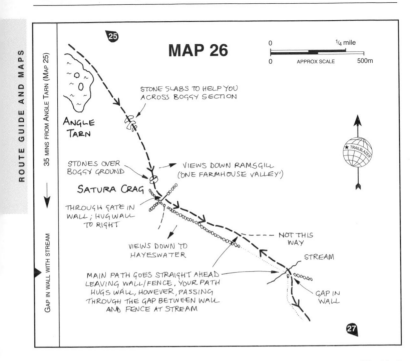

MAP 26

STONE SLABS TO HELP YOU
ACROSS BOGGY SECTION

ANGLE TARN

STONES OVER
BOGGY GROUND

VIEWS DOWN RAMSGILL
('ONE FARMHOUSE VALLEY')

SATURA CRAG

THROUGH GATE IN
WALL; HUG WALL
TO RIGHT

VIEWS DOWN TO
HAYESWATER

NOT THIS
WAY

STREAM

MAIN PATH GOES STRAIGHT AHEAD
LEAVING WALL/FENCE, YOUR PATH
HUGS WALL, HOWEVER, PASSING
THROUGH THE GAP BETWEEN WALL
AND FENCE AT STREAM

GAP IN
WALL

35 MINS FROM ANGLE TARN (MAP 25)

GAP IN WALL WITH STREAM

ROUTE GUIDE AND MAPS

eyrie of England's last **golden eagle**. This male bird is the only bird of its kind left in England, and conservationists are hoping a female from Scotland can be attracted down to mate.

Furthermore, there is also the **Measand Forces** (Map 29), a small waterfall running into the Haweswater Reservoir and a wonderful place to stretch out your weary limbs and rest awhile; while the amble through the wooded glade along Haweswater Beck is an unequivocal delight. The small village of **Burnbanks** (Map 30) at the head of the reservoir has nothing to offer the walker except for a very infrequent bus service (Stagecoach No 111) to Bampton and Penrith (see public transport map and services pp43-5).

Bampton offers two excellent accommodation possibilities: *Mardale Inn* (off Map 30, p124; ☎ 01931 713244, 🖳 www.mardaleinn.co.uk; 4D or T, 3 en suite; £70 per room; food served 6-9pm daily); or, in nearby **Bampton Grange**, the equally recommended *Crown and Mitre* (☎ 01931 713225; 2S/2D/1T/2F; £28 per person). Note, however, that while both these places are lovely, they don't actually shorten the day's walking by that much.

And then, towards the end of the stage, there's **Shap Abbey** (see box p125 and Map 32), an atmospheric ruin set in a peaceful spot by the River Lowther. It's just unfortunate that, by the time you get there, you'll be *(cont'd on p125)*

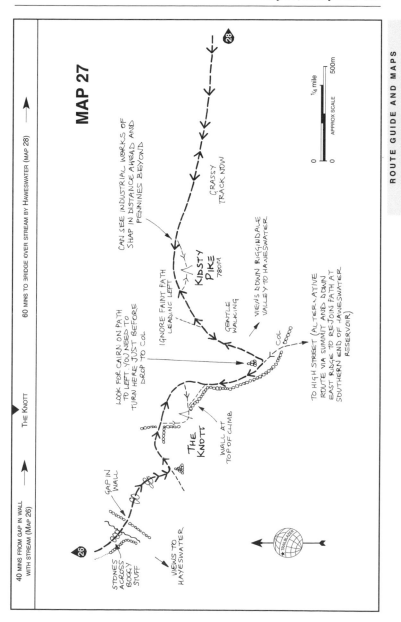

40 MINS FROM GAP IN WALL
WITH STREAM (MAP 26) →

THE KNOTT ►

60 MINS TO BRIDGE OVER STREAM BY HAWESWATER →

MAP 27

CAN SEE INDUSTRIAL WORKS OF
SHAP IN DISTANCE AHEAD AND
PENNINES BEYOND

GRASSY
TRACK NOW

IGNORE FAINT PATH
LEADING LEFT

KIDSTY
PIKE
780M

GENTLE
WALKING

VIEWS DOWN RIGGINDALE
VALLEY TO HAWESWATER

COL

LOOK FOR CAIRN ON PATH
TO LEFT, YOU NEED TO
TURN HERE JUST BEFORE
DROP TO COL

TO HIGH STREET (ALTERNATIVE
ROUTE VIA SUMMIT AND DOWN
EAST RIDGE TO REJOIN PATH AT
SOUTHERN END OF HAWESWATER
RESERVOIR)

GAP IN
WALL

THE
KNOTT

WALL AT
TOP OF CLIMB

STONES
ACROSS
BOGGY
STUFF

VIEWS TO
HAYESWATER

TRAIL BLAZER

0   1/4 mile

0   500m
APPROX SCALE

ROUTE GUIDE AND MAPS

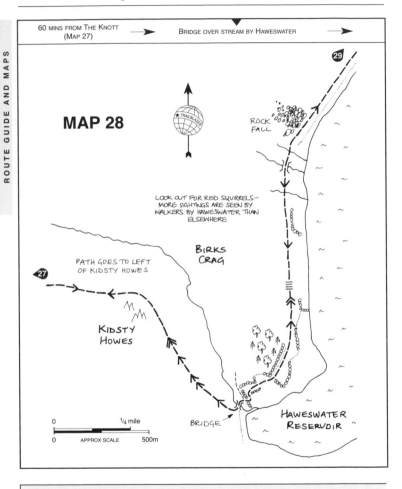

60 MINS FROM THE KNOTT
(MAP 27) →

BRIDGE OVER STREAM BY HAWESWATER →

29

MAP 28

★ TRAILBLAZER

ROCK
FALL

LOOK OUT FOR RED SQUIRRELS—
MORE SIGHTINGS ARE SEEN BY
WALKERS BY HAWESWATER THAN
ELSEWHERE

BIRKS
CRAG

PATH GOES TO LEFT
OF KIDSTY HOWES

27

KIDSTY
HOWES

0   ¼ mile

0   APPROX SCALE   500m

BRIDGE

HAWESWATER
RESERVOIR

❏ Haweswater Reservoir

What is now one of Cumbria's largest bodies of water was once a small and fairly unassuming lake stuck on the eastern edge of the national park. In 1929, however, a bill was passed authorizing the use of Haweswater as a reservoir to serve the needs of the population of Manchester. A concrete dam, 470m wide and 35m high, was constructed at the northern edge of the lake, raising the depth of the lake by over 30m and increasing the surface area to four miles long by half a mile wide (6k by 1km).

This project was not without its opponents. In particular, many protested at the loss of the settlements that had existed on Haweswater's shore for centuries. The

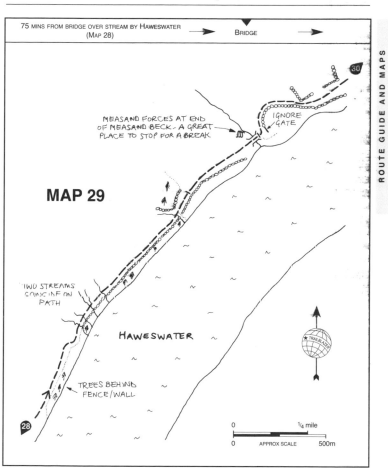

75 MINS FROM BRIDGE OVER STREAM BY HAWESWATER (MAP 28) → BRIDGE →

30

MEASAND FORCES AT END OF MEASAND BECK - A GREAT PLACE TO STOP FOR A BREAK

IGNORE GATE

MAP 29

TWO STREAMS COINCIDE ON PATH

HAWESWATER

TRAILBLAZER

TREES BEHIND FENCE/WALL

28

0   ¼ mile

0   APPROX SCALE   500m

largest of these was Mardale Green on Haweswater's eastern shore (near the pier). Before the village was flooded, coffins were removed from the graveyard and buried elsewhere and the 18th-century Holy Trinity Church was pulled down. Some of the windows from this church are now in the reservoir tower. Even today, during times of drought when the water level is low, the walls of Mardale emerge from the reservoir. This last happened in 2003. Despite man's interference the lake is still something of a wildlife haven. Swimming in the waters are wild brown trout, char, gwyniad and perch, while Riggindale is an RSPB haven, with wheatear, raven, ring ouzel and peregrine.

ROUTE GUIDE AND MAPS

50 MINS FROM BRIDGE (MAP 29) TO ROSGILL BRIDGE (MAP 31) →

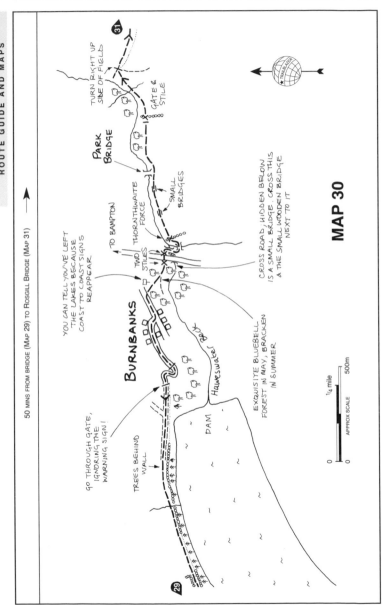

MAP 30

TURN RIGHT UP
SIDE OF FIELD

GATE &
STILE

PARK
BRIDGE

SMALL
BRIDGES

THORNTHWAITE
FORCE

TO BAMPTON

TWO
STILES

CROSS ROAD, HIDDEN BELOW
IS A SMALL BRIDGE. CROSS THIS
& THE SMALL WOODEN BRIDGE
NEXT TO IT

YOU CAN TELL YOU'VE LEFT
THE LAKES BECAUSE
COAST TO COAST SIGNS
REAPPEAR

BURNBANKS

EXQUISITE BLUEBELL
FOREST IN MAY, BRACKEN
IN SUMMER

Haweswater

DAM

GO THROUGH GATE,
IGNORING THE
WARNING SIGN!

TREES BEHIND
WALL

¼ mile

0   500m

0   APPROX SCALE

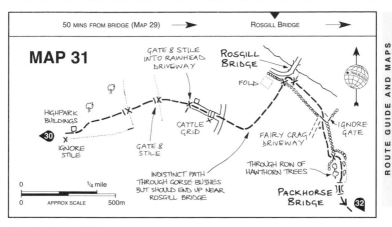

(cont'd from p120) in no mood to appreciate it, your thoughts having turned long ago from holy orders to hot showers. From the abbey, it's a straightforward trudge along roads to **Shap**.

And that's it; you've left the Lakes behind. Little of what you will encounter from here on in will be as wild – or as steep – as that which has gone before. But as much as you may be relieved now, it's those lakes and fells you'll be missing most when the walk is over.

SHAP   MAP 33 p125 & MAP 34 p128
Shap is a thin, narrow village huddled around one long, wide street. That street is the A6, in former times one of the main routes north to Scotland and still the high-est main road in the country. The road used to supply Shap's traders with enough passing trade to make a living and the village grew on the proceeds. But then they built the M6, less than a mile to the east, and at a

❑ **Shap Abbey**
Shap Abbey (see Map 32 p126) has the distinction of being the last abbey to be founded in England, in 1199. It was built by the French Premonstratensian order founded by St Norbert at Prémontré in Northern France, who were also known as the White Canons after the colour of their habits.

The abbey also enjoys the distinction of being the last one dissolved by Henry VIII, in 1540. Presumably Henry's henchmen would have had plenty of practice in dissolving monasteries by this time, which is perhaps why the abbey is today in such a ruinous state. The best-preserved section is the **western belltower**, built around 1500. Information boards provide details of the layout of the abbey. Since its demise, the abbey has had to suffer the further indignity of having some of its best carved stonework purloined by the locals for use in their own buildings. The cottage by the abbey, for example, clearly used a couple of remnants of the abbey in its construction, albeit to good effect, while Shap's 17th-century market hall, just by the NatWest Bank, is built largely from abbey stone. Even some of the local stone walls contain abbey stones.

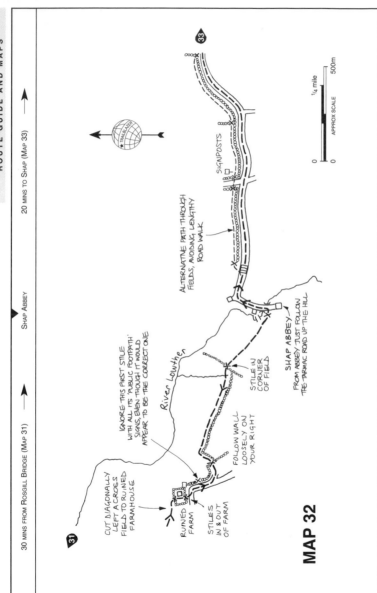

MAP 32

IGNORE THIS FIRST STILE WITH ALL ITS 'PUBLIC FOOTPATH' SIGNS, EVEN THOUGH IT WOULD APPEAR TO BE THE CORRECT ONE

River Lowther

CUT DIAGONALLY LEFT ACROSS FIELD TO RUINED FARMHOUSE

RUINED FARM

STILES IN & OUT OF FARM

FOLLOW WALL LOOSELY ON YOUR RIGHT

STILE IN CORNER OF FIELD

ALTERNATIVE PATH THROUGH FIELDS, AVOIDING LENGTHY ROAD WALK

SIGNPOSTS

SHAP ABBEY – FROM ABBEY JUST FOLLOW THE TARMAC ROAD UP THE HILL

TRAILBLAZER

31

33

APPROX SCALE

0   ¼ mile

0   500m

stroke in 1970 the lifeblood of traffic through Shap was siphoned away for good, and the village slipped into a gentle decline. Which is pretty much how you find it today.

There are some attractive features, including a 17th-century market hall built with masonry from the abbey, but overall the place is pretty plain. However, the fact that it lies at the end of a hard day's walk, offers the first accommodation since Patterdale, and has a chippy and a couple of pubs that offer platefuls of filling grub, are reasons enough to love this place.

Services

There isn't much in the way of services in Shap though the village has its own website (🖳 www.shapcumbria.co.uk). By the **post office** (Mon-Thu 9am-12.30pm, 1.30-5.30pm; Fri 9am-12.30pm; Sat 9am-noon) is the **Co-op**, open late (Mon-Sat 8am-8pm) and good for provisions; it also has a Link **cash machine** (£1.20). There's another cash machine in the Bull's Head (£1.50 charge). There is also a **general store** (Map 34; Mon-Wed 7.30am-3.30pm, Thurs 7am-4pm, Fri 6.45am-5pm, Sat 7-11am).

There's a NatWest **bank** (Mon & Fri only 10.45am-12.45pm) opposite the school and a **newsagent** (Mon-Sat 5am-5.30pm, Sun 7.30am-1pm) opposite the memorial park.

Where to stay

The *Bull's Head* (☎ 01931 716678) is a busy locals' pub with a small beer garden where you can **camp** for £5 (with a 25% discount off one of their filling bar meals if you have prebooked, which they recommend campers do).

The *King's Arms* (Map 34; ☎ 01931 716277, 🖳 www.thekingsarmsatshap.co .uk; 2D/3T all en suite, 2F) charges £70 for two sharing, single occupancy £40. Bar meals are served daily 6-8.30pm.

Built at the beginning of the 18th century, *New Ing Farm* (☎ 01931 716719; 2S/1D/1T/2F) won plaudits from all who stayed here though at the time of writing it had been taken over by new owners so things may change. Look for the pillar in reception which, the previous owners

thought, may have been salvaged from the abbey. The tariff of £25 was terrific value but the rate may change. Over the road, the smart *Hermitage* (☎ 01931 716671; 1S/2D or T/1F, mostly en suite) is just as good value and has also been recommended by readers. The house itself is over 300 years old yet the rooms come with all mod cons including TV, and tea- and coffee-making facilities. Rates start at £28, with single occupancy from £30.

Right at the far end of town, the *Greyhound* (Map 34; ☎ 01931 716474, 🖳 www.greyhoundshap.co.uk; 2S/6D or T/1F, all en suite) is very welcoming and the rooms are very comfy. B&B starts at around £35 (£38 sgl). *Fell House* (Map 34; ☎ 01931 716343, 🖳 www.fellhouse.com; 2T/3D/2F) is now under new ownership following an extensive refurbishment. The

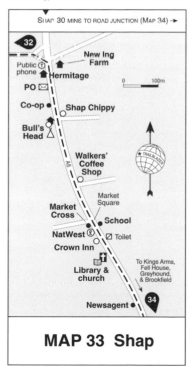

SHAP 30 MINS TO ROAD JUNCTION (MAP 34) →

MAP 33 Shap

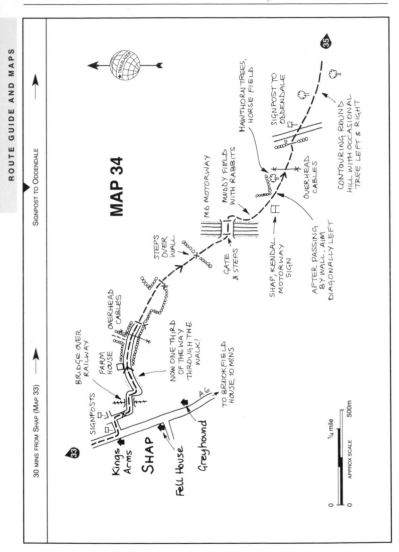

MAP 34

30 MINS FROM SHAP (MAP 33)

SIGNPOST TO OODENDALE

33

Kings Arms

SHAP

Fell House

Greyhound

A6

SIGNPOSTS

BRIDGE OVER RAILWAY

FARM HOUSE

OVERHEAD CABLES

NOW ONE THIRD OF THE WAY THROUGH THE WALK!

TO BROOKFIELD HOUSE, 10 MINS

STEPS OVER WALL

GATE & STEPS

M6 MOTORWAY

SHAP, KENDAL MOTORWAY SIGN

AFTER PASSING BY WALL, AIM DIAGONALLY LEFT

MUDDY FIELD WITH RABBITS

HAWTHORN TREES, HORSE FIELD

SIGNPOST TO OODENDALE

OVERHEAD CABLES

CONTOURING ROUND HILL WITH OCCASIONAL TREE LEFT & RIGHT

35

¼ mile

500m

APPROX SCALE

0

0

(Opposite)   The precarious Striding Edge, as viewed from near the top of Helvellyn, England's third highest peak (see p113).

(Overleaf)   **Top**: Looking down Greenup, on the trail between Borrowdale and Grasmere; Skiddaw in the distance. **Bottom**: Wordsworth's Dove Cottage (see p107) in the quintessential Lakeland village of Grasmere.

rooms are smart and comfy, the breakfasts hearty and, perhaps best of all, the lady of the house is a qualified masseuse (£30 for half an hour). All rooms come with tea- and coffee-making facilities and some are en suite. Rates are from £25 per person, £30 for single occupancy.

Finally, there's *Brookfield House* (☎ 01931 716397, 🖳 www.brookfieldshap.co .uk; 1S/1D or T/1D, some en suite), where B&B is from £25 (per person for two sharing) to £28.50 (per person in an en suite); the single costs £27.50. The breakfasts are good here, and whilst some readers have said the woman owner is intimidating, she is also very attentive to her guests' needs, with one couple saying that she even did their washing free of charge.

Where to eat
The *Greyhound* (see p127) is reputed to cook the best grub in town and most trekkers are more than happy with their fare. The menu consists of mainly local dishes including a decent-sized plate of Cumberland sausage with mash or chips (£6.50). Unfortunately, the Greyhound's location at the very southern end of town is mightily inconvenient for those staying at the Hermitage or New Ing Farm B&B, for whom a walk of over a mile is necessary. More convenient is the *Bull's Head* which does decent British food (daily noon-2pm, 6.30-9pm) either in their restaurant or in the bar. They also claim to have the cheapest beer in the Lake District.

The *King's Arms* (see p127; food served daily noon-2pm, Mon-Fri 5-8pm, Sat & Sun 6-8pm) has a 'happy hour' for their food between 5 and 6pm Monday to Friday, when two meals cost £10.

The fourth village pub, the *Crown Inn* (☎ 01931 716229), serves food daily 12 noon-8.30pm, with a 'snack' menu of sandwiches on offer noon-6pm and more substantial fare in the evenings.

Nearer the centre, there's *Shap Chippy* (☎ 01931 716388; Mon-Sat 9am-1.30pm, daily 4.30-8pm) opposite the Bull's Head (isn't it curious that it is only now, a four- or five-day walk from the nearest sea, that we come across the first fish and chip shop on our route?) and a little further south stands the *Walkers' Coffee Shop* (☎ 01931 716238, 🖳 www.walkerscoffeeshop.co.uk; Tues-Fri 10-4pm, Sat 10am-5pm, Sun noon-4.30pm) which is good for quiches and sandwiches but which is also, alas, usually closed by the time the Coast to Coasters trickle into town.

Transport (see also pp43-5)
Bus No 106 operated by Stagecoach and others calls here 7/day Mon-Sat en route between Kendal and Penrith. The buses leave from Shap's Market Square. The bus takes 30 minutes from Shap to reach Penrith (and 12 minutes to Orton), 45 minutes from Shap to Kendal. The last service from Shap connects at Penrith with the No 563 to Kirkby Stephen.

STAGE 6: SHAP TO KIRKBY STEPHEN   MAPS 34-43

Introduction
Those who struggled to complete the previous stage will be less than delighted to hear that today's hike is, at **21 miles (33km, 7hr)**, even longer. Indeed, for many it will be the longest day on the entire route. Thankfully, there is again a chance to break this stage into two, this time by taking the short diversion into Orton, either to stay overnight or merely to rest awhile in one of the tearooms, indulging in the produce of the local chocolate factory as you do so. If you've got the time, we recommend you do.

This stage of the walk is also renowned for the **prehistoric sites** that crop up with reasonable regularity throughout the day. From stone circles to giants' graves and unearthed settlements, there's plenty to distract you from any nascent

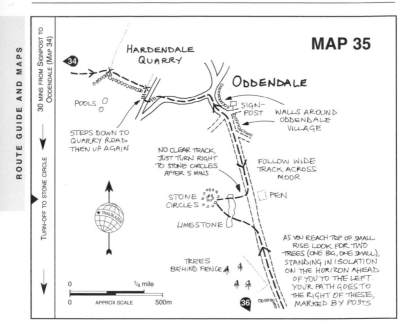

blisters and sore feet, though it's fair to say that none of the sites will make your jaw drop in amazement.

The route

The first prehistoric site occurs about an hour into the walk, just past the mysteriously isolated, walled village of **Oddendale** (Map 35) where, just five minutes off the path to the right (west), lie two **concentric stone circles**. As with just about every prehistoric site on the trail, both their age and purpose are unknown. This stage's second prehistoric site, indicated by a signpost pointing off the path, is **Robin Hood's Grave** (Map 37), a large cairn in a shallow fold in the moor and not a grave at all (and certainly not the grave of the man who, on your walk so far, has already had a promontory named after him, and who gives his name to the bay that is our ultimate destination; both of which, as far as we know, also have nothing to do with him).

Eventually the trail drops down past a quarry and crosses the road, bending south to a junction with the B6260, leaving it to the left to drop down past a wonderfully preserved **limekiln** to Broadfell Farm. Those visiting Orton, whose white churchtower has been clearly visible since the brow of the hill, should continue down the hill through the farm from here; those who wish to carry on with their march should join the farm's driveway and continue east round Orton Scar. Incidentally, look up occasionally on this drop into Orton; more than one hiker has noted that the birdlife around here is surprisingly rich and varied.

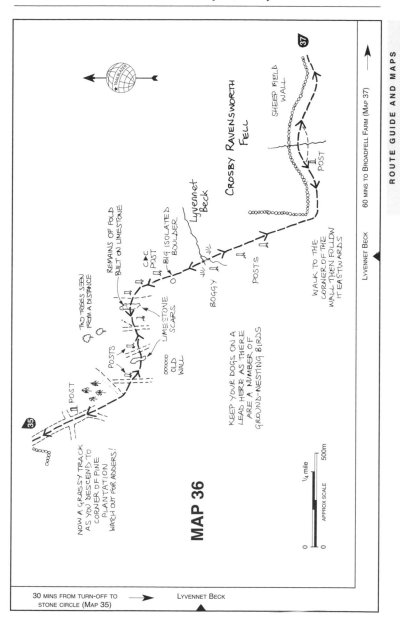

MAP 36

NOW A GRASSY TRACK AS YOU DESCEND TO CORNER OF PINE PLANTATION WATCH OUT FOR ADDERS!

POST

TWO TREES SEEN FROM A DISTANCE

POSTS

LIMESTONE SCARS

OLD WALL

REMAINS OF FOLD BUILT ON LIMESTONE

CPC POST

BIG ISOLATED BOULDER

Lyvennet Beck

BOGGY

POSTS

CROSBY RAVENSWORTH FELL

SHEEP FIELD WALL

POST

KEEP YOUR DOGS ON A LEAD HERE AS THERE ARE A NUMBER OF GROUND-NESTING BIRDS

WALK TO THE CORNER OF THE WALL THEN FOLLOW IT EASTWARDS

¼ mile
APPROX SCALE
0   500m

★ TRAILBLAZER

30 MINS FROM TURN-OFF TO STONE CIRCLE (MAP 35) → LYVENNET BECK

LYVENNET BECK 60 MINS TO BROADFELL FARM (MAP 37)

ROUTE GUIDE AND MAPS

ROUTE GUIDE AND MAPS

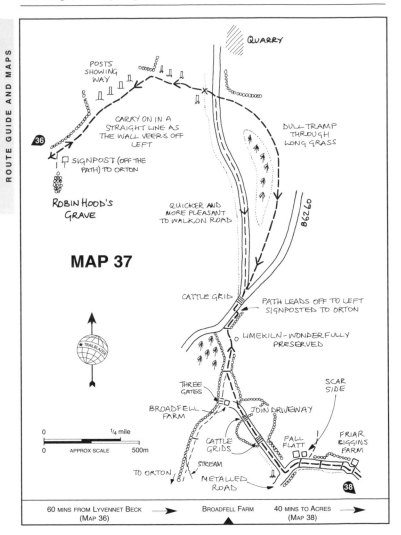

QUARRY

POSTS SHOWING WAY

CARRY ON IN A STRAIGHT LINE AS THE WALL VEERS OFF LEFT

DULL TRAMP THROUGH LONG GRASS

36

SIGNPOST (OFF THE PATH) TO ORTON

ROBIN HOOD'S GRAVE

QUICKER AND MORE PLEASANT TO WALK ON ROAD

B6260

MAP 37

★ TRAILBLAZER

0   ¼ mile

0   APPROX SCALE   500m

CATTLE GRID

PATH LEADS OFF TO LEFT SIGNPOSTED TO ORTON

LIMEKILN - WONDERFULLY PRESERVED

THREE GATES

BROADFELL FARM

SCAR SIDE

JOIN DRIVEWAY

CATTLE GRIDS

FALL FLATT

FRIAR BIGGINS FARM

TO ORTON

STREAM

METALLED ROAD

38

60 MINS FROM LYVENNET BECK ──→ (MAP 36)

BROADFELL FARM

40 MINS TO ACRES ──→ (MAP 38)

ORTON   see map opposite

Orton is typical of the quaint little villages in which the Coast to Coast specializes, but one with a couple of surprises in store for walkers who bother to make the short diversion off the trail. For one thing there's the church, built way back in 1293 though altered much since. Then there are the pillories below the church, used once upon a time (and who knows, maybe still today?) to restrain wrongdoers and teach them the error of their ways. Down the hill is a further surprise, **Kennedy's**, the chocolate factory (more of a kitchen really).

The **post office** and **shop** (post office hours: Mon, Tue, Fri 9am-1pm, 2-5pm; Wed & Sat 9am-noon; store open 8am-6pm) are nearby. Stagecoach's **Bus No 106** (Kendal to Penrith and vice versa) stops in the village; see pp43-5 for details.

Where to stay and eat

Recommended time and again by Coast to Coasters, *Barn House* (☎ 015396 24259, 💻 www.barnhouse-orton.freeserve.co.uk; 1D/2T all en suite) on the Raisbeck Road has just three rooms but each is supremely comfortable and equipped with TV and tea- and coffee-making facilities. One guest described the breakfasts as spectacular, too, with fresh fruit and do-it-yourself muesli, where you mix the ingredients yourself. Rates start at £28 per person, or £32 for single occupancy. The recently refurbished *George Hotel* (☎ 015396 24229, 💻 www .thegeorgehotelorton.co.uk; 1S/2D/3T/1F) is in the centre of town. Rates start at £25 (£27.50 for the single).

Two places that have received mixed reviews from walkers are: *Mostyn House* (☎ 015396 24258, 💻 iv_bland@hotmail .com; 1D en suite/2T shared bathroom), which charges £30/pp in the en suite room and £25 in a twin, with a single occupancy supplement of £5 (a packed lunch costs £4); and *New House Farm* (Map 38; ☎ 015396 24324; 1D or T/1T) where **camping** (£5, plus £1 for shower) is allowed (though the reviews from Coast to Coasters have been less than flattering about the campsite facilities, despite the fact that there's a static caravan (£24) you can use if it's wet. B&B starts at £23. Campers can also order breakfast and/or an evening meal (£14). New House Farm is best reached from Knott

Lane (see map 38). Follow Knott Lane south to the T Junction. Turn (left) and continue for five minutes. The farm is on the right-hand side.

You can sample *Kennedy's* (Mon-Sat 9am-5pm; Sun & bank hols 11am-5pm; café shuts 30 minutes before closing) products in their attached coffee house and ice-cream parlour. For a chocoholic overdose, try their scrumptious chocolate cake and wash it down with a hot chocolate, made with pure chocolate and topped with grated chocolate too. *New Village Tearooms* (☎ 015396 24886; Apr-Oct 10am-5pm, Nov-Mar 10.30am-4.30pm) serve some lovely home-made biscuits and cakes; we think it's one of the best tearooms on the route. For pub grub, *The George Hotel* (see column opposite) in the village centre serves lunches (12 noon-2.30pm, Sun to 3pm) and dinner (6-9pm) daily; the roast lamb jennings in Cumberland sauce (£10.95) is mighty fine.

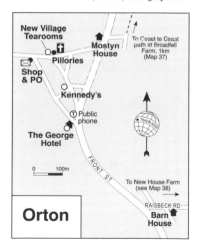

New Village Tearooms

Mostyn House

To Coast to Coast path at Broadfell Farm, 1km (Map 37)

Pillories

Shop & PO

Kennedy's

ⓣ Public phone

The George Hotel

TRAILBLAZER

0   100m

To New House Farm (see Map 38)

RAISBECK RD

Barn House

FRONT ST

Orton

(see map 38) ... (Map 37) ... (see Map 38)

There's a second and more impressive **stone circle** (Map 38) a mile to the east of Orton on the Coast to Coast path. It can be reached, for those who didn't take the Orton detour, via a driveable track running east from Broadfell Farm. (Those who *did* visit Orton can rejoin this track at the stone circle by taking the Raisbeck road east and heading up Knott Lane).

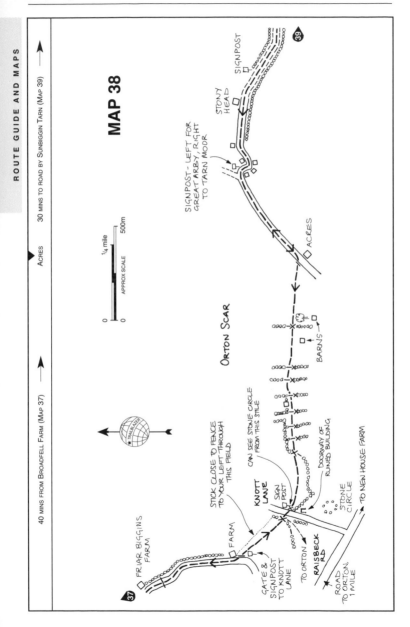

40 MINS FROM BROADFELL FARM (MAP 37) ⟶   ACRES   30 MINS TO ROAD BY SUNBIGGIN TARN (MAP 39) ⟶

MAP 38

¼ mile

0   500m

APPROX SCALE

FRIAR BIGGINS FARM

FARM

GATE & SIGNPOST TO KNOTT LANE

TO ORTON

RAISBECK RD

ROAD TO ORTON, 1 MILE

TO NEW HOUSE FARM

STONE CIRCLE

KNOTT LANE

SIGN POST

STICK CLOSE TO YOUR LEFT THROUGH THIS FIELD

CAN SEE STONE CIRCLE FROM THIS STILE

DOORWAY OF RUINED BUILDING

ORTON SCAR

BARNS

ACRES

SIGNPOST - LEFT FOR GREAT ARBY, RIGHT TO TARN MOOR

STONY HEAD

SIGNPOST

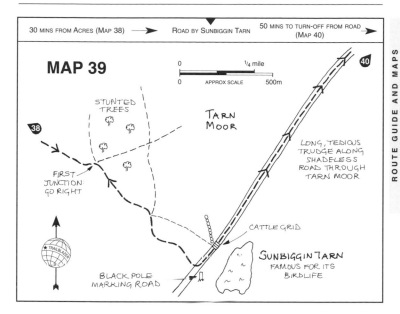

30 MINS FROM ACRES (MAP 38) ⟶   ROAD BY SUNBIGGIN TARN   50 MINS TO TURN-OFF FROM ROAD (MAP 40)

MAP 39

0   ¹/₄ mile

0   APPROX SCALE   500m

STUNTED TREES

TARN MOOR

38

LONG, TEDIOUS TRUDGE ALONG SHADELESS ROAD THROUGH TARN MOOR

FIRST JUNCTION: GO RIGHT

40

CATTLE GRID

★ TRAILBLAZER

SUNBIGGIN TARN FAMOUS FOR ITS BIRDLIFE

BLACK POLE MARKING ROAD

After this, the trail continues east through yet more fields and on to **Tarn Moor** (Map 39). All being well, by continuing south-east you'll emerge from the moor at **Sunbiggin Tarn**, an important bird sanctuary.

There now follow three miles/5km of tedious road walking (Maps 39-40), perhaps the dullest section of the Coast to Coast. (Incidentally, with the introduction of the 'Right to Roam' law, there is now a path running to the south of the tarn that avoids all this tedious road rambling. Look out for signposts that indicate the course of this path.) The two paths reunite before ***Bents Farm*** (Map 41; bookings ☎ 01946 758198, 🖳 www.bentscampingbarn.co.uk); they have a camping barn which sleeps 12-14 (bed £6) and permit camping for £3 per person.

The next prehistoric site lies a short way past the farm where, having crossed a stile, a signpost urges you to stick to the recognized path running alongside the wall so as not to disturb the archaeological site. This will probably come as something of a surprise, not least because, no matter how hard you look, there seems to be no archaeological site anywhere. However, this field plays host to the **Severals Village settlement** which, believe it or not, is considered to be one of the most important prehistoric sites in the whole of Britain. And the fact that it remains unexcavated does nothing to diminish this, or to quell the archaeologists' enthusiasm for the place. Without leaving the path, try to notice irregular or unnatural depressions and bumps in the land here; it is these undulations that have so excited the archaeologists.   *(cont'd on p139)*

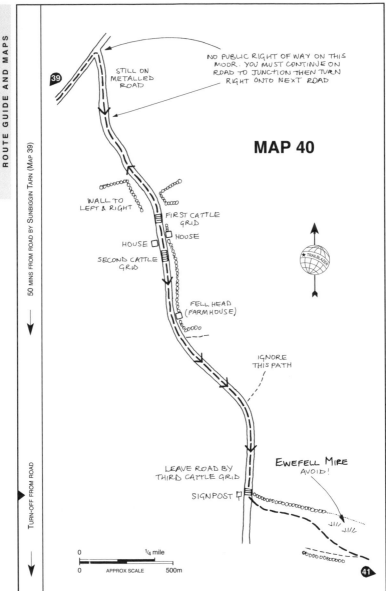

MAP 40

NO PUBLIC RIGHT OF WAY ON THIS MOOR. YOU MUST CONTINUE ON ROAD TO JUNCTION THEN TURN RIGHT ONTO NEXT ROAD

39

STILL ON METALLED ROAD

WALL TO LEFT & RIGHT

FIRST CATTLE GRID

HOUSE HOUSE

SECOND CATTLE GRID

FELL HEAD (FARMHOUSE)

IGNORE THIS PATH

LEAVE ROAD BY THIRD CATTLE GRID

SIGNPOST

EWEFELL MIRE
AVOID!

50 MINS FROM ROAD BY SUNBIGGIN TARN (MAP 39)

TURN-OFF FROM ROAD

0   1/4 mile
0   APPROX SCALE   500m

41

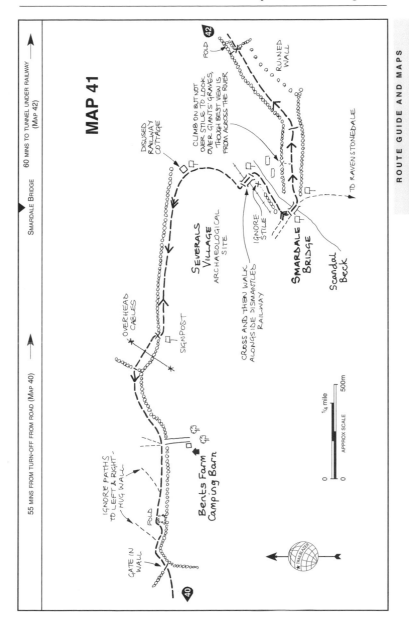

55 MINS FROM TURN-OFF FROM ROAD (MAP 40)

SMARDALE BRIDGE

60 MINS TO TUNNEL UNDER RAILWAY (MAP 42)

MAP 41

DISUSED RAILWAY COTTAGE

CLIMB ON BUT NOT OVER STILE TO LOOK OVER GIANTS' GRAVES, THOUGH BEST VIEWS IS FROM ACROSS THE RIVER

FOLD

42

RUINED WALL

OVERHEAD CABLES

SEVERALS VILLAGE ARCHAEOLOGICAL SITE

SIGNPOST

IGNORE STILE

TO RAVENSTONEDALE

CROSS AND THEN WALK ALONGSIDE DISMANTLED RAILWAY

SMARDALE BRIDGE

Scandal Beck

IGNORE PATHS TO LEFT & RIGHT - HUG WALL

FOLD

Bents Farm Camping Barn

¼ mile

500m

APPROX SCALE

0

0

GATE IN WALL

40

TRAILBLAZER

ROUTE GUIDE AND MAPS

60 MINS FROM SMARDALE BRIDGE (MAP 41) →   ↑   TUNNEL UNDER RAILWAY ▶

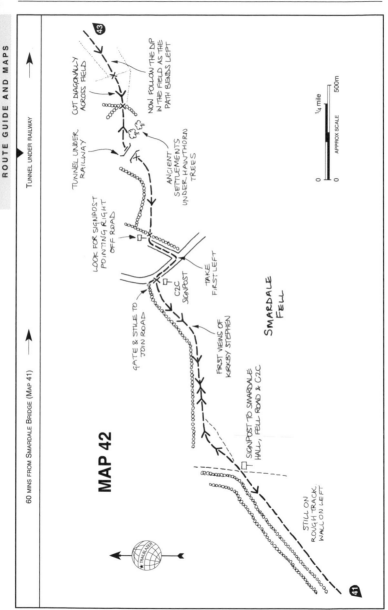

MAP 42

TRAILBLAZER

STILL ON ROUGH TRACK. WALL ON LEFT

SIGNPOST TO SMARDALE HALL, FELL ROAD & C2C

SMARDALE FELL

FIRST VIEWS OF KIRKBY STEPHEN

GATE & STILE TO JOIN ROAD

C2C SIGNPOST

TAKE FIRST LEFT

LOOK FOR SIGNPOST POINTING RIGHT OFF ROAD

ANCIENT SETTLEMENTS UNDER HAWTHORN TREES

TUNNEL UNDER RAILWAY

CUT DIAGONALLY ACROSS FIELD

NOW FOLLOW THE DIP IN THE FIELD AS THE PATH BENDS LEFT

43

41

0   ¼ mile
0   500m
APPROX SCALE

On the opposite side of Scandal Beck lies the final ancient site on this stage, the so-called **Giants' Graves** (called pillow mounds on OS maps), a series of long narrow mounds which, some say, may have been prehistoric rabbit enclosures. Climbing to the crest of **Smardale Fell**, the Nine Standards now appears on the horizon for the first time – another prehistoric feature, but one for which you'll have to wait until the next stage.

By now, however, those who are attempting this walk from Shap in one go will not be thinking of such distant prospects, but will be concentrating more on the delights that await them in the valley below – a valley, appropriately enough, that goes by the name of Eden.

KIRKBY STEPHEN   See map p143

Kirkby Stephen (usually pronounced 'Kirby Stephen' without the second 'k') vies with Richmond as the biggest town on the route, though don't let that fool you into thinking that this place is a metropolis. In fact, Kirkby Stephen is a pleasant market town built along the A685 with a population of around 1600, a figure that's swollen considerably during the summer months by walkers, runners, cyclists and other holidaymakers.

The focus of the town is its market square. There have been markets in Kirkby Stephen since at least 1361 when it was granted a market charter. Note the cobbled outline on the square's floor; it marks the outer limits of the old bull-baiting area, a popular pastime in the town up until 1820 when a bull broke free and ran amok, killing a number of bystanders.

The main tourist attraction in Kirkby Stephen is the 13th-century **St Hedda church** (see box p140).

Other sites of note include the old and much-photographed **signpost** at the top end of town, where the distances are given in miles and furlongs (see column opposite); and the curious but attractive **stone seats** in the form of sheep, that stand by the door of the tourist office. Carved by artist Keith Alexander, they are reputed to increase the fertility of any who sit upon them.

Frank's Bridge is a pretty double-arched stone footbridge, a quiet place to sit by the grassy riverbank and feed the ducks. It is thought to be named after a local brewer called Frank Birkbeck who lived in the 19th century.

One other item of note is the **flock of parrots** owned by a local resident that fly around the town during the day, before returning home at dusk. The **Masonic Hall** is now the location for the Acoustic Tearoom's concerts (see p142).

Services

Kirkby Stephen has become the spiritual (though it's not *quite* the geographical) heart of the Coast to Coast path. A couple of the baggage courier services (see pp20-1) operate out of the town, and those who opt to take advantage of their taxi service will spend the night in Kirkby Stephen before heading to St Bees the next morning.

The **tourist office** (☎ 017683 71199, Easter-Oct Mon-Sat 9.30am-5.30pm, Sun 10am-4pm, Oct-Easter Mon 10am-noon, 2-4pm, Tues-Sat 10am-noon) is crammed with brochures and leaflets and the staff seem knowledgeable. There's also a **website**, 🖳 www.kirkby-stephen.com.

Old roadsign with distances in miles and furlongs. In case you have forgotten eight furlongs equals one mile.

❏ St Hedda Church

The church is separated from the market square by the peaceful lawn of the **cloisters**. On entering the main gate, on your right is the **Trupp Stone**, resembling a stone tomb or table, where until 1836 the locals' tithes were collected. Take half an hour or so to wander around inside the church, which is known locally as the Cathedral of the Dales. It is built on the site of a Saxon church, though the earliest feature (the nave) of the present structure dates only to 1220.

Features to look out for include the 17th-century **font**, a great stone lump at the rear of the church, and the nearby **bread shelves**, used for distributing bread to the poor. There's also a **Norman coffin** by the north wall, unearthed in 1980 during restoration work, and a glass display cabinet, also by the north wall, housing 16th- and 17th-century Bibles and, curiously, a **boar's tusk**, said to belong to the last wild boar shot in England. It was killed by the first Sir Richard Musgrave (died 1464), who was buried with the tusk in Hartley Chapel, to the south of the chancel. (The place where Sir Richard shot the boar, by the way, the appropriately named Wild Boar Fell, lies to the south of Kirkby Stephen.)

The church's most interesting feature, however, is the 8th-century **Loki Stone** facing the main door, a metre-high block carved by the Vikings with the horned figure of the Norse god Loki. A bit of a prankster, one of Loki's tricks backfired and resulted in the death of Odin's son, which led to Loki being bound in chains and thrown into a subterranean dungeon. When the church was built the locals interpreted the carving as a representation of a demon. The stone was thus placed in the church to remind parishioners of the terrifying creatures that awaited non-believers in the afterlife.

Indeed, demons still play a big part in the folklore of Kirkby Stephen. At 8pm every day step outside to hear if they are still ringing the **Taggy Bell**, a warning to those who are still on the streets that Taggy, the local demon, now stalks the town looking for prey.

For details about St Hedda himself, see box p216.

Just down Market St a little way is the library (☎ 017683 71325; Mon & Wed 10am-12.30pm, 1.30-6pm, Fri 10am-12.30pm, 1.30-5pm; Sat 10am-1pm) with **internet** connection (50p for 15 minutes). There are two **banks** with **cash machines** while on the other side of the road is the **post office** (Mon-Fri 9am-5.30pm, Sat 9am-12.30pm), and opposite is the best **supermarket** in the town centre, the Co-op (Mon-Sat 8am-10pm, Sun 9am-10pm). There's also a Spar (daily 8am-10.30pm) further up the street.

Eden Outdoors (☎ 017683 72431; Mon-Fri 9am-5pm; Sat 9.30am-4.30pm) is the only **hiking shop** but it's a pretty good one, with plenty of cheap army surplus gear as well as regular trekking stuff. The owners say that, for emergencies, they will open up out-of-hours if you call them at home

and you'll usually find their numbers written in a notice on the door. Blister kits are also on sale at the Green Tree **pharmacy** (Mon-Fri 9am-5.30pm; Sat 9am-1pm).

Near the bottom of North Rd (the continuation of Market St), at No 37, is a **holistic health centre** (☎ 017683 72482), with a sauna, Jacuzzi and treatments such as Indian-head massage, perfect for sore muscles.

Where to stay

The Pennine View Caravan and Camping Park (Map 43; ☎ 017683 71717) is a smart spot for campers just outside town near the Croglin Castle pub, with a laundry room, sinks for washing up and a clean shower and toilet block (complete with piped music). It costs £6 per person with free showers.

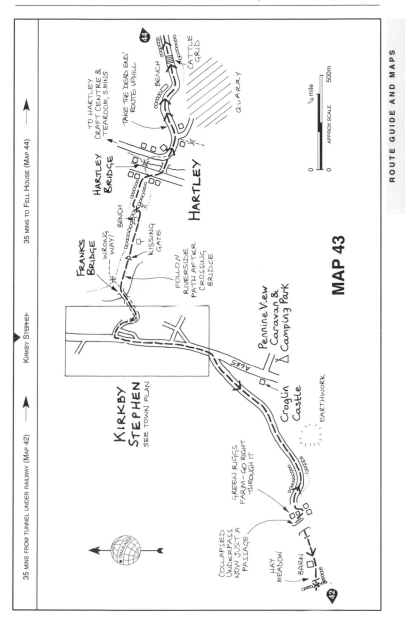

35 MINS FROM TUNNEL UNDER RAILWAY (MAP 42)

KIRKBY STEPHEN

35 MINS TO FELL HOUSE (MAP 44)

MAP 43

¼ mile

500m

APPROX SCALE

0

0

TO HARTLEY CRAFT CENTRE & TEAROOM, 5 MINS

TAKE THE DEAD END ROUTE UPHILL

BENCH

CATTLE GRID

QUARRY

44

HARTLEY BRIDGE

HARTLEY

BENCH

FRANKS BRIDGE

WRONG WAY!

KISSING GATE

FOLLOW RIVERSIDE PATH AFTER CROSSING BRIDGE

KIRKBY STEPHEN

SEE TOWN PLAN

PENNINE VIEW CARAVAN & CAMPING PARK

A685

CROGLIN CASTLE

EARTHWORK

GREEN RIGGS FARM - GO RIGHT THROUGH IT

COLLAPSED UNDERPASS NOW JUST A PASSAGE

HAY MEADOW

BARN

42

Kirkby Stephen Hostel (☎ 0781 771 0311; 40 beds) is housed in a converted Methodist chapel in the centre of town. Given up by the YHA, it's recently been opened by a highly entertaining gentleman who seems to delight in his own eccentricity. The hostel reflects the owner's larger-than-life character, including his collection of portraits hanging from the walls. According to one guest, it's a lot more fun than your average hostel. Rates start at £17 and the hostel is self-catering only.

Of the B&Bs on the walk, I've received more recommendations for the *Old Croft House* (☎ 017683 71638, ⬚ www.oldcrofthouse.co.uk; 1S with private bathroom, 1D/2D or T, all en suite; closed January) than any other place. It is a lovely old Georgian townhouse, made all the better by the extraordinary warmth and generosity of the owners who advertise their establishment as a B&B run by walkers for walkers. And they seem to know what trekkers want, welcoming guests with freshly baked scones and even supplying foot spas! They also now offer food in the evenings, with a choice of menus for £15 (the 'Walker's menu') or £19.50. The breakfasts are great (thanks in part to the homemade bread and jams) and overall this place scores top marks in every area. From 2008, however, dogs will no longer be accepted. Rates start at £25 each for two sharing, single occupancy £28-30.

Next to the hostel, *Fletcher House* (☎ 017683 71013, ⬚ www.fletcherhousecumbria.co.uk; 1S/2D/1T/1F all en suite) is another Georgian house, with TV in every room, that charges from £27.

At 63 High St the *Jolly Farmers Guest House* (☎ 017683 71063; 4D/4T, all en suite) has the added attraction of hydro-spa baths in some of the rooms, which should help take those aches away. Rates start at £27 per person, £30 single occupancy.

Back in the centre near the square, the *Kings Arms* (☎ 017683 71378, ⬚ www.kingsarmskirkbystephen.co.uk; 1S/7D or T/1F, 5 en suite) is a seventeenth-century former posting inn with many antiques in the rooms. Rates are £25/22.50 sgl/dbl, £32.50/26.25 en suite. To the east of the

main road is the grand 17th-century *Manor House* (☎ 017683 72757, ⬚ www.manorhouse.netfirms.com; 2D/1F all en suite) with exposed beams in the rooms and plenty of cats strolling around the grounds. Rates are £27 per person, £32 single occupancy.

Other places to stay include *The Black Bull Hotel* (☎ 017683 71237, ⬚ www.blackbullkirkbystephen.co.uk; 2S/5D/2F, all en suite), 38 Market Sq, which charges £32/27 per person sgl/dbl; and *Croglin Castle* (Map 43; ☎ 017683 71389; 2T/3D/1F), South Rd, now under new management, where B&B costs £30 per person and, beautifully, there is no single supplement.

Where to eat

On the main street there are no fewer than three **chippies** including the *Coast to Coast* (Mon, Thurs, Fri & Sat 11.30am-1.30pm, 4.30-7pm, Sun 4.30-7pm) that features in Wainwright's video.

As for tearooms, our favourite is the *Pink Geranium* (☎ 017683 71586; Wed-Sat 9am-4.30pm, Sun 9am-4pm) which gives you a great big pot of tea, and whose food is some of the most imaginative and generous around. *Pendragon* (Mon-Wed & Fri 10am to at least 4pm, Sat & Sun 9.30am-4pm), by the church, is slightly more rough and ready but still very friendly and good value.

Rattan & Rush (☎ 017683 72123; Tue-Sat 9am-5pm) is a tearoom which is particularly popular for its live folk music sessions (*The Acoustic Tearoom* ⬚ www.acoustictearoom.co.uk) in the evening. However, the latter are now held in the Masonic Hall approximately twice a month. Tickets are usually around £10 for entry to the show, or £22 for a two-course meal and the show.

The Mulberry Bush (☎ 01683 71572, ⬚ www.the-mulberry-bush.co.uk) is yet another pleasant Kirkby Stephen café (daily 9.15am-4pm), though one that turns itself into a smart Bistro-style restaurant (Thur-Sun 5-10pm; low season Fri-Sat only) in the evenings serving modern British and European cuisine.

For a picnic lunch to eat by the river, call in at *The Bread Shop* (Mon-Sat 8am-

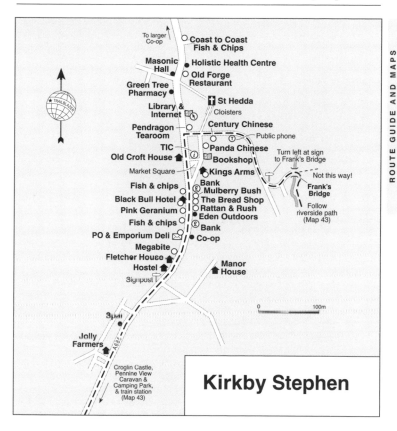

To larger Co-op

Coast to Coast Fish & Chips

Masonic Hall

Holistic Health Centre

Green Tree Pharmacy

Old Forge Restaurant

Library & Internet

St Hedda

Cloisters

Pendragon Tearoom

Century Chinese

Public phone

TIC

Panda Chinese

Turn left at sign to Frank's Bridge

Old Croft House

Bookshop

Market Square

Kings Arms

Not this way!

Fish & chips

Bank

Frank's Bridge

Mulberry Bush

Black Bull Hotel

The Bread Shop

Pink Geranium

Rattan & Rush

Eden Outdoors

Follow riverside path (Map 43)

Fish & chips

Bank

PO & Emporium Deli

Co-op

Megabite

Fletcher House

Manor House

Hostel

Signpost

3pm

Jolly Farmers

Croglin Castle, Pennine View Caravan & Camping Park, & train station (Map 43)

0   100m

Kirkby Stephen

5pm, Sun 9.30am-3.30pm) or try *Megabite* (☎ 017683 72984; Mon-Sat 9am-2.30pm, Sun 10.30am-2.30pm), an unpretentious takeaway specializing in baguettes (from £2.10) with wonderful fillings. Another good place to pick up supplies is *The Emporium Deli* (Mon-Fri 9am-5.30pm, Sat 9am-2pm), in the front of the post office building, with a great selection of the world's finer foodstuffs.

For evening meals, if you're up near the campsite (see p140) *Croglin Castle* (Wed-Sun noon-2pm, daily 6-9pm) is a convenient stop with good lunchtime offers (currently £5.95 for two courses). In the

town centre the *Kings Arms* (see opposite; daily 12noon-2pm) has a fine reputation and a fair vegetarian selection; the moussaka (£6.25) here is tasty, while the grilled Lakeland lamb chops are good value at £6.95. Of the other pubs the *Black Bull* (see opposite) does locally inspired meals including the ubiquitous Cumberland sausage for £6.75.

The most exclusive evening meals are at the intimate, some might say tiny, *Old Forge Restaurant* (☎ 017683 71832; Tue-Sun 6.30pm-late) which has a reputation for excellent food such as chick pea and potato curry with spiced mushrooms and bulgar wheat (£10.50) and steaks (from £13.50). For something more exotic, both the *Panda Chinese Takeaway* (☎ 017683 71283; Sun-Thu 5.30-11.30pm; Fri-Sat 5.30pm-12 midnight) and the *Century Chinese Restaurant* (☎ 017683 72828; Tue-Sat 12 noon-2pm, 5-11.30pm; Sun 5-11.30pm) serve up the usual array of Oriental fare. The latter also has a sit-in restaurant.

Transport (see also pp43-5)

The **train** station – the only one, apart from St Bees, on the Coast to Coast path – lies over a mile to the south of the town centre. Kirkby Stephen is on the Carlisle to Leeds line, with 5-6/day trains in each direction Mon-Sat, and 2-3/day on Sunday.

As for **buses**, Stagecoach's No 563 runs to Penrith and back from the Market Square Mon-Sat (journey time around an hour), while the No 564 runs from both the Market Square and the railway station to Kendal four times a day Mon-Sat, a journey of 60-75 minutes.

Finally, for a **taxi** Steady Eddie's Taxis (☎ 017683 72036) are said to be reliable, or call Prima **taxis** on ☎ 017683 72557.

STAGE 7: KIRKBY STEPHEN TO KELD   MAPS 43-50

Introduction

This **13-mile (21km, 4¹/₂-5¹/₂hr)** stage is something of a red-letter day, full of major landmarks. Not only do you cross the mighty **Pennines** – the backbone of the British Isles – but in doing so you cross the watershed; from now on, all rivers flow eastwards, where before they flowed west to the Irish Sea. This is also the stage where you pass from the county of Cumbria, your home for the past week or so, to **Yorkshire**, your home for the rest of the trek. And finally, by the end of this stage you are virtually at the halfway point, completing more than 95 miles out of approximately 192 (153km out of 307).

Yet in spite of the importance of today, the one thing that most walkers remember about this stage is not the number of landmarks they achieve but the bogs they have to negotiate along the way. If you've heard the stories about Coast-to-Coasters falling into waist-deep mud it is during this stage that they probably did it. The maps point out where the boggiest sections are. If you do succumb to one of the deeper mires, cheer yourself up with the thought that, at the end of the stage, you'll be spending the night in the gentle pastoral scenery of Swaledale, Yorkshire's most northerly dale, and perhaps its loveliest.

Note that, due to severe trail erosion, there are now **three paths** (see pp145-50) across the Pennines to Keld, the exact route you take depending upon what time of year you are walking. These three paths are marked on Maps 45a, 46 and 47 as well as on modern OS maps, and are colour coded. All are about the same length, but walking times vary due to terrain. Briefly: the **green route** is for those walking in winter (December to April) or in particularly bad weather and does not actually take you up to the Nine Standards. The other two routes, **red** (May to July) and **blue** (August to November) both climb up to Nine Standards before going their separate ways down on the other side.

(Opposite) The church at Muker (see p163) in exquisite Swaledale.

The route

To begin, from Kirkby Stephen you cross Frank's Bridge (Map 43) up to **Hartley**. The path climbs the hill and skirts around a working quarry on a fairly steep metalled road. At the end lies a wide dirt track up Hartley Fell, where the path splits (Map 45): the red and blue routes head up the hill to Nine Standards, while the green route continues to hug the stone wall that has accompanied you for most of your walk up Hartley Fell so far. The three routes are described below.

The three routes to Keld

● **Green Route (Dec-Apr; Maps 45, 45a, 48-49; 3hr 25mins from where the route separates from the Red and Blue routes)** This is the simplest route and perhaps in very inclement weather the best one, regardless of season. The disadvantage is that it doesn't actually visit the Nine Standards, instead

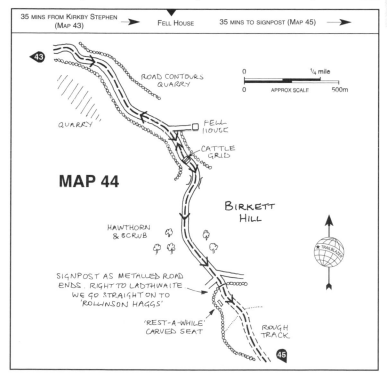

35 MINS FROM KIRKBY STEPHEN (MAP 43) → FELL HOUSE   35 MINS TO SIGNPOST (MAP 45) →

ROAD CONTOURS QUARRY

0 .... ¼ mile
0 ...... APPROX SCALE 500m

QUARRY

FELL HOUSE

CATTLE GRID

MAP 44

BIRKETT HILL

HAWTHORN & SCRUB

SIGNPOST AS METALLED ROAD ENDS. RIGHT TO LADTHWAITE WE GO STRAIGHT ON TO 'ROLLINSON HAGGS'

'REST-A-WHILE' CARVED SEAT

ROUGH TRACK

TRAILBLAZER

(Opposite) **Top**: Made it at last! The Nine Standards (see p147) mark the end of the climb up the Pennines. **Bottom**: A row of pretty terraced cottages in Richmond (see p177), the largest town on the walk.

ROUTE GUIDE AND MAPS

ROUTE GUIDE AND MAPS

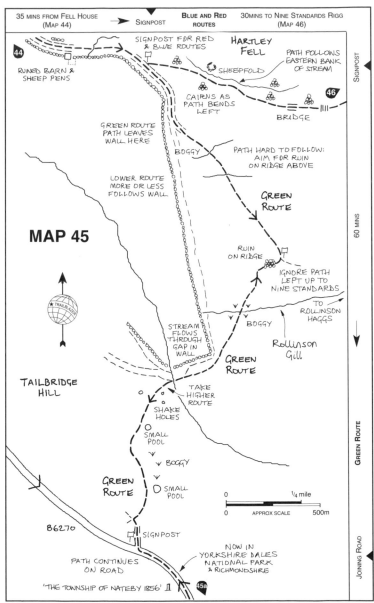

35 MINS FROM FELL HOUSE (MAP 44) → SIGNPOST

BLUE AND RED ROUTES

30MINS TO NINE STANDARDS RIGG (MAP 46)

44

RUINED BARN & SHEEP PENS

SIGNPOST FOR RED & BLUE ROUTES

HARTLEY FELL

SHEEPFOLD

PATH FOLLOWS EASTERN BANK OF STREAM

SIGNPOST

CAIRNS AS PATH BENDS LEFT

BRIDGE

46

GREEN ROUTE PATH LEAVES WALL HERE

BOGGY

PATH HARD TO FOLLOW: AIM FOR RUIN ON RIDGE ABOVE

LOWER ROUTE MORE OR LESS FOLLOWS WALL

GREEN Route

60 MINS

MAP 45

★ TRAILBLAZER

RUIN ON RIDGE

IGNORE PATH LEFT UP TO NINE STANDARDS

TO ROLLINSON HAGGS

STREAM FLOWS THROUGH GAP IN WALL

BOGGY

Rollinson Gill

GREEN Route

TAILBRIDGE HILL

TAKE HIGHER ROUTE

SHAKE HOLES

SMALL POOL

BOGGY

GREEN Route **GREEN Route**

SMALL POOL

0   ¼ mile
0   APPROX SCALE   500m

B6270

SIGNPOST

NOW IN YORKSHIRE DALES NATIONAL PARK & RICHMONDSHIRE

JOINING ROAD

PATH CONTINUES ON ROAD

'THE TOWNSHIP OF NATEBY 1856'

45a

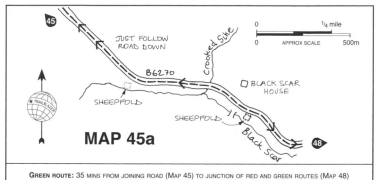

GREEN ROUTE: 35 MINS FROM JOINING ROAD (MAP 45) TO JUNCTION OF RED AND GREEN ROUTES (MAP 48)

continuing south along the farm wall towards Rollinson Haggs and on to the B6270, before diverting east to Ravenseat. As it follows a wall or road for most of the way and does not climb up to the same altitude as the others it is, all in all, a little dreary.

● **Red Route (May-July; Maps 45-49; 3hr 35 mins from where the green route separates)** You will already have seen glimpses since Kirkby Stephen of the 3m-high piles of slate and stones that are the **Nine Standards**. Though they continue to disappear temporarily behind the curves and folds of Hartley Fell as you head uphill, the path itself is straightforward enough and, all being well, you should reach the Standards just 30 minutes after leaving the junction with the green route.

At the top enjoy sumptuous views west over the Eden Valley to the Lakeland fells. Take your time. From now on, things get a little muddy as the route continues south up to the crest of **White Mossy Hill**. There, all being well, you should be able to make out a large **pile of stones** (resembling a ruin) in the distance due south of you; once there you should be able to see a well-constructed **pillar** standing among millstones to the south-south-east. From here you drop to the road and, turning left, walk on to the farm at **Ravenseat**, situated by a weir.

● **Blue Route (Aug-Nov; Maps 45-49; 3hr 20mins from where the green route separates)** Up to Nine Standards this route is identical to the red route, but

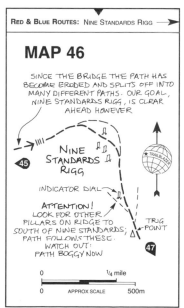

RED & BLUE ROUTES: NINE STANDARDS RIGG ⟶

MAP 46

SINCE THE BRIDGE THE PATH HAS BECOME ERODED AND SPLITS OFF INTO MANY DIFFERENT PATHS. OUR GOAL, NINE STANDARDS RIGG, IS CLEAR AHEAD HOWEVER

NINE STANDARDS RIGG

INDICATOR DIAL

ATTENTION! LOOK FOR OTHER PILLARS ON RIDGE TO SOUTH OF NINE STANDARDS; PATH FOLLOWS THESE. WATCH OUT: PATH BOGGY NOW

TRIG POINT

ROUTE GUIDE AND MAPS

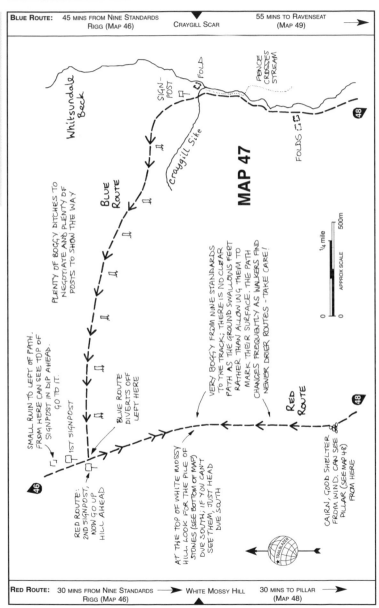

BLUE ROUTE: 45 MINS FROM NINE STANDARDS RIGG (MAP 46) — CRAYGILL SCAR — 55 MINS TO RAVENSEAT (MAP 49) →

MAP 47

Whitsundale Beck

SIGN-POST

FOLD

FENCE CROSSES STREAM

Craygill Sike

BLUE ROUTE

FOLDS

48

¼ mile   500m

0   APPROX SCALE   0

PLENTY OF BOGGY DITCHES TO NEGOTIATE AND PLENTY OF POSTS TO SHOW THE WAY

VERY BOGGY FROM NINE STANDARDS TO THE TRACK; THERE IS NO CLEAR PATH AS THE GROUND SWALLOWS FEET RATHER THAN ALLOWING THEM TO MARK THEIR SURFACE. THE PATH CHANGES FREQUENTLY AS WALKERS FIND NEWER DRIER ROUTES -TAKE CARE!

RED ROUTE

48

SMALL RUIN TO LEFT OF PATH. FROM HERE CAN SEE TOP OF SIGNPOST IN DIP AHEAD. GO TO IT.

1ST SIGNPOST

BLUE ROUTE DIVERTS OFF LEFT HERE

46

RED ROUTE: 2ND SIGNPOST, NOW GO UP HILL AHEAD

AT THE TOP OF WHITE MOSSY HILL, LOOK FOR THE PILE OF STONES (SEE BOTTOM OF MAP) DUE SOUTH; IF YOU CAN'T SEE THEM, JUST HEAD DUE SOUTH

CAIRN, GOOD SHELTER FROM WIND. CAN SEE PILLAR (SEE MAP 48) FROM HERE

TRAILBLAZER

RED ROUTE: 30 MINS FROM NINE STANDARDS RIGG (MAP 46) → WHITE MOSSY HILL — 30 MINS TO PILLAR (MAP 48) →

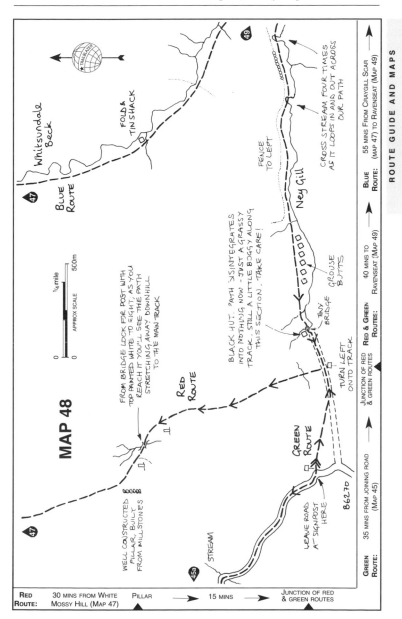

MAP 48

WHITSUNDALE BECK

FOLD & TIN SHACK

BLUE ROUTE

RED ROUTE

FROM BRIDGE LOOK FOR POST WITH TOP PAINTED WHITE TO RIGHT, AS YOU REACH IT YOU'LL SEE THE PATH STRETCHING AWAY DOWNHILL TO THE MAIN TRACK

½ mile
APPROX SCALE
500m

WELL CONSTRUCTED PILLAR, BUILT FROM MILLSTONES

CROSS STREAM FOUR TIMES AS IT LOOPS IN AND OUT ACROSS OUR PATH

FENCE TO LEFT

NEY GILL

BLACK HUT. PATH DISINTEGRATES INTO NOTHING NOW - JUST A GRASSY TRACK. STILL A LITTLE BOGGY ALONG THIS SECTION. TAKE CARE!

GROUSE BUTTS

TINY BRIDGE

TURN LEFT ONTO TRACK

GREEN ROUTE

B6270

LEAVE ROAD AT A SIGNPOST HERE

STREAM

| **Red Route:** | 30 mins from White Mossy Hill (Map 47) | Pillar | 15 mins | Junction of Red & Green Routes |

| **Green Route:** | 35 mins from joining road (Map 45) | Junction of Red & Green Routes | **Red & Green Routes:** | 40 mins to Ravenseat (Map 49) | **Blue Route:** | 55 mins from Craygill Scar (Map 47) to Ravenseat (Map 49) |

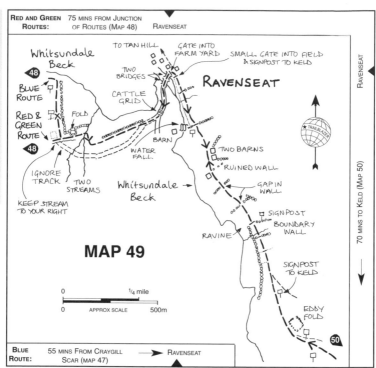

RED AND GREEN ROUTES: 75 MINS FROM JUNCTION OF ROUTES (MAP 48) RAVENSEAT

Whitsundale Beck

TO TAN HILL

GATE INTO FARM YARD

SMALL GATE INTO FIELD & SIGNPOST TO KELD

TWO BRIDGES

RAVENSEAT

BLUE ROUTE

CATTLE GRID

RED & GREEN ROUTE

FOLD

BARN

WATER FALL

TWO BARNS

RUINED WALL

IGNORE TRACK

TWO STREAMS

Whitsundale Beck

GAP IN WALL

KEEP STREAM TO YOUR RIGHT

SIGNPOST

BOUNDARY WALL

RAVINE

MAP 49

SIGNPOST TO KELD

0 ¼ mile

0 APPROX SCALE 500m

EDDY FOLD

BLUE ROUTE: 55 MINS FROM CRAYGILL SCAR (MAP 47) → RAVENSEAT

RAVENSEAT

70 MINS TO KELD (MAP 50)

near the ruin at the end of the ridge this route takes an eastern course *around*, rather than over, White Mossy Hill. Regular posts (often every 30m or so) ensure that you can't get lost as you make your way to Whitsundale Beck, which you follow south to a reunion with the other two paths.

From **Ravenseat** the path drops south through farms lining **Whitsundale Beck**, a picturesque little river punctuated with some fairly impressive waterfalls and ravines. Passing the farmhouse of **Smithy Holme** (Map 50), you can join the B6270 immediately by crossing the bridge, or take the path above **Cotterby Scar**. (For once we recommend the road, as it allows you to visit Wainwath Force.) The two paths reunite by the bridge before *Park House* (☎ 01748 886549; a campsite charging £4 per person) from where it's a gentle stroll to Keld, near enough the halfway point on the Coast to Coast.

KELD   **MAP 50, opposite**
Keld sits at the head of Swaledale, its houses huddled together against the often inclement weather. It's tiny today, at first sight merely a pretty village of little consequence save that it marks, almost, the halfway point on our trek and is also the only place on both the Coast to Coast and Pennine Way walks. However, in common with the rest of Swaledale, in the mid-19th

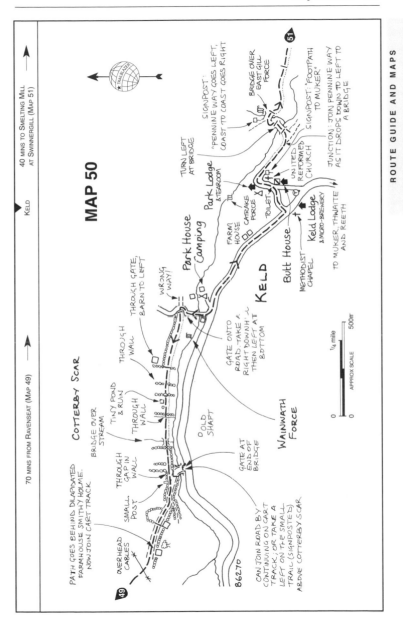

MAP 50

70 MINS FROM RAVENSEAT (Map 49) ⟶   ▶ KELD   40 MINS TO SMELTING MILL AT SWINNERGILL (MAP 51)

PATH GOES BEHIND DILAPIDATED FARMHOUSE SMITHY HOLME. NOW JOIN CART TRACK

COTTERBY SCAR

BRIDGE OVER STREAM

THROUGH WALL

TINY POND & RUIN

THROUGH WALL

THROUGH GAP IN WALL

SMALL POST

OVERHEAD CABLES

49

OLD SHAFT

GATE AT END OF BRIDGE

WAINWATH FORCE

B6270

CAN JOIN ROAD BY CONTINUING ON CART TRACK, OR TAKE A LEFT ON THE SMALL TRAIL (SIGNPOSTS) ABOVE COTTERBY SCAR

THROUGH GATE, BARN TO LEFT

WRONG WAY!

Park House Camping

FARM HOUSE

CATRAKE FORCE

GATE ONTO ROAD - TAKE A RIGHT DOWN H...L THEN LEFT AT BOTTOM

TURN LEFT AT BRIDGE

Park Lodge & TEAROOM

TOILETS

KELD

Butt House

Keld Lodge & MICRO-BREWERY

METHODIST CHAPEL

UNITED REFORMED CHURCH

SIGNPOST: "PENNINE WAY GOES LEFT, COAST TO COAST GOES RIGHT

BRIDGE OVER EAST GILL FORCE

51

SIGNPOST: "FOOTPATH TO MUKER"

JUNCTION: JOIN PENNINE WAY AS IT DROPS DOWN TO LEFT TO A BRIDGE

TO MUKER THWAITE AND REETH

TRAILBLAZER

1/4 mile

0   500m

APPROX SCALE

century Keld stood at the heart of the lead-mining industry in the area. Many of the buildings were constructed at this time, as a quick survey of the construction dates written above the doors of the houses will confirm. The village's two **Methodist chapels** (one next to Keld Lodge, the second in the heart of the village) were also built then.

Keld is more about water than lead today. The name means 'spring' in Norse and the **Swale River** (dyed brown by the peat) rushes through town. Do take the opportunity to visit some of the small nearby waterfalls – more accurately called cascades or, locally, **forces** – including Catrake Force, just above the village, and East Gill Force below it.

There are few places to stay in Keld but don't be too hard on yourself if you fail to book in time and as a consequence can't find a room. Further down the valley are Thwaite and Muker, both with some accommodation, and the walk down to both is wonderful. Indeed, such are the sumptuous charms of Swaledale's gentle rolling scenery, dotted here and there with the valley's distinctive, cubic laithes – stone barns for housing hay and livestock – that many hikers are persuaded to forego the 'official' Coast to Coast path via Swinner and Gunnerside gills (see p156) in favour of a gentle stroll down the valley, joining up with the path again only towards the end of Swaledale at Reeth. And even if you *are* staying in Keld, do take the time to stroll (or take a **bus** – see opposite) down to these villages. (However, check when the last bus goes back to Keld from Muker as it's a fairly long uphill walk.)

The only services here are a **public toilet** and **phone**. For more details on Keld and the rest of Swaledale visit the **website**, 🖥 www.swaledale.net.

Where to stay and eat

It seems almost ironic that **Keld**, virtually the halfway point and thus a place where you'd want to celebrate, is the only village at the end of a stage with no pub, though Keld Lodge (see column opposite) has a bar that's usually lively; Butt House also has a licence and Park Lodge sells beer and wine.

There are two **campsites**, both with showers and both charging £4 per person. *Park House* lies on the road on the way into the village, while *Park Lodge* (🕿 01748 886274, 🖥 www.rukins-keld.co.uk; open all year) is at the bottom of the village, though their actual campsites are located in several different places, including below Butt House and right by the river. They also have a lovely little **tearoom** (Easter to end Sep; daily 9am-6pm) in the farmhouse with tables and chairs in the garden out front. There are bacon rolls for £2.50 and they have a limited selection of supplies for sale but it does include beer and wine, which can be a godsend for drinkers who are only too aware of the lack of a pub in the village. They also serve an extra pot of hot water when you order tea – always a sign of a good tearoom in our opinion.

The rather wonderful *Keld Lodge* (🕿 01748 886259, 🖥 www.keldlodge.com; 3S/4T or F/4D, en suite except for 2S) not only has its own bar (the first in Keld since the closure of the Cat Hole pub in 1953) but has also established a micro-brewery, named Kelder, next door. Formerly the old youth hostel, and prior to that a shooting lodge, Keld Lodge offers some wonderfully smart accommodation, from the compact single 'pods' (that have their own toilet and hand basin) to the fully en suite, super-swish doubles and twins, with every room boasting a TV and most having wonderful views as well. But it's the *restaurant* (open to non residents) that is really establishing the Lodge's reputation, with a good vegetarian selection (one of the owners is a veggie) and an extensive wine list. Food is available daily all day but light meals are served at lunch time. Wi-fi is promised in the near future too. Rates are £35 per person, or £30 in one of the single pods. If anything can silence the critics who bemoan the closure of the hostel, or feel that the Lodge is out of character in somewhere as small as Keld, this place can.

Butt House (🕿 01748 886374, 🖥 www.coasttocoastguides.co.uk; 3D/1F en suite), run by the formidable, no-nonsense Doreen Whitehead, author of an accommodation guide to the Coast to Coast (see p39), lies just a few metres down the hill, below the phone box. Unfortunately, at the time of writing Doreen and her husband were planning to sell up and move. We wish them both well; it feels as if a part of the Coast to Coast history will disappear with them. However, they expect the new owners to continue doing B&B so it's worth ringing to find out the latest.

A further B&B, *East View* (☎ 01748 886776, or 01484 681381 from Oct to Apr; 🖳 www.keldholidaycottages.co.uk; 1S or D/1D or T) lies tucked away at the bottom of the hill opposite the church. Open Easter to the end of September, they insist on serving dinner as well as providing B&B and charge £38 per person, £39 in the single.

Transport
The Little Red **Bus** No 30 goes from Keld to Reeth and Richmond via Thwaite, Muker and all the Swaledale villages twice a day at 10.30am and 2.55pm Mon-Sat (not bank hols); see pp43-5 for further details.

THWAITE   OFF MAP 50
Kearton Country Hotel (☎ 01748 886277, 🖳 www.keartoncountryhotel.co.uk; 6D/5T/ 1F, all en suite; Feb-Dec) is a good-looking place. Rates are £31.50 per night plus £9.50 for dinner; rates are reduced for longer stays. Their smart *restaurant* is open to non-residents. Local specialities are prominent on the menu, though vegetarians are only catered for with advance notice; dinner is served 6.30-7.30pm.

STAGE 8: KELD TO REETH   MAPS 50-56

Introduction
The walk from Keld begins at the foot of the village – a bit of a pain to those who have spent the night at Thwaite or Muker and who must now return uphill to Keld to rejoin the path. There are two ways around this problem: the first is the valley walk alternative to Reeth as described on pp160-4 (Thwaite is actually off the low-level trail, but it's simple to walk down to Muker and join the trail from there).

But if, instead, you wish to take the high-level route – which is the one described in Wainwright's book – you could catch the bus back up to Keld. There is one morning service (No 30) a day Monday to Saturday from Muker (at the time of writing it left from near the Farmer's Arms at 10.11am) to Keld via Thwaite. Note that on this high-level route there is nowhere to buy any food or drink: come prepared.

The 'official' path
The wildlife along this **11-mile (17.5km, 4½hr)** walk is abundant, so try to set off as early as possible to increase your chances of seeing deer, rabbits and pheasants. However, as with the walk from Shap to Kirkby Stephen, this high-level route is mainly about archaeology and the evidence of man's existence in the far north of England. But, unlike that stage where we encountered a number of prehistoric sites, the precise purposes of which remain the subject of much speculation to the present day, this stage is all about uncovering the region's well-documented recent history, and the evidence on the ground is easy to interpret. For today's walk takes us through a part of Yorkshire that has been forever altered and scarred by the activities of the lead-mining industry.

The first evidence of this is **Crackpot Hall** (Map 51), 30 minutes from Keld along a gloriously pretty trail high above the Swale. Though there has been a house here since the 16th century, the ruin you see today actually dates from the

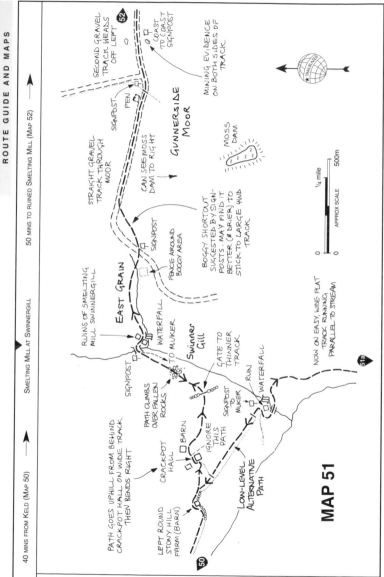

MAP 51

SECOND GRAVEL TRACK HEADS OFF LEFT

52

COAST TO COAST SIGNPOST

GUNNERSIDE MOOR

MINING EVIDENCE ON BOTH SIDES OF TRACK

SIGNPOST

PEN

STRAIGHT GRAVEL TRACK THROUGH MOOR

CAN SEE MOSS DAM TO RIGHT

MOSS DAM

SIGNPOST

FENCE AROUND BOGGY AREA

BOGGY SHORTCUT SUGGESTED BY SIGN-POSTS. MAY FIND IT BETTER (& DRIER) TO STICK TO LARGE 4WD TRACK

RUINS OF SMELTING MILL SWINNERGILL

EAST GRAIN

WATERFALL

TO MUKER

SWINNER GILL

GATE TO THINNER TRACK

NOW ON EASY, WIDE FLAT TRACK RUNNING PARALLEL TO STREAM

SIGNPOST

PATH CLIMBS OVER FALLEN ROCKS

SIGNPOST TO MUKER

RUIN

WATERFALL

51A

PATH GOES UPHILL FROM BEHIND CRACKPOT HALL ON WIDE TRACK THEN BENDS RIGHT

CRACKPOT HALL

BARN

IGNORE THIS PATH

LOW-LEVEL ALTERNATIVE PATH

LEFT ROUND STONY HILL FARM (BARN)

50

TRAILBLAZER

¼ mile

APPROX SCALE

500m

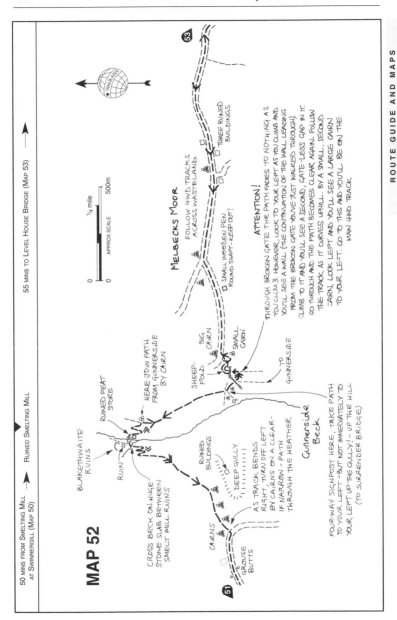

MAP 52

50 MINS FROM SMELTING MILL AT SWINNERGILL (MAP 50) ──▶ RUINED SMELTING MILL ──▶ 55 MINS TO LEVEL HOUSE BRIDGE (MAP 53) ──▶

BLAKETHWAITE RUINS

RUINED PEAT STORE

HERE JOIN PATH FROM GUNNERSIDE BY CAIRN

RUIN

CROSS BECK ON HUGE STONE SLAB BETWEEN SMELT MILL RUINS

SHEEP FOLD

BIG CAIRN

SMALL CAIRN

TO GUNNERSIDE

RUINED BUILDINGS

DEEP GULLY

Gunnerside Beck

AS TRACK BENDS RIGHT, TURN OFF LEFT BY CAIRNS ON A CLEAR-IF NARROW - PATH THROUGH THE HEATHER.

CAIRNS

GROUSE BUTTS

FOUR-WAY SIGNPOST HERE; TAKE PATH TO YOUR LEFT - BUT NOT IMMEDIATELY TO YOUR LEFT UP THE GULLY! - UP THE HILL (TO SURRENDER BRIDGE)

MELBECKS MOOR

FOLLOW 4WD TRACKS ACROSS WASTELANDS

SMALL WOODEN PEN ROUND SHAFT - KEEP OUT!

THREE RUINED BUILDINGS

ATTENTION!

THROUGH BROKEN GATE THE PATH FADES TO NOTHING AS YOU CLIMB. HOWEVER, LOOK TO YOUR LEFT AS YOU CLIMB AND YOU'LL SEE A WALL (THIS CONTINUATION OF THE WALL LEADING FROM THE BROKEN GATE YOU'VE JUST WALKED THROUGH.) CLIMB UP TO IT AND YOU'LL SEE A SECOND, GATE-LESS GAP IN IT. GO THROUGH AND THE PATH BECOMES CLEAR AGAIN. FOLLOW THE TRACK AS IT CURVES UPHILL. BY A SMALL, SECOND CAIRN, LOOK LEFT AND YOU'LL SEE A LARGE CAIRN TO YOUR LEFT. GO TO THIS AND YOU'LL BE ON THE MAIN 4WD TRACK

0 ───── ¼ mile
0 ───── 500m
APPROX SCALE

53

51

❏ Lead mining in Swaledale

According to the best estimates, lead has been mined in Swaledale since at least Roman times, and very possibly there was some small-scale mining back in the Bronze Age. A couple of pigs (ingots) of lead, including one discovered in Swaledale with the Roman name 'Hadrian' marked upon it, have been found. A versatile metal, lead is used in plumbing (indeed the word 'plumbing' comes from the Latin for lead), ship-building, roofing as well as in the manufacture of glass, pottery and paint. During medieval times lead was much in demand by the great churches and castles that were being built at that time.

The onset of the Industrial Revolution caused mining in Swaledale to become more organized and developed from the end of the 17th century. The innovation of gunpowder blasting, too, led to a sizeable increase in production, and the Yorkshire mines were at the centre of the British mining industry. Indeed, during the mid-19th century Britain was producing over half the world's lead, and the mines in Yorkshire were producing 10 per cent of that.

But while some of the mine owners grew fabulously wealthy on the proceeds, the workers themselves suffered appalling conditions, often staying for a week or more at the mine, spending every daylight hour inside it. Deaths were common as the mines were rarely built with safety in mind, and as the mines grew ever deeper as technology progressed, so conditions became ever more hazardous. Illnesses from the cramped, damp and insanitary conditions were rife. As if to rub salt into the wounds, many of the workers did not even own their own tools, but instead hired them from an agent.

The industry continued to prosper throughout much of the 19th century until the opening of mines in South America lead to an influx of cheaper imports and a fall in price, sending many British mines into bankruptcy. Many workers drifted away, usually to the coal mines around Durham, or to London and North America, in search of better prospects. By the early 20th century many of the villages were struggling to survive. Indeed, in the words of one resident of Reeth, when the mines closed the village became a 'City of the Dead'. Thankfully, tourism today has gone some way to securing the future of these attractive mining villages, and with the establishment of the Yorkshire Dales National Park, the future looks a lot brighter for the villages of Swaledale.

18th century and, while not directly connected to the mining industry, the farmhouse was once owned by one of the mine's managers. Quiet and ruined now, the location, with views down the valley, is perfect. As a plaque poignantly puts it, remember that this hall used to echo to the sound of children laughing. 'Crackpot', by the way, means 'Deep hole or chasm that is the haunt of crows', and is not a comment on the mental stability of the people who once lived here.

The path bends north now from behind the Hall to the remains of **Swinnergill mines**, including the ruins of a smelt mill, and on over **Gunnerside Moor**. Passing **Moss Dam** (a small body of water to your right) and various mineshafts and spoil heaps to left and right, you then continue down to the next extensive set of ruins at **Blakethwaite** (Map 52) in the valley of Gunnerside Beck, a good place to stop for a picnic lunch. While sitting on the grassy bank behind the large ruined peat store with its impressive arched windows (peat was used to heat the furnace to smelting), look for the flue coming down from the hill, finishing near the kiln on the western banks.

From here the path continues east up to the top of **Melbecks Moor**. Most people lose their way on this ascent, but not to worry: everybody eventually hits the path to Gunnerside, and by following it north the trail across the moor is joined once more. The landscape at the top is a bit of a shock. Whereas the mining relics you have encountered thus far have been rather neat and charming, what confronts you now is a gravel wasteland almost entirely devoid of life; a landscape that more or less exactly conforms to the definition of the word 'desolate'. This devastation is, it won't surprise you to discover, the work of man. The area was artificially stripped of any vegetation by water which would be dammed up above the site, then released by the miners to reveal the minerals underneath. This stripped land is known as a *hush*. While few will fall in love with the tedious monotony of the place, it does at least have its own intrinsic interest, showing how easily man can alter the landscape for good – or rather, for bad. It also serves to remind Coast to Coast trekkers, jaded, perhaps, by a week or more of incredible scenery, just what ugliness looks like. Furthermore, though you may feel melancholy walking through such lifeless terrain, you'll probably be pleased to know that during it you pass the trek's hundred-mile mark.

At the end of your 'moon walk' lies **Level House Bridge** (Map 53), where you cross **Hard Level Gill** before following it down to the ruined **Old Gang**

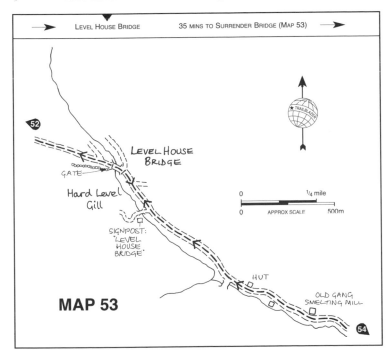

ROUTE GUIDE AND MAPS

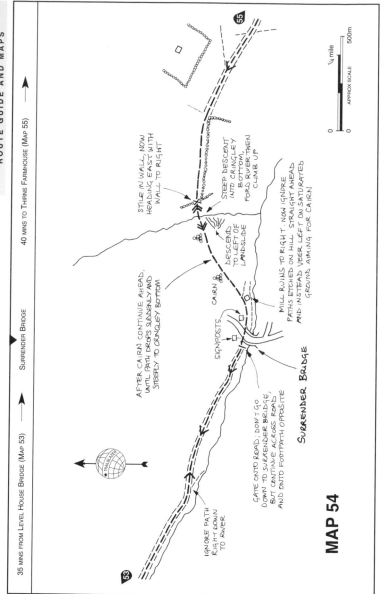

TRAIL BLAZER

IGNORE PATH RIGHT DOWN TO RIVER

AFTER CAIRN CONTINUE AHEAD, UNTIL PATH DROPS SUDDENLY AND STEEPLY TO CRINGLEY BOTTOM

STILE IN WALL, NOW HEADING EAST WITH WALL TO RIGHT

STEEP DESCENT INTO CRINGLEY BOTTOM, FORD RIVER THEN CLIMB UP

DESCENT TO LEFT OF LANDSLIDE

CAIRN

SIGNPOSTS

MILL RUINS TO RIGHT, NOW IGNORE PATHS ETCHED ON HILL STRAIGHT AHEAD AND INSTEAD VEER LEFT ON SATURATED GROUND AIMING FOR CAIRN

GATE ONTO ROAD; DON'T GO DOWN TO SURRENDER BRIDGE, BUT CONTINUE ACROSS ROAD AND ONTO FOOTPATH OPPOSITE

SURRENDER BRIDGE

MAP 54

APPROX SCALE
0 — ¼ mile
0 — 500m

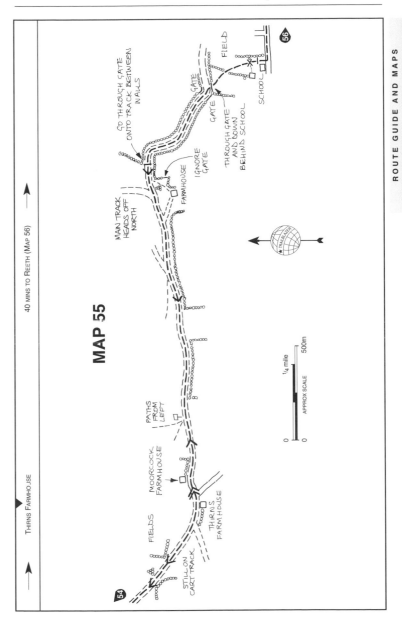

MAP 55

40 MINS TO REETH (MAP 56)

THIRNS FARMHOUSE

GO THROUGH GATE ONTO TRACK BETWEEN WALLS

MAIN TRACK HEADS OFF NORTH

IGNORE GATE

FARMHOUSE

GATE

GATE

THROUGH GATE AND DOWN BEHIND SCHOOL

SCHOOL

FIELD

PATHS FROM LEFT

MOORCOCK FARMHOUSE

FIELDS

THIRNS FARMHOUSE

STILL ON CART TRACK

TRAILBLAZER

¼ mile

APPROX SCALE

0   500m

0

ROUTE GUIDE AND MAPS

Smelting Mill, the most extensive set of ruins yet and one now protected by a preservation order. At **Surrender Bridge** (Map 54) you cross the road and continue past another smelt-mill ruin, traversing the excellently named **Cringley Bottom** and a great deal of farmland (Map 55) on your way to Reeth.

The Swaledale Valley alternative   Maps 51a-e, 56

The disadvantage with this walk is that it does make this stage rather short (about 4½hrs) and simple, and you may well end up in Reeth soon after lunch. You could, if time is pressing, walk on to Richmond, though that would be an awful lot to tackle in one day and it would be a shame to bypass Reeth and all

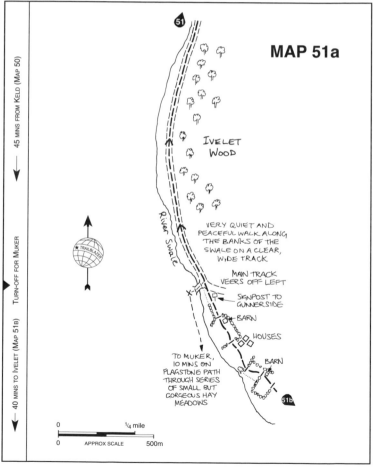

MAP 51a

IVELET WOOD

River Swale

VERY QUIET AND PEACEFUL WALK ALONG THE BANKS OF THE SWALE ON A CLEAR, WIDE TRACK

MAIN TRACK VEERS OFF LEFT

SIGNPOST TO GUNNERSIDE

BARN

HOUSES

BARN

TO MUKER, 10 MINS ON FLAGSTONE PATH THROUGH SERIES OF SMALL BUT GORGEOUS HAY MEADOWS

★ TRAILBLAZER

0   ¼ mile
0   APPROX SCALE   500m

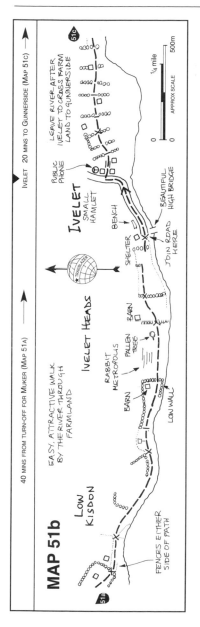

MAP 51b

40 MINS FROM TURN-OFF FOR MUKER (MAP 51A) →

IVELET 20 MINS TO GUNNERSIDE (MAP 51c) →

EASY, ATTRACTIVE WALK BY THE RIVER THROUGH FARMLAND

LOW KISDON

FENCES EITHER SIDE OF PATH

IVELET HEADS

RABBIT METROPOLIS

BARN

FALLEN TREE

LOW WALL

BARN

SHELTER

BENCH

IVELET SMALL HAMLET

PUBLIC PHONE

BEAUTIFUL HIGH BRIDGE

JOIN ROAD HERE

LEAVE RIVER AFTER IVELET TO CROSS FARM LAND TO GUNNERSIDE

0   ¼ mile
0   500m
APPROX SCALE

51b

51c

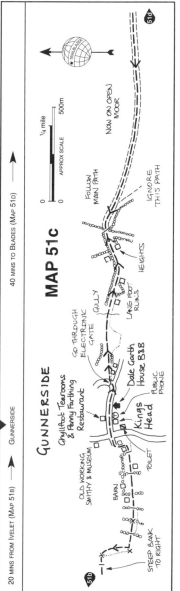

MAP 51c

40 MINS TO BLADES (MAP 51D) →

NOW ON OPEN MOOR

FOLLOW MAIN PATH

IGNORE THIS PATH

HEIGHTS

LANE FOOT RUINS

GULLY

GO THROUGH ELECTRONIC GATE

Dale Garth House B&B

PUBLIC PHONE

GUNNERSIDE

Ghyllfoot Tearooms & Penny Farthing Restaurant

OLD WORKING SMITHY & MUSEUM

BARN

Kings Head

TOILET

STEEP BANK TO RIGHT

0   ¼ mile
0   500m
APPROX SCALE

51b

51d

20 MINS FROM IVELET (MAP 51B) →   GUNNERSIDE   ←→

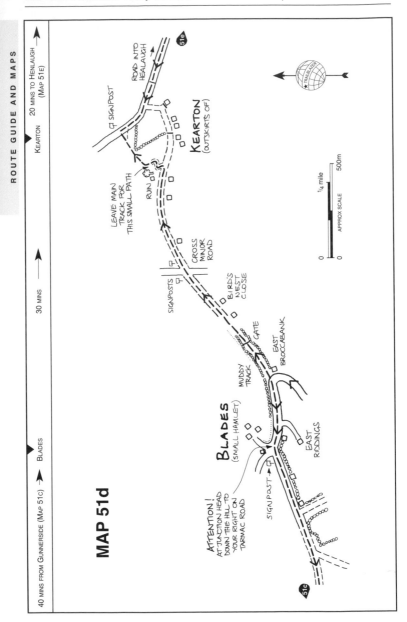

MAP 51d

ATTENTION!
AT JUNCTION HEAD
DOWN THE HILL TO
YOUR RIGHT ON
TARMAC ROAD

SIGNPOST

BLADES
(SMALL HAMLET)

EAST
RIDDINGS

EAST
BROCCABANK

GATE

MUDDY
TRACK

SIGNPOSTS

BIRD'S
NEST
CLOSE

CROSS
MINOR
ROAD

LEAVE MAIN
TRACK FOR
THIS SMALL PATH

RUN

KEARTON
(OUTSKIRTS OF)

SIGNPOST

ROAD INTO
HEALAUGH

51e

51c

APPROX SCALE
0   ¼ mile
0   500m

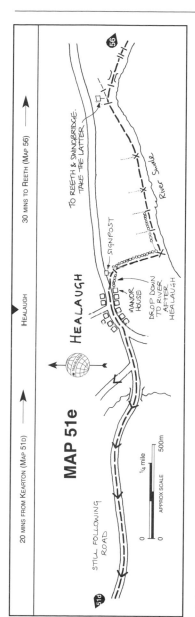

MAP 51e

HEALAUGH

20 MINS FROM KEARTON (MAP 51d)

HEALAUGH

30 MINS TO REETH (MAP 56)

TO REETH & SWINGBRIDGE: TAKE THE LATTER

SIGNPOST

River Swale

MANOR HOUSE

DROP DOWN TO RIVER AFTER HEALAUGH

STILL FOLLOWING ROAD

¼ mile

500m

APPROX SCALE

its pubs without spending at least one night there. Our advice? Enjoy the walk at a leisurely pace, stop frequently to admire the valley, take the diversion to Muker – and silence the voices in your head that insist that you haven't done enough today with a pint or two of Old Peculier in one of Reeth's hostelries.

The advantage of this walk is that it is beautiful, particularly in the early morning before the crowds arrive. Indeed, it's a rare trekker who doesn't prefer this to Wainwright's original high-level trail. The path is so easy and unstrenuous that you can fully appreciate your surroundings without distraction and spend time looking for riparian wildlife such as herons, ducks and, so it is said, otters.

The villages passed on the way are a joy too. **Muker** (off Map 51a and actually slightly off the route) is a very pleasant little place and one of James Herriot's (see p164) favourites. It has a church and a pub, the *Farmers Arms* (☎ 01748 886297), which serves food daily noon-2.30pm and 6-8.45pm. It has also been the home for 30 years of **Swaledale Woollens** (🖥 www.swa ledalewoollens.co.uk), its products made from the wool of Swaledale sheep, a hardy breed whose tough wool is considered ideal for carpets. The shop boasts that it actually saved the village following the depression caused by the collapse of the mining industry. Following a meeting in the local pub, a decision was made to set up a local cottage industry producing knitwear, and today 30 home workers are employed in knitting the jumpers, hats and many other items available in the store.

Muker Village Store and Teashop (☎ 01748 886409, 🖳 www.mukervillage
.co.uk) comprises the village shop, a tearoom (Easter to end Oct, Wed-Mon
11am-ish to when it goes quiet; weekends only in winter) and **B&B** (1D or T;
£30 per person). Accommodation is also available at *Chapel House* (☎ 01748
886822, 🖳 www.mukerchapel.co.uk; 1D), just up from Swaledale Woollens,
where the room costs £30 per night with a £5 single occupancy supplement;
the eighteenth-century *Swale Farm* (☎ 01748 886479, 🖳 www.dalesand
valeswalks.co.uk/swalefarm.html; 1D/1T en suite), near the shop, offers B&B
for £25 per person with no extra charge for single occupancy.

Ivelet (Map 51b), a small hamlet, has a public phone.

Then there's **Gunnerside** (🖳 www.gunnerside.info; Map 51c, p161)
which has a post office, public toilet and public phone, and even an old **smithy**
with attached museum (Easter-Oct 11am-5pm, closed Mon; £2.50).

The excellent *Ghyllfoot Tearooms* (☎ 01748 886239; 10.30am-5pm,
closed Tue) transforms into the *Penny Farthing Restaurant* (Mar to Oct only)
serving meals on Wednesday and Saturday evenings and Sunday lunch; a
pleasant pub, the *Kings Head* (☎ 01748 886261, 🖳 www.kingsheadgunner-
side.co.uk), which serves pub grub (Apr-Nov daily noon-3pm and 6-9pm) that
they describe, accurately, as hearty rather than flashy.

There's accommodation at *Dalegarth House* (☎ 01748 886275, 🖳 www
.dalegarthhousebandb.co.uk; 1T en suite) on the way out of the village towards
Reeth, with one twin room for £23, or £25 single supplement.

From Gunnerside the path crosses moor and farmland, eventually dropping down to fair **Healaugh** (Map 51e, p163), from where it returns to the
river to continue to Reeth, which it enters via the raised pavement of the
Quaker Road.

REETH   see map opposite

Reeth, the 'capital' of Swaledale, is the
archetypal Yorkshire dale village: flanked
to north and south by mine-scarred valley
walls, at its heart lies a village green surrounded on all sides with examples of those
twin institutions of Yorkshire hospitality:
the **tearoom** (of which it has five), and the
pub (three at the last count). As if to under-
line its Yorkshire credentials still further, it
also has a renowned brass band. Hardly
surprising, therefore, that the village was
used as a location for many of the episodes
of the quintessential Yorkshire series *All
Creatures Great and Small* by James
Herriot.

Mentioned in the Domesday survey of
1086, the village grew in prominence, as
did everywhere else in Swaledale, on the
profits of the mining industry, though
unlike other villages it could always claim
a second string to its bow as the main market town for Swaledale (the market is held

on the Green on Fridays). Thankfully, after
the mines had closed, tourism gave Reeth a
new lease of life and today the town is host
to a number of B&Bs and hotels, as well as
some good **gift shops** (Pots'n'Presents,
Garden House and Dales Centre) and a
small **museum** (see p168).

Services

The **tourist office** and **National Park centre** (☎ 01748 884059, 🖳 www.yorkshire
dales.org; Apr-Oct, daily 10am-5pm, Nov-
Mar Fri, Sat & Sun 10am-4pm) is to the
west of the Green in Hudson House.

On the other side of the Green is the
post office (Mon-Fri 9am-5.30pm, Sat
9am-12.30pm) whose **general store** is
open Mon-Sat 9am-5.30pm, Sun 10am-
4pm. Or there are **cash machines** (charging
a fee) in both the Black Bull (£1.50) and the
newsagents (Mon-Fri 7am-7.30pm, Sat
7.30am-7pm, Sun 8am-4pm; £1.85) at the
bottom of the hill on the way out of town.

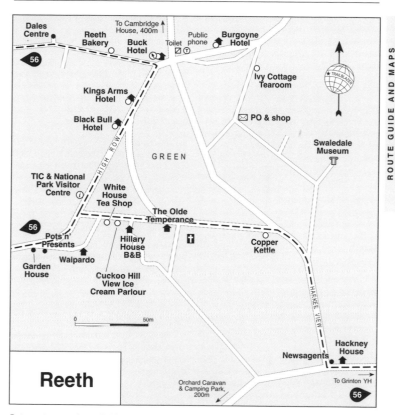

Reeth

Internet access is available at Buck Hotel (see p166).

Several **buses** pass through Reeth, including Little Red Bus No 30 which travels up to Keld 2/day Mon-Sat, and 6/day to Richmond; see pp43-5 for details. For a **taxi** call ☎ 01748 884553.

Where to stay

Grinton Lodge YH (off Map 56; ☎ 0870 770 5844, 🖳 grinton@yha.org.uk; 71 beds; £14), a former shooting lodge, is the nearest hostel; meals are served, it is licensed and it has a TV, games room and internet access. However, it is an exhausting 1¼ miles (about 2km) further along the road (and off the trail) so we recommend that

you take a **B&B** here tonight. Alternatively, you could **camp** at *The Orchard Caravan Park* (☎ 01748 884475; check in at the house signed 'Warden Enquiries'), open April-Oct; book in advance in peak season. The enthusiastic new owners have helped to transform the place and, though still dominated by caravans, it's a much improved site. You can camp here for £5 and, wonderfully, if it's raining they'll allow you to shelter in one of their old caravans for the same price.

Of the B&Bs, *Hackney House* (☎ 01748 884302; 1S/2D/1T/1F), Bridge Terrace, at the bottom of town is an unassuming terraced house, though the breakfasts are big and the welcome friendly. With rates starting at just £27/22-25 sgl/dbl, this is great value.

Another place to try is *Walpardo* (☎ 01748 884626, ✉ walpardoreeth@aol .com; 1S/1T), just off the Green on Anvil Square, where B&B is just £20. *Hillary House* (☎ 01748 884171, 1D/1T), 4 Hillary Terrace, offers B&B for £20 per person (£25 single occupancy) and comes recommended. *The Olde Temperance* (☎ 01748 884401, 1S/1D/1F) charges £20 for a one-night stay (£18 for three nights or more) and is situated above a Christian bookshop.

Across the Green, *Ivy Cottage* (☎ 01748 884418, ✉ www.ivycottagereeth.co .uk; 2D/1T) has en suite only rooms at £55, or £37.50 single occupancy.

Buck Hotel (☎ 01748 884210, ✉ www .buckhotel.co.uk; 1S/6D/2T/1F, all en suite) is the only place in town with **internet access** (£1.50 for 30 minutes). Per person rates range from £25.25 in the family room to £37.50 for the single.

The Black Bull (☎ 01748 884213; 3D/3T/1F all en suite) dates back to 1680 and has rooms overlooking the Green and down Swaledale; prices start at £30.

The *Kings Arms* (☎ 01748 884259, ✉ www.thekingsarms.com; 1T/8D/1F), next door is 50 years younger, the stone above the door testifying to a construction date of 1734. They charge £35 for their rear bedrooms, £40 for those overlooking the Green, and £45 for the room with a four-poster.

The smartest place in town, *The Burgoyne Hotel* (☎ 01748 884292, ✉ www .theburgoyne.co.uk; 5D/3T all en suite), dominates the north side of the Green, though you may feel a little out of place in such salubrious surroundings. Rooms come with TVs, DVDs and wi-fi connections, and rates start at £117.50 for a twin or double room or £175 for four-poster extravagance.

Cambridge House (☎ 01748 884633, ✉ www.cambridge-house-reeth.co.uk; 1S/3D/1T), Arkengarthdale Rd, lies about a quarter of a mile outside the village; head north from the public toilets and Buck Hotel and you'll find it on the left. It's a charming place, an early twentieth-century building constructed on the site of a much older property and stuffed full of antiques, where the considerate owners care so much about the comfort of the guests that all the rooms are south facing with ravishing views down to Reeth, and where they've taped pillows to the ceiling beams so guests don't hurt themselves when they bash their heads! Rates are £33 per person.

Where to eat
Reeth Bakery (☎ 01748 884735; open summer Mon-Sat 10am-4pm, Sun 11am-5pm; winter Fri & Sat 10am-4pm, Sun 11am-5pm plus most holiday periods), on Silver St on the way into Reeth, is a little treasure. In previous editions we have waxed lyrical about this bakery, run by the friendly, unassuming John Crofter and selling home-baked bread made with organic flour from the water mill at Little Salkeld; in addition they have a great selection of Swaledale cheeses and chutneys, as well as short-breads, flapjacks and other cakes. Suffice to say, nothing has changed. Indeed, I once spent an extra day in Reeth purely on the strength of this man's fruit loaf!

If you can't squeeze into the three-table tearoom take your purchases out onto the green. Because, to put it bluntly, if you don't sample anything here you must really hate yourself – or at least, you soon will do.

Just because we rate the bakery so highly, however, doesn't mean the other tearooms aren't also worthy of praise. The *Copper Kettle* (☎ 01748 884748; Apr-Sep Sat-Thur 10am-8.30pm, Fri 10am-3pm; Mar & Oct 10.30am-5pm) is a pleasant, traditional sort of place serving such delights as a proper cream tea (£2.70) and Swaledale high teas (£5.75). It also opens in the evening to serve more substantial fare, with most dishes around the £7.25 mark including beef lasagne and lamb moussaka.

The *White House Tea Shop* (☎ 01748 884763; Mar-Jan, Fri-Tue 10.30am-4.30pm), on the corner of Anvil Square, sells ice cream and filling lunches. However, they have built up such a loyal clientele that you would be incredibly lucky to get a table on a Sunday.

You may get more joy at the *Ivy Cottage Tearoom* (open Tue, Wed, Fri-Sun; noon-5pm) which serves hot baguettes, soups and sandwiches as well as the usual cream teas etc.

Cuckoo Hill View (☎ 01748 884929; daily in summer 11.30am-5pm, occasionally up to 8pm, weekends only in winter though for obvious reasons their hours depend slightly on the weather) is a very welcome addition to the food scene in Reeth, an ice-cream parlour at the foot of the Green serving such unusual delights as 'cranberry crush' and 'black cherry whim wham'.

For an evening meal (6-9pm), the *Buck Hotel* does a good spread, while the *Black Bull* is known for its homemade pies (from £7.25) and serves food daily between noon and 2.30pm and 6-9.30pm. Turn up early and you should be able to get a seat at the Old Draper's Shop at the centre of the pub, which is quieter than the rest of it. Next door, *The Kings Arms* also serves food daily noon-2.30pm and 6-9.30pm. The smartest place to eat is the *Burgoyne* (see opposite) but it's a little pricey. (The contact details for all these are opposite.)

ROUTE GUIDE AND MAPS

❏ Drystone walls

I am a Dry Stone Waller
All day I Dry Stone Wall
Of all appalling callings
Dry Stone Walling's worst of all
Pam Ayres, 1978

Along the Coast to Coast path you'll pass hundreds of drystone walls. Beautiful and photogenic, particularly when covered in a layer of velvety green moss, they are probably the most ubiquitous feature of northern England's landscape. That said, few walkers give much thought to who built them, nor have any idea just how much skill and effort goes into making these walls. Drystone walls, so called because they are built without mortar, have been around since Elizabethan times when, as now, they were used to demarcate the boundaries between one farmer's land and another. Many others were built during the Enclosure Acts between 1720 and 1840, when previously large fields shared between a number of farmers were divided into strips of land. A very few of these 18th-century walls are still standing: those nearest to a village tend to be the oldest, as it was this land that was divided and enclosed first. The fact that the walls have lasted so long is largely due to the care that goes into building each one.

The first step to building a drystone wall is to dig some deep, secure foundations. That done, the next step is to build the wall itself, or rather walls, for a typical drystone wall is actually made up of two thinner walls built back to back. This design helps to make the wall as sturdy as possible. Every so often, a row of 'through-stones' are built into the wall that serve to bind the two halves together. It is estimated that one tonne of stone is required for one square yard of wall. Each stone is chosen carefully to fit exactly: a bad choice can upset the pressure loading, leading to an early collapse. Smaller chippings are used to fill the gaps.

Despite the walls' longevity, or perhaps because of it, drystone walling is becoming something of a lost art. The wire fence is a cheaper, simpler and just as effective way of dividing land, and while the existing drystone walls have to be repaired occasionally, more often than not the farmer would rather do it himself than call in a professional. As a result, the industry is in decline. In Swaledale there is said to be only one full-time drystone waller left.

For those who wish to try drystone walling for themselves, a one-day course has recently been set up. The cost is £45 per day and you'll be in a group of no more than six people. To join, call (☎ 0792 8628181; ✉ forecast@kt.dinternet.com).

ROUTE GUIDE AND MAPS

What to see

Swaledale Museum (☎ 01748 884118, 🖳 www.swaledalemuseum.org), open Easter-Oct, Wed-Fri, Sun & bank hols 10.30am-5.30pm and at other times by prior arrangement; £3) is housed in the old nineteenth-century Methodist School Room. It holds some surprisingly good exhibits and is well worth an hour or so of anyone's time, particularly if you want to learn more about the local mining and farming industries. The drystone wallers' craft (see box p167) is examined, and the museum also looks at the social history of the area in some detail, attempting through its exhibits to show how the locals used to live a hundred or more years ago.

STAGE 9: REETH TO RICHMOND   MAPS 56-61

Introduction

There are a couple of lovely tracts of woodland on this **10¹/₂-mile (17km, 3¹/₂hr)** stage, a simple and short one that should, if you set off early enough, allow you time to enjoy the sights of Richmond at the end of it.

A couple of charming villages are passed on the way too, as well as the remains of an old priory. Overall, not a spectacular day but, if the weather's OK, an exceedingly pleasant one.

The route

Marrick Priory (Map 57) and its ruins lie just 40 minutes outside Reeth; it is reached by taking the turn-off on the main road signposted towards Marrick, Marske and Hurst. Though it's visible from a distance away, casual visitors are not now allowed to visit the ruins which have been incorporated within **Marrick Priory Outdoor Education and Residential Centre**. Nevertheless, workers there are pretty used to seeing people walking down the drive to inspect the exterior of the place and seem pretty relaxed about it. The abbey was founded by local noble, Roger de Aske, for Benedictine nuns who numbered 17 at the priory's dissolution in 1540. There are a couple of tomb slabs in the grounds, including one by the entrance belonging to a Thomas Peacock who died in 1762 at the grand old age of 102.

Those disappointed with not being able to explore the ruins thoroughly will find some consolation in the walk up to Marrick village, an incredibly pretty uphill amble through the first of this stage's woods, known as **Steps Wood**. The path you are walking on is known as the **Nuns' Steps**, so-called because the nuns are said to have constructed the 375 steps as a walkway to the abbey. At the top, through a couple of fields, lies the village that gave Marrick Priory its name.

❏ **Important note – walking times**

Unless otherwise specified, **all times in this book refer only to the time spent walking.** You will need to add 20-30% to allow for rests, photography, checking the map, drinking water etc. When planning the day's hike count on 5-7 hours' actual walking.

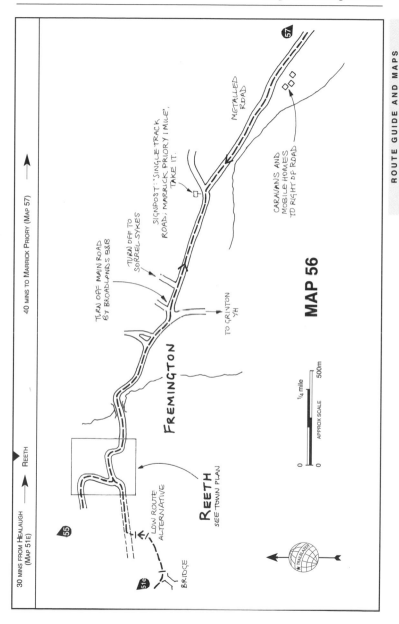

30 MINS FROM HEALAUGH (MAP 51E)

◄ REETH ►

40 MINS TO MARRICK PRIORY (MAP 57) ►

55

51E

BRIDGE

LOW ROUTE ALTERNATIVE

REETH
SEE TOWN PLAN

FREMINGTON

TURN OFF MAIN ROAD
BY BROADLANDS B&B

TURN OFF TO
SORREL SYKES

TO GRINTON YH

SIGNPOST 'SINGLE TRACK
ROAD, MARRICK PRIORY 1 MILE'
TAKE IT.

57

METALLED ROAD

CARAVANS AND
MOBILE HOMES
TO RIGHT OF ROAD

MAP 56

0 ¼ mile
0 500m
APPROX SCALE

TRAILBLAZER

MARRICK — MAP 57, opposite

Mentioned in *The Domesday Book* as Mange and Marig, the derivation of the name Marrick is something of a mystery. According to one school of thought it has something to do with marshes; according to another, it means something like 'The Habitation of Mary'. Still others believe it to mean Horse or Boundary Ridge from old Norse.

There are no pubs or shops here, in fact very little save for some 25 houses, a public phone and a village institute, but there is a delightful B&B, *The Lodge* (☎ 01748 884474, ☐ http://members.aol.com/marricklodge/marricklodge.html; 1D/1T), tucked down a driveway. The owners are a wonderfully welcoming couple who'll ply you with tea and flapjacks as soon as you walk in; the house itself is a country-cottage delight filled with interesting knick-knacks and furniture. They also have a small lawn for **camping** (£5) nearby. All in all, highly recommended. Rates are from £22.50, the three-course dinner is £12.50.

From Marrick the trail begins a long north-easterly march up to Marske through farmland punctuated by any number of stiles and gates. Look out for *Elaine's Teas* (Map 57; ☎ 01748 884266; opening times vary but approximately daily 9am-late), a farmhouse serving snacks and drinks which also has a **campsite** for £4 per person. They also do an evening meal for campers (with the meat coming from their farm), for just £11 for a main course and sweet. Even if you're not camping here, it's worth stopping just to try the cakes which are so good they are often entered into local competitions.

At the end of this march through the pastures the road to **Marske**, with impressive Marske Hall (Map 58) on the right, is joined. Continuing up through Marske, you pass the crenellated **Church of St Edmund the Martyr**, built on the site of an earlier church dating back to 1090, of which the north and south doors and hexagonal supporting pillars survive. St Edmund, incidentally, was a Saxon king put to death by the Danes in AD870.

Half a mile out of the village the road is once again forsaken in favour of pasture as the trail continues its relentless march north-east, bending east only when the farm track to West Applegarth (Map 59), below **Applegarth Scar**, is reached.

The farms Low and High Applegarth are passed before the trail reaches a third farm at East Applegarth where, high above the wooded valley, there is *Richmond Camping Barn* (☎ 01748 822940; the nearest camping option to Richmond), a beautifully rustic place open April to October. There are 12 beds (£6.50 per person) and a small grassy patch for **camping** (£3). Facilities are limited, but there is a kitchen and at the time of writing they were installing a shower.

The trail continues into enchanting **Whitecliffe Wood**, emerging 15 minutes later at High Leases Farm with its free-range chickens. A road walk follows before you eventually pass through the suburbs and into Richmond.

(cont'd on p175)

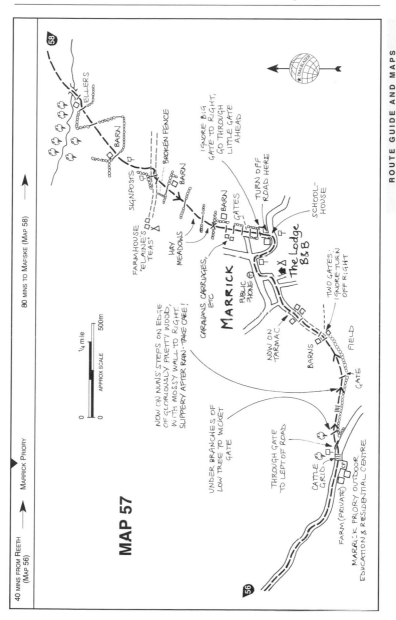

MAP 57

¼ mile
500m
0
0 APPROX SCALE

56

MARRICK PRIORY OUTDOOR EDUCATION & RESIDENTIAL CENTRE

FARM (PRIVATE)

CATTLE GRID

THROUGH GATE TO LEFT OF ROAD

UNDER BRANCHES OF LOW TREE TO WICKET GATE

NOW ON NUNS' STEPS ON EDGE OF GLORIOUSLY PRETTY WOOD, WITH MOSSY WALL TO RIGHT. SLIPPERY AFTER RAIN-TAKE CARE!

CARAVANS, CARRIAGES, ETC.

MARRICK

PUBLIC PHONE

NOW ON TARMAC

BARNS

FIELD

GATE

TWO GATES: IGNORE TURN OFF RIGHT

The Lodge B&B

SCHOOLHOUSE

TURN OFF ROAD HERE

IGNORE BIG GATE TO RIGHT, GO THROUGH LITTLE GATE AHEAD

GATES

BARN

HAY MEADOWS

BARN

BROKEN FENCE

SIGNPOSTS

FARMHOUSE "ELAINE'S TEAS"

BARN

ELLERS

58

TRAILBLAZER

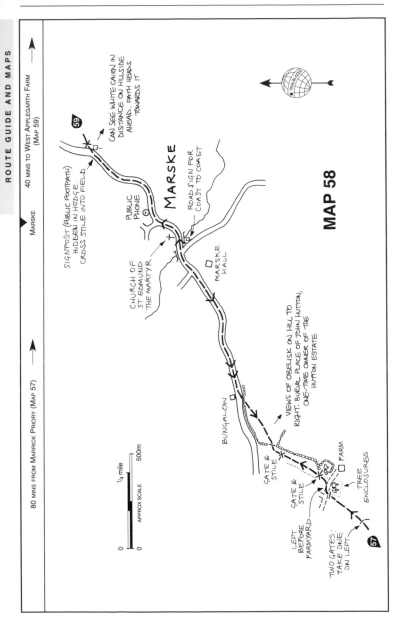

80 MINS FROM MARRICK PRIORY (MAP 57) ———→

MARSKE ► 40 MINS TO WEST APPLEGARTH FARM (MAP 59) ———→

SIGNPOST (PUBLIC FOOTPATH) HIDDEN IN HEDGE. CROSS STILE INTO FIELD

CAN SEE WHITE CAIRN IN DISTANCE ON HILLSIDE AHEAD. PATH HEADS TOWARDS IT

TRAILBLAZER

MARSKE

PUBLIC PHONE

ROADSIGN FOR COAST TO COAST

CHURCH OF ST EDMUND THE MARTYR

MARSKE HALL

MAP 58

BUNGALOW

VIEWS OF OBELISK ON HILL TO RIGHT, BURIAL PLACE OF JOHN HUTTON, ONE-TIME OWNER OF THE HUTTON ESTATE

GATE & STILE

FARM

TREE ENCLOSURES

GATE & STILE

LEFT BEFORE FARMYARD

TWO GATES; TAKE ONE ON LEFT

57

¼ mile

500m

APPROX SCALE

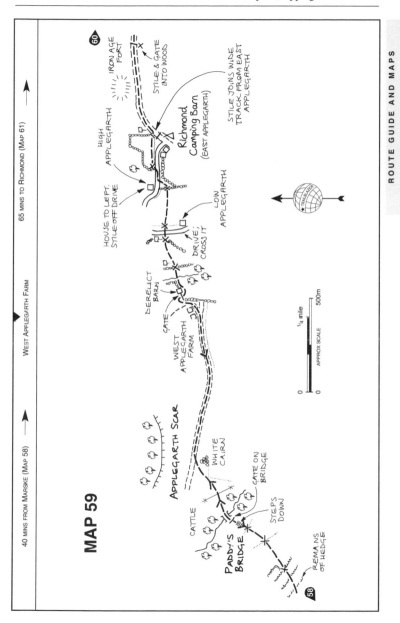

MAP 59

40 MINS FROM MARSKE (MAP 58)

WEST APPLEGARTH FARM

65 MINS TO RICHMOND (MAP 61)

60

IRON AGE FORT

STILE & GATE INTO WOODS

STILE JOINS WIDE TRACK FROM EAST APPLEGARTH

HIGH APPLEGARTH

Richmond Camping Barn (EAST APPLEGARTH)

HOUSE TO LEFT, STILE OFF DRIVE

LOW APPLEGARTH

DRIVE; CROSS IT

DERELICT BARN

GATE

WEST APPLEGARTH FARM

APPLEGARTH SCAR

WHITE CAIRN

GATE ON BRIDGE

STEPS DOWN

CATTLE

PADDY'S BRIDGE

REMAINS OF HEDGE

TRAILBLAZER

¼ mile

APPROX SCALE

0   500m

58

ROUTE GUIDE AND MAPS →

65 MINS FROM WEST APPLEGARTH FARM (MAP 59) TO RICHMONDSHIRE CRICKET CLUB (MAP 61)

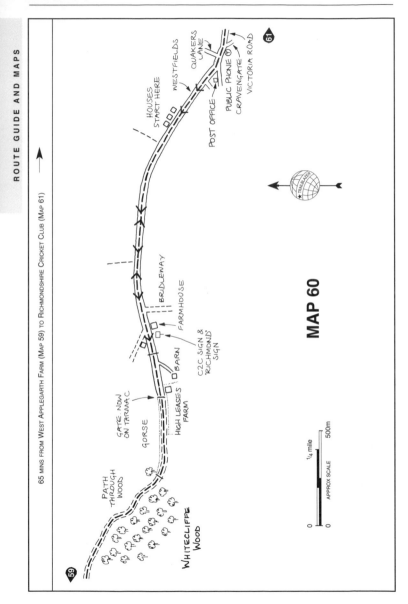

MAP 60

QUAKERS LANE

WESTFIELDS

HOUSES START HERE

PUBLIC PHONE
CRAVENGATE
VICTORIA ROAD

POST OFFICE

BRIDLEWAY

FARMHOUSE

C2C SIGN & RICHMOND SIGN

BARN

GATE NOW ON TARMAC

HIGH LEASES FARM

GORSE

PATH THROUGH WOOD

WHITECLIFFE WOOD

TRAILBLAZER

¼ mile

500m

APPROX SCALE

RICHMOND   MAP 61, p177

Up above a castle! Down below a stream!
Up above a ruin! Down below a dream!
Man made the castle, rude, forbidding, bare.
God made the river, swift, eternal, fair.
From the recollections of **Mr M Wise** as recorded in *Richmond Yorkshire in 1830s* (Wenham Publishers 1977).

This is the largest settlement on the Coast to Coast and feels like it too. Richmond is a busy market town that grew parasitically around the **castle**, built by one Alan the Red in the 11th century.

As the castle fell into disrepair over time some of its stones were pillaged to build the surrounding houses, giving the entire town the same sombre hue as the castle. As that castle, and the reason for the town's existence, disintegrated still further, Richmond discovered a new source of prosperity as, curiously, the foremost cabinet-making town in the country during the Georgian era at the end of the 18th century. Many of the buildings leading off the main market-place date back to this era (indeed, the town museum is housed in a former cabinet-maker's workshop), and in addition there's a **Georgian theatre**, said to be the finest in the country, particularly following its restoration in 2003.

Dominating the centre of the town is its large cobbled **market-place**, while off it run small winding alleys, known as *wynds*. Most of the town's attractions can be found on or near this market-place, though a couple of the ruins nearby also warrant further investigation.

The size and scale of the town – to say nothing of the noise, the bustle and the traffic – may come as something of a shock to Coast to Coasters used to smaller and more genteel settlements. It can also get a little rowdy in the evenings, particularly at weekends. But Richmond does have its advantages too, particularly in terms of the facilities it provides, as well as enough sights to keep amused those who decide to rest for a day in the town.

Services

The **tourist office** (☎ 01748 850252, 🖳 www.yorkshiredales.org; open Easter to end Oct daily 9.30am-5.30pm, Nov-Easter Mon-Sat 9.30am-4.30pm), on the junction of Victoria and Queens roads, is extremely helpful and stocks all manner of souvenirs, books and brochures about nearby attractions. There's also a Richmond **website** (🖳 www.richmond.org.uk) that's worth checking out before you arrive in town.

On the subject of the internet, the **library** (Mon, Tue, Fri 9.30am-7pm, Thu 9.30am-5pm, Sat 9.30am-4pm; closed Wed and Sun) has an **internet** service and ten terminals, though alas they now charge a rather cheeky £1.25 for 30 minutes to non-members.

The **post office** (Mon, Tues & Fri 9am-7pm, Thur 9.30am-5pm, Sat 9.30am-4pm) does foreign exchange and all the major **banks** are represented on the main square and have cashpoints. Having got your money you'll then want something to spend it on. The **trekking shop**, Yeoman's (Mon-Sat 9am-5.30pm, Sun 10am-5pm), on Finkle St, is worth checking out for replacement equipment; Stepping Out is an outdoor clothes and shoes shop nearby. There's a Boots on the main square and a second **pharmacy**, Richmond Pharmacy, can be found on King St.

Castle Hill **Bookshop**, below the castle, has a good selection on local history. For **food shopping** there's a Somerfield (Mon-Sat 8am-10pm, Sun 9am-6pm) between the Kings Head and Castle Tavern on the main square, and a Co-op superstore (Mon-Fri 8am-10pm, Sat 8am-8pm, Sun 11am-5pm) to the north of Grey Friars Tower.

Where to stay

There are no hostels in Richmond and the nearest campsite is the **camping barn** at Applegarth (see p170). The only realistic option, therefore, is to take a room at a B&B or hotel. If you haven't pre-booked, your best bet is the tourist office which runs a free accommodation-booking service.

There's a good chance you'll end up staying on Frenchgate, which has several B&Bs. *Willance House* (☎ 01748 824467, 🖥 www.willancehouse.com; 1D/2D or T), at No 24 is an oak-beamed house (or rather, three houses) dating back to the 17th century. It's named after the first alderman of Richmond and stands just a few yards off the main square. Now under new management and recently refurbished, all rooms are en suite and rates start at £31 per night, £30 thereafter.

Further up this road, away from the square is *Frenchgate Guesthouse* (☎ 01748 823421, 0788 976 8696; 2D/1T), 66 Frenchgate, which, like the others, has thrilling views down to and across the Swale. Other features include TVs and free wi-fi access; rates start at £35 per person, or singles are a steep £60, or an even steeper £70 at weekends. Whack another £3 on top if paying by credit card.

Almost opposite Willance House is the smart *Frenchgate Restaurant & Hotel* (☎ 01748 822087, 🖥 www.thefrenchgate .co.uk; 2S/2D/3T or D/1F), 59-61 Frenchgate, describes itself as a hotel for the 'executive walker' – and when you catch a glimpse of the marble floor, stone walls and oak beds you'll understand why! A lovely place that the new owner is justifiably proud of, they charge £58 for the single, £98 for the family room, and from £98 for the doubles and twins.

Across town from Frenchgate, two other great options stand near each other close to the bridge. *Restaurant on the Green* (☎ 01748 826229; 1D/1T), 5-7 Bridge St, is a handsome Grade II William and Mary house that was rebuilt in 1689 and which has some wonderful features including two magnificent 18th-century sundials. Rates here start at £29. Evening meals are served but to guests only.

On the other side of the small Green is *The Old Brewery Guesthouse* (☎ 01748 822460, 🖥 www.oldbreweryguesthouse .com; 1S/3D/2T), another Grade II Georgian building and the nerve centre for Sherpa Van (see p21). Run by a lady whom one couple described as lovely, there's a wide choice of breakfasts including smoked salmon and scrambled egg in a bagel. Most rooms are en suite and rates start at £30 for a single (not en suite) and £30-32.50 per person for two sharing.

On the square itself is *The Kings Head* (☎ 01748 850220, 🖥 www.kingsheadrich mond.co.uk; 30 rooms), probably the smartest hotel in town though it doesn't look like much on the outside. All rooms are en suite and start at £82/58-71 sgl/dbl per room for B&B.

Moat House (☎ 01748 823285; 1D/ 10D or T/2F), 9 Castle Hill, is like a tardis, a seemingly average-sized place that's surprisingly huge inside. Under new management, they charge £25 per person per night; only one of the rooms is en suite.

Another excellent choice is *Nuns Cottage* (☎ 01748 822809, 🖥 www.nuns cottage.co.uk; 1D/1T), 5 Hurgill Rd, which is actually three cottages converted into one Grade II listed house. The house is lovely and filled with antiques and guests are welcomed with a sherry and find fresh fruit in the room and a video recorder (with videos); nevertheless, the favourite part for most trekkers is the enclosed garden surrounded by high stone walls, a wonderfully tranquil sanctuary from the hubbub outside. B&B here costs £65-80 per room.

The Buck (☎ 01748 822259, 🖥 www .thebuck-richmond.co.uk; 1D or T/5F) on Newbiggin is an unpretentious, friendly place with six en suite rooms. Parts of the inn date back to the fourteenth century. Rates start at £65 in a double or twin, the price dropping if staying more than one night.

There are a couple of other places to stay on Pottergate, including the friendly *Pottergate Guesthouse* (☎ 01748 823826; 1S/2D/2T/1F, £30 per person in one of the three en suite rooms, £25 in a room with shared bathroom), 4 Pottergate; and the relatively new *Rosedale Guest House* (☎ 01748 823926, 07854 698027, 🖥 www .richmondbedandbreakfast.co.uk; 2T/2D/ 1D or F), quite a neat and tidy place with en suite only rooms charging £65 for a double or twin, £35-40 for single occupancy.

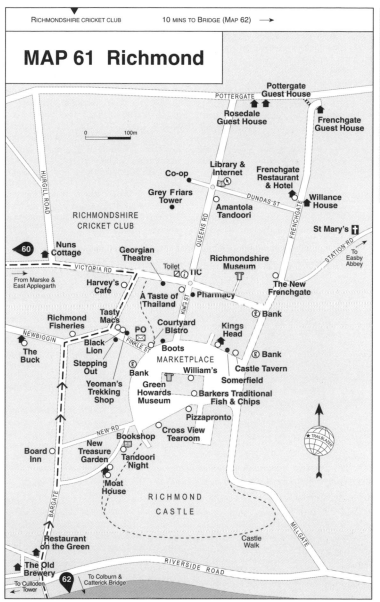

RICHMONDSHIRE CRICKET CLUB   10 MINS TO BRIDGE (MAP 62) →

MAP 61 Richmond

POTTERGATE

Pottergate
Guest House

Rosedale
Guest House

Frenchgate
Guest House

0   100m

Library &
Internet

Co-op

Frenchgate
Restaurant
& Hotel

Willance
House

Grey Friars
Tower

DUNDAS ST

Amantola
Tandoori

St Mary's

RICHMONDSHIRE
CRICKET CLUB

FRENCHGATE

60

Nuns
Cottage

Georgian
Theatre

VICTORIA RD

Toilet

Richmondshire
Museum

STATION RD

To
Easby
Abbey

From Marske &
East Applegarth

Harvey's
Café

TIC

The New
Frenchgate

QUEENS RD

A Taste of
Thailand

Pharmacy

KING ST

Bank

Tasty
Mac's

Richmond
Fisheries

Courtyard
Bistro

Kings
Head

NEWBIGGIN

PO

Bank

Black
Lion

FINKLE ST

Boots

The
Buck

Stepping
Out

MARKETPLACE

Castle Tavern

Bank

William's

Somerfield

Yeoman's
Trekking
Shop

Green
Howards
Museum

Barkers Traditional
Fish & Chips

Pizzapronto

NEW RD

Bookshop

Cross View
Tearoom

Board
Inn

New
Treasure
Garden

Tandoori
Night

BARGATE

Moat
House

RICHMOND

CASTLE

TRAILBLAZER

Castle
Walk

MILLGATE

Restaurant
on the Green

The Old
Brewery

62

To Colburn &
Catterick Bridge

RIVERSIDE ROAD

To Culloden
Tower

HURGILL ROAD

ROUTE GUIDE AND MAPS

Where to eat

Of the many tea shops that decorate Richmond's streets, **Moat House** (see p176; 10am-8pm) is probably the best place for a full English breakfast (£4.50), though the cheapest option is to go for one at a Wetherspoon's pub, of which there are a couple in town.

For lunch, **Harvey's Café** (☎ 01748 829505; Mon, Tue, Thur-Sat 10am-4pm), on Rosemary Lane, does a great pensioner's special of £5.25 for two courses, including roasts, yorkshire pudding and five different vegetables; vegetarian options are also available.

A more modern, swish tearoom, **Williams** (☎ 01748 824052, 🖳 www.williamsdeli.co.uk; daily 9am-4.30pm in summer, depending on demand in winter) stands in the centre of the square and serves a tasty roast Yorkshire beef sandwich for £4.15. More traditional and unfussier, **Cross View Tearooms** (☎ 01748 825897, Mon-Sat 9am-5pm, Sun 10am-5pm) is friendly and cheap.

Richmond is well-served by fish and chip shops, the most popular of which is probably **Richmond Fisheries** (☎ 01748 822937) just off the main square at 4 Newbiggin and open daily. All manner of food is served here, including the unfussy nosh boxes, where for £2.30 you get a plastic carton filled with chips and kebab meat.

For a quick bite of a different kind there are pizzas to takeaway at **Pizzapronto** (☎ 01748 826265; daily 5-11.30pm) on the square and an excellent sandwich shop, **Tasty Macs** (☎ 01748 822597; Mon-Sat 10am-3pm), with a menu the size of a wall, on Finkle St.

Our favourite eatery is the **New Frenchgate** (☎ 01748 824949, 🖳 www .frenchgatecafe.co.uk), on Frenchgate, open Mon-Sat 11.30am to 3pm and daily 6pm to late, with the menu offering such unusual items as sautéed mushrooms in Swaledale blue cheese sauce for £4.50. In our opinion it's also the best place for vegetarians.

Food is served in the **Black Lion** (☎ 01748 826217) Mon-Sat 11am-2.30pm and Tue-Sun 5.30-9.30pm, on the Market Square, including such tasty and unusual dishes as rabbit casserole.

For more exotic flavours, there's an Indian restaurant, **Amantola Tandoori** (☎ 01748 826070; Sun-Thur 4.45-11.45pm, Fri-Sat 4.45pm-12.15am), on Queen's Rd, and another, **Tandoori Night** (☎ 01748 826677, daily 5.30pm-midnight), on Castle Hill, while **New Treasure Garden** (☎ 01748 826085, 825827 after 6pm; Wed-Mon 6-11pm), 7 Castle Hill, is a good Cantonese restaurant with an interesting Szechuan selection; if you're unfamiliar with this spicy Chinese fare, you may care to try the Szechuan House special (£8 per person, which has a sample of every dish (including dishes made from chicken, squid, bean curd, duck and pork), much of it covered with a special sauce made with chillies, garlic, 'five spicy powder' and yellow bean sauce.

A Taste of Thailand (☎ 01748 829696, daily 5-11pm), on King St, has been recommended and has everybody's favourite Thai dish, green curry, for £6-8, and operate a BYOB (Bring Your Own Booze) with £1 corkage.

The smartest place to eat on the square is the restaurant at the **Kings Head** (see p176; open daily 7-9.15pm, Sun noon-2pm) where you can dine on such fancy dishes as supreme of duck with caper mash and orange sauce (£15.95). They also do meals at the bar (noon-2pm, 6-9.15pm) which are more reasonable.

Just as good, **Courtyard Bistro** (Mon-Sat 9.30am-5pm, Sun 10am-4pm, Fri & Sat 7-10pm) is a fair-value place, doing a reasonable 'workers' lunch' of sandwiches, crisps and tea or coffee for £4.95 during the day, and smarter dishes in the evening from £10.95 including a tasty poached salmon in Hollandaise sauce (£13.95).

The **Frenchgate Restaurant and Hotel** (see p176; daily 7-9pm) is another good, if expensive, choice for a relaxed evening's dining with guinea fowl and sea bass on the menu. Prices are £25 for two courses, £29 for three.

For drinking, there are plenty of pubs lining the main square, though often they are extremely noisy and a couple seem to cater largely to groups of local youths looking for a fight. Nevertheless the *Castle Tavern* is quieter during the day and does cheap pub grub. A more pleasant option is *The Buck* (food daily noon-2.30pm, Mon-Thur 6-8.30pm), on Newbiggin, which, though it still has loud music playing, is a lot more friendly and relaxed and has great views across the river. Further down on Bargate is the *Board Inn*, a quiet freehouse.

What to see and do

Richmond is a great town to walk around, with plenty of twisting wynds to explore and plaques installed here and there that point out places of interest and detail the history of certain buildings. The following sights are all listed at ⌨ www.rich mond.org.uk.

● **Richmond Castle** (☎ 01748 822493) Without Richmond Castle it is arguable that there would be no Richmond and while it ceased performing the proper duties of a castle years ago, in the middle of the 18th century it found alternative employment as a tourist attraction and has been welcoming visitors ever since. The castle is open daily from 1 April to 30 September 10am-6pm (1 Oct-31 Mar, 10am-4pm), and charges £4 adult, £3 with concessions, £1.80 children, under 5s free, family ticket £9.

Visitors are advised not to rush headlong to the ruins, but instead should take time to visit the **exhibition** in the reception building first; it gives a thorough account of the history of the castle and the town – and how historians have pieced this history together – as well as a display on how the castle was built. There's also an interesting section on conscientious objectors (absolutists) who refused to fight and were held captive here during the First World War. Their poignant graffiti still exists on the cell walls, though for protection these cells are today kept locked; copies of the graffiti, however, have been made and can be seen in the exhibition.

Advancing to the ruins themselves, you may be a little disappointed at first by the lack of surviving structures within the castle walls, though by being patient and

reading thoroughly the information boards dotted around, you should get a reasonable idea of how the castle once looked.

Scholars will be excited by the ruins of **Scolland Hall**, the finest ruins left from Alan the Red's time; most visitors, however, will find the views from the **keep** overlooking the town far more engrossing.

● **Richmondshire Museum** (☎ 01748 825611, ⌨ www.communigate.co.uk/ne /richmondshiremuseum) Another surprisingly absorbing local museum, similar in terms of content to Reeth's Swaledale Museum (see p168), though bigger and with even more impressive exhibits, the Richmondshire Museum is open daily from Good Friday to 31 October (closed the rest of the year) 10.30am to 4pm and has an entrance fee of £2.50/1.50. Highlights include **Cruck House**, a 15th-century building moved wholesale from Ravensworth in 1985, an exhibition tracing the history of transport (including an original penny farthing), and, most popular of all, the set of the surgery from the TV version of James Herriot's *All Creatures Great and Small*.

● **Green Howards Museum** (☎ 01748 826561; ⌨ www.greenhowards.org.uk) Richmond has a long military association and is the garrison town of Catterick (now, surprisingly, larger than Richmond itself!). The town's regiment, the Green Howards, have their own museum and **headquarters** (Mon-Sat 10am-4.30pm; £3.30/3 adults/ concs) in the heart of the town in the former Holy Trinity Church, right in the middle of the market-place. With a history spanning the Crimean and Boer wars, as well as military engagements on the North-West Frontier of India plus, of course, more modern battles, the story of the regiment is a fascinating one and it is clearly and interestingly recounted in the museum. Highlights include the staggering 3750-strong medal collection awarded to members of the regiment.

● **Easby Abbey** Formerly and more properly known as **St Agatha's Monastery**, Easby Abbey lies about a mile to the east of Richmond Castle. You get a distant view of it from across the Swale during the next

ROUTE GUIDE AND MAPS

stage's walk, but if you've got the time we strongly advise you pay a proper visit. Like those at Shap, the ruins at Easby were once part of a Premonstratensian Abbey, this one built in 1152, just 31 years after the founding of the order by St Norbert in Prémontré. The monastery served the community for almost 400 years (unlike many other orders who deliberately cut themselves off from the outside world, the Premonstratensians saw it as their duty to administer and serve the laity) until the reign of Henry VIII and the dissolution. Unwilling to bow to Henry's demands that the monastery be closed, the monks joined the Pilgrimage of Grace in 1536, the most popular rebellion against Henry. Many monasteries were briefly restored by the rebels – St Agatha's at Easby among them – though after they were defeated, Henry set about exacting a chilling revenge on those monasteries who had dared to defy his orders, instructing his forces in the north to

'*cause such dreadful execution upon a good number of inhabitants, hanging them on trees, quartering them and setting their heads and quarters in every town, as shall be a fearful warning*'.

While visiting, be sure to check out the parish church here at Easby, which has survived in remarkable condition and plays host to some wonderful 13th-century **wall paintings**. Look out, too, for the 12th-century **panel of glass** depicting St John.

Other sights There are a couple of magnificent ruined towers. The first you'll come across is **Grey Friars Tower**, in the gardens behind the tourist office. This was once part of a Franciscan monastery, founded in 1258, though the tower itself wasn't built until sometime around 1500. The second, clearly visible to the west of town from Richmond Castle, is **Culloden Tower**, a folly dating back to 1746. Amazingly, it is now a novelty holiday cottage let out by the Landmark Trust (🖳 www.landmark trust.org.uk).

Transport (see also pp43-5)

The nearest **railway station** is in Darlington, but there are plenty of **buses** from the market-place. Arriva's buses Nos 34 and X59 run to Darlington, taking around 45 mins. The Little Red Bus No 30 runs back up the Swaledale Monday to Saturday, calling at Reeth (6/day), Gunnerside (4-day) and Keld (2/day). Cheaters who wish to skip some of the next section can catch one of the many buses to Catterick Bridge or Brompton-on-Swale. There are plenty of other services (X26, 27, X27, 28) to nearby villages and towns; ask at the tourist office for details.

National Express do not operate to Richmond, though services go from Darlington to a number of cities in Britain including Edinburgh, Liverpool, Newcastle and London; you can book tickets at Richmond tourist office.

For a **taxi** call Star Cars (☎ 01748 835559) or Aklipse Taxis (☎ 01748 821414).

STAGE 10: RICHMOND TO INGLEBY CROSS   MAPS 61-72

Introduction

This is another long stage, so long that we strongly advise you break it up with a night at Danby Wiske. True, there is something to be said for completing the walk across the **Vale of Mowbray** that separates Swaledale from the Cleveland Hills as quickly as possible. It is, after all, a fairly uneventful trudge by the lofty standards of the Coast to Coast, much of it conducted on roads. Indeed tackling it all in one go is what Wainwright recommends. It's true, too, that the terrain is largely flat and though **23 miles (37km, 8³/₄hr)**, the distance between Richmond and Ingleby Cross, sounds a long way, it's actually very achievable.

But when Wainwright was researching his book, facilities in Danby Wiske were scarce; in his own words, '*you might, with luck, get a bag of crisps at the inn but certainly not a meal or a sandwich*'. Things have obviously changed for the better, however, and now there are not only two great B&Bs but the pub is an absolute treat. So if you have the time, in our opinion there's a lot to be said for spending a morning ticking off a couple more sights in Richmond, before heading on to Danby Wiske in the afternoon.

Besides, this first stage is not without its charms, from the brief woodland stroll outside Richmond to the riverbank meanderings near Catterick, where rabbits hop freely in the fields and kingfishers swoop from branch to branch above the water. So don't dismiss this stage as one to endure rather than enjoy; after all, any walk with kingfishers in it is a walk worth doing.

The route

Starting off with a quick riverside stroll from the southern side of Richmond Bridge, you join the A6136, leaving it by following a lane to the left that leads to the sewage works and then into a gorgeous stretch of riparian woodland. At the top of the woods are the ruins of **Hagg Farm** and, a little way further on, the village of **Colburn** (Map 63). Saxon for 'Cold Brook', Colburn's two dozen houses – plus one enormous stately home, Colburn Hall – are all built, literally, within a stone's throw of the river. This, so the story goes, is because the location of each house was determined by a man throwing stones from the river: where each stone landed, a house was built.

This interesting if implausible story aside, Colburn has little of fascination to the average hiker, though it does play host to the ***Hildyard Arms*** (☎ 01748 832353, Mon-Sat 6.30-11pm, Sun to 10.30pm, Sat/Sun 12-3pm) which permits **camping** on their lawn free of charge but there are no facilities except the toilets in the pub (available in the evenings only). Also, the pub does not serve food.

From Colburn the path skirts the eastern side of the last cottage, crosses two fields and then heads towards, and follows the course of, the Swale. At one point the path skirts above the former site of **St Giles Hospital** that flourished by the river around 800 years ago. Across the field from the hospital site is *St Giles Farm* (☎ 01748 811372; 1T/1D/1F; booking advisable) which does B&B for £27.50-30, £30 single supplement, and **camping** in the garden for £5 per person with shower.

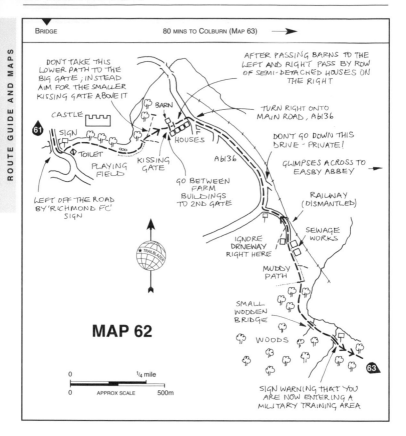

BRIDGE   80 MINS TO COLBURN (MAP 63)   ⟶

AFTER PASSING BARNS TO THE LEFT AND RIGHT PASS BY ROW OF SEMI-DETACHED HOUSES ON THE RIGHT

DON'T TAKE THIS LOWER PATH TO THE BIG GATE; INSTEAD AIM FOR THE SMALLER KISSING GATE ABOVE IT

CASTLE

BARN

TURN RIGHT ONTO MAIN ROAD, A6136

61

SIGN

HOUSES

DON'T GO DOWN THIS DRIVE - PRIVATE!

TOILET

KISSING GATE

A6136

GLIMPSES ACROSS TO EASBY ABBEY ⟶

PLAYING FIELD

GO BETWEEN FARM BUILDINGS TO 2ND GATE

RAILWAY (DISMANTLED)

LEFT OFF THE ROAD BY 'RICHMOND FC' SIGN

SEWAGE WORKS

IGNORE DRIVEWAY RIGHT HERE

★ TRAILBLAZER

MUDDY PATH

SMALL WOODEN BRIDGE

MAP 62

WOODS

63

0   1/4 mile

0   APPROX SCALE   500m

SIGN WARNING THAT YOU ARE NOW ENTERING A MILITARY TRAINING AREA

From here the path continues above the river past ***Thornborough Farm*** (Map 64; ☎ 01748 811421) where **camping** is possible but very basic (£2.50 per person, toilet block but no shower, hot water available from the farmhouse), and under the A1 to **Catterick Bridge**. Famous now for its giant racecourse, the name Catterick comes from the Roman name *Cataracta*, meaning waterfall, and a Roman town lies buried underneath the modern settlement. By the bridge is ***Bridge House Hotel*** (☎ 01748 818331; 🖳 www.bridgehousehotelcatterick .com; 3S/6D/3T/3F), with origins dating back to the fifteenth century. Rates are £50 for a single room, £80 in the double/twin and family rooms.

Further evidence of the Romans can be seen across the bridge where, having taken the riverside path to the right after crossing the Swale, you walk by an ancient wall that many believe was once some kind of Roman embankment. The hamlet of **Bolton-on-Swale** (Map 65) is the next place of note. *(cont'd on p188)*

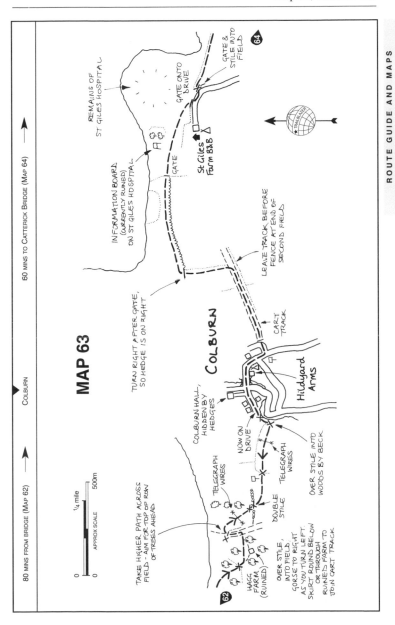

MAP 63

REMAINS OF ST GILES HOSPITAL

INFORMATION BOARD (CURRENTLY RUINED) ON ST GILES HOSPITAL

GATE

St Giles Farm B&B

GATE ONTO DRIVE

GATE & STILE INTO FIELD

64

TRAILBLAZER

TURN RIGHT AFTER GATE, SO HEDGE IS ON RIGHT

LEAVE TRACK BEFORE FENCE AT END OF SECOND FIELD

COLBURN

COLBURN HALL, HIDDEN BY HEDGES

CART TRACK

Hildyard Arms

NOW ON DRIVE

TELEGRAPH WIRES

OVER STILE INTO WOODS BY BECK

TELEGRAPH WIRES

DOUBLE STILE

TAKE HIGHER PATH ACROSS FIELD - AIM FOR TOP OF ROW OF TREES AHEAD

0 ¼ mile
0 500m
APPROX SCALE

HAGG FARM (RUINED)

OVER STILE, INTO FIELD, GORSE TO RIGHT AS YOU TURN LEFT. SKIRT ROUND BELOW OR THROUGH RUINED FARM TO JOIN CART TRACK

62

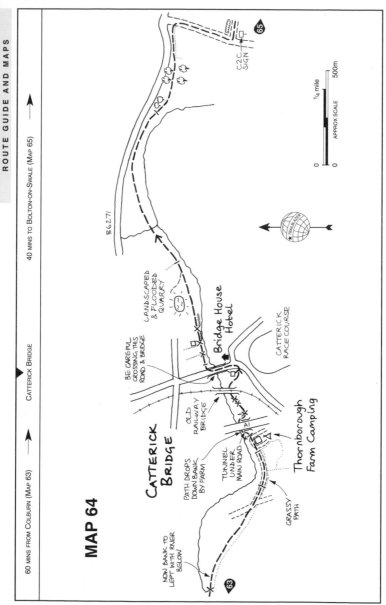

MAP 64

CATTERICK BRIDGE

NOW BANK TO LEFT WITH RIVER BELOW

63

PATH DROPS DOWN BANK BY FARM

GRASSY PATH

TUNNEL UNDER MAIN ROAD

Thornborough Farm Camping

A1

OLD RAILWAY BRIDGE

BE CAREFUL CROSSING THIS ROAD & BRIDGE

LANDSCAPED & FLOODED QUARRY

Bridge House Hotel

CATTERICK RACE COURSE

B6271

C2C SIGN

65

¼ mile

APPROX SCALE   500m

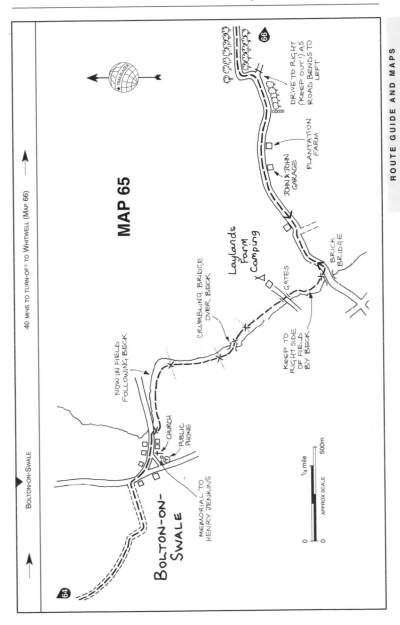

MAP 65

40 MINS TO TURN-OFF TO WHITWELL (MAP 66) →

64

BOLTON-ON-SWALE

MEMORIAL TO HENRY JENKINS

CHURCH

PUBLIC PHONE

NOW IN FIELD FOLLOWING BECK

CRUMBLING BRIDGE OVER BECK

Laylands Farm Camping

GATES

KEEP TO RIGHT SIDE OF FIELD BY BECK

BRICK BRIDGE

JOHN X JOHN GARAGE

PLANTATION FARM

DRIVE TO RIGHT (KEEP OUT!) AS ROAD BENDS TO LEFT

66

¼ mile

500m

APPROX SCALE

0

0

ROUTE GUIDE AND MAPS

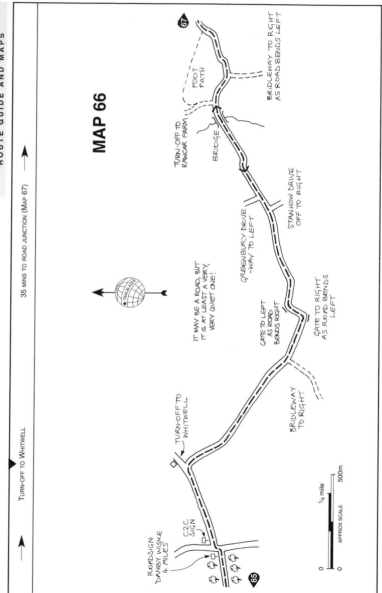

← TURN-OFF TO WHITWELL

35 MINS TO ROAD JUNCTION (MAP 67) →

MAP 66

ROADSIGN: DANBY WISKE 4 MILES

C2C SIGN

65

TURN-OFF TO WHITWELL

IT MAY BE A ROAD, BUT IT IS AT LEAST A VERY, VERY QUIET ONE!

GATE TO LEFT AS ROAD BENDS RIGHT

GREENBURY DRIVE -WAY TO LEFT

GATE TO RIGHT AS ROAD BENDS LEFT

BRIDLEWAY TO RIGHT

STANHOW DRIVE OFF TO RIGHT

TURN-OFF TO RANCAR FARM

FOOT PATH

BRIDGE

BRIDLEWAY TO RIGHT AS ROAD BENDS LEFT

67

¼ mile

500m

APPROX SCALE

0
0

TRAILBLAZER

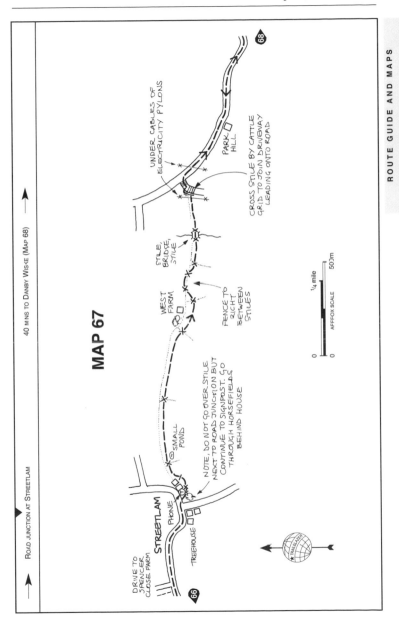

MAP 67

ROAD JUNCTION AT STREETLAM

40 MINS TO DANBY WISKE (MAP 68)

DRIVE TO
SPENCER
CLOSE FARM

STREETLAM

PHONE

TREEHOUSE

66

SMALL
POND

NOTE, DO NOT GO OVER STILE
NEXT TO ROAD JUNCTION BUT
CONTINUE TO SIGNPOST. GO
THROUGH HORSEFIELDS
BEHIND HOUSE

WEST
FARM

FENCE TO
RIGHT
BETWEEN
STILES

STILE,
BRIDGE,
STILE

UNDER CABLES OF
ELECTRICITY PYLONS

CROSS STILE BY CATTLE
GRID TO JOIN DRIVEWAY
LEADING ONTO ROAD

PARK
HILL

68

APPROX SCALE

0   ¼ mile

0   500m

(cont'd from p182) Don't look for refreshments here – you'll do so in vain – but do visit the churchyard, famous for the **monument to Henry Jenkins**, a local man who lived an unremarkable life; unremarkable that is, except for its length: he was 169 when he died. The church itself is even older, dating back to the fourteenth century, with Norman and Saxon ancestors; you can see various bits of masonry from these earlier churches inside, including part of an Anglo-Danish cross shaft in the vestry and part of a pointed arch in the vestry roof.

More unexceptional field-walking ensues on your way to *Laylands Farm* (Map 65; ☎ 01748 811491, **camping** possible from £4), followed by the longest stretch of road-walking on the entire trail (Maps 65-8). Though the roads are quiet and the flanking hedges alive with birdsong, you'd be forgiven for dreaming of public transport to help you along this section. Dream on: there is no public transport around here. At **Streetlam** (Map 67) there is an opportunity to leave the road for more fields of pasture and livestock. Negotiate these and rejoin the road leading into Danby Wiske.

DANBY WISKE   MAP 68, opposite

It may be only a small place with little to see save for a 11th-century Norman church, but the quality of the accommodation alone justifies spending a night here. It's as if the village, on reading Wainwright's book and his hurtful comments about Danby Wiske, went out of its way to prove him wrong.

The Manor House (☎ 01609 774662, 🖳 m.sanders79@btinternet.com; 2S/1D/1T), on the way to the church, is both the most upmarket place in town and the place with the most history, being a listed building dating back to around 1600, that was built on a base that was possibly part of an old Yorkshire longhouse and is therefore much older. B&B starts from only £22.

The former owners of the local pub, the White Swan, have transferred the humour and hospitality which made the pub so popular in the first place and brought it to their new venture, *The Old School* (☎ 01609 774227; 1S/1D/2T; Easter to end Sep). A 19th-century schoolhouse, all the rooms are bright, neat and smart and all but one twin are en suite; it's a lovely place.

Another good choice, the efficiently run *Ashfield* (☎ 01609 771628; 2T en suite, one with private facilities; Apr-Sep) also provides some smart, bright rooms with TV and tea-/coffee-making facilities. Reluctant to do simply B&B without an evening meal too, unless it's a group booking, they charge £38 for a three-course dinner, bed and break-fast, £25 for simple B&B. Washing and drying facilities are £4, a packed lunch £3.

The pub, *The White Swan* (☎ 01609 770122; 1S/2D/2T/1F), is both the geographic and social heart of the village. It has one en suite room and five others with shared bathroom. Rates are £65 for the room in the en suite, £55 otherwise. Note, however, that they do not allow pets. They also offer **camping** (£5 per person) on the lawn, campers have use of shower and toilet facilities. The bar has an **internet** terminal (£1.50 for 30 mins). Food is served in the bar Mon-Fri 11.30am-4pm, Sat & Sun 12noon-3pm, daily 7-9pm (order by 7.30pm). Service can be slow; the food is nothing to write home about.

As for the **church** – one of the very few in England that has no known dedication – only the solid oak door and the font are 11th-century originals, though much of the north aisle is only slightly younger. Look above the main door at the tympanum and you should be able to make out the outlines of three badly weathered figures. They have been interpreted as follows: the central figure is the Angel of Judgement who weighs the soul of the figure on the right using the scales that he holds in his other hand. Though the evil deeds in one of the scale's pans outweigh the good ones in the other, the third figure, the Angel of Mercy (Jesus Christ), has slipped his fingers under the pan containing the bad deeds, thus causing the good deeds to seem heavier.

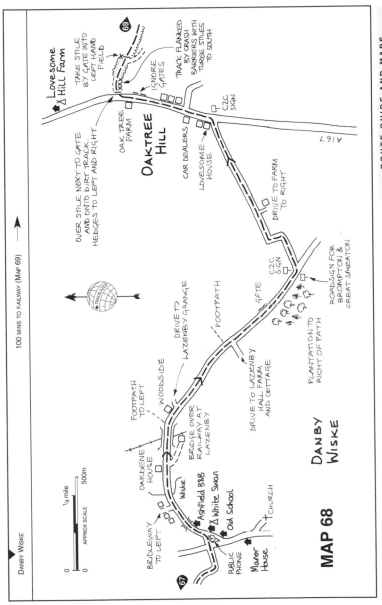

DANBY WISKE

100 MINS TO RAILWAY (MAP 69)

MAP 68

DANBY WISKE

Lovesome Hill Farm

TAKE STILE BY GATE INTO LEFT HAND FIELD

TRACK FLANKED BY CRASH BARRIERS WITH THREE STILES TO SOUTH

IGNORE GATES

C2C SIGN

OVER STILE NEXT TO GATE AND ONTO DIRT TRACK. HEDGES TO LEFT AND RIGHT

OAK TREE FARM

OAKTREE HILL

CAR DEALERS

LOVESOME HOUSE

DRIVE TO FARM TO RIGHT

A167

C2C SIGN

DRIVE TO LAZENBY GRANGE

FOOTPATH

GATE

ROADSIGN FOR BROMPTON & GREAT SMEATON

PLANTATION TO RIGHT OF PATH

FOOTPATH TO LEFT

WOODSIDE

DRIVE TO LAZENBY HALL FARM AND COTTAGE

OAKDENE HOUSE

BRIDGE OVER RAILWAY AT LAZENBY

Wiske

Ashfield B&B

White Swan

Old School

BRIDLEWAY TO LEFT

PUBLIC PHONE

Manor House

CHURCH

¼ mile

500m

0

APPROX SCALE

67

69

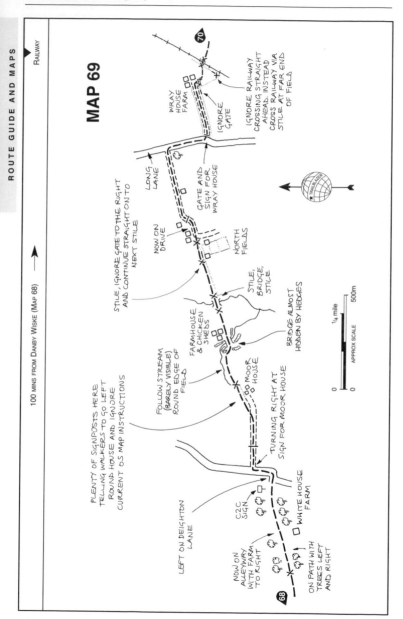

ROUTE GUIDE AND MAPS

RAILWAY

100 MINS FROM DANBY WISKE (MAP 68) →

MAP 69

70

IGNORE RAILWAY
CROSSING STRAIGHT
AHEAD. INSTEAD
CROSS RAILWAY VIA
STILE AT FAR END
OF FIELD

WRAY
HOUSE
FARM

IGNORE
GATE

LONG
LANE

GATE AND
SIGN FOR
WRAY HOUSE

STILE, IGNORE GATE TO THE RIGHT
AND CONTINUE STRAIGHT ONTO
NEXT STILE

NOW ON
DRIVE

NORTH
FIELDS

STILE,
BRIDGE,
STILE

FARMHOUSE
& CHICKEN
SHEDS

BRIDGE ALMOST
HIDDEN BY HEDGES

FOLLOW STREAM
(BARELY VISIBLE)
ROUND EDGE OF
FIELD

PLENTY OF SIGNPOSTS HERE
TELLING WALKERS TO GO LEFT
ROUND HOUSE AND IGNORE
CURRENT OS MAP INSTRUCTIONS

MOOR
HOUSE

TURNING RIGHT AT
SIGN FOR MOOR HOUSE

LEFT ON DEIGHTON
LANE

C2C
SIGN

WHITE HOUSE
FARM

NOW ON
ALLEYWAY
WITH FARM
TO RIGHT

ON PATH WITH
TREES LEFT
AND RIGHT

68

¼ mile
APPROX SCALE
500m
0   0

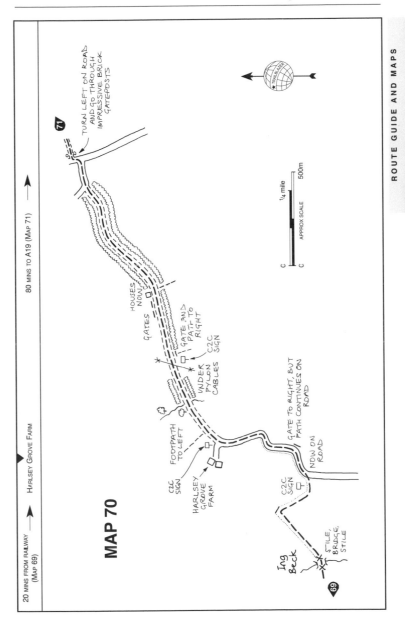

20 MINS FROM RAILWAY (Map 69) → ── ▶ HARLSEY GROVE FARM ── 80 MINS TO A19 (MAP 71) →

MAP 70

Ing Beck

STILE, BRIDGE, STILE

C2C SIGN

NOW ON ROAD

GATE TO RIGHT, BUT PATH CONTINUES ON ROAD

C2C SIGN

HARLSEY GROVE FARM

FOOTPATH TO LEFT

UNDER PYLON CABLES

C2C SIGN

GATE AND PATH TO RIGHT

GATES

HOUSES NOW

TURN LEFT ON ROAD AND GO THROUGH IMPRESSIVE BRICK GATEPOSTS

TRAILBLAZER

¼ mile · 500m
APPROX SCALE

ROUTE GUIDE AND MAPS

A19

80 MINS FROM HARLSEY GROVE FARM (MAP 70)

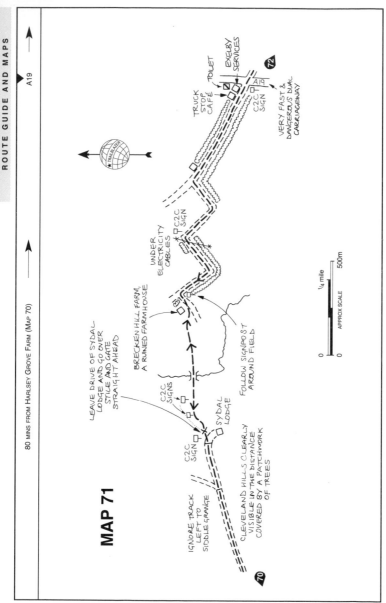

MAP 71

IGNORE TRACK
LEFT TO
SIDDLE GRANGE

CLEVELAND HILLS CLEARLY
VISIBLE IN THE DISTANCE
COVERED BY A PATCHWORK
OF TREES

C2C
SIGN

C2C
SIGNS

SYDAL
LODGE

LEAVE DRIVE OF SYDAL
LODGE AND GO OVER
STILE AND GATE
STRAIGHT AHEAD

BRECKEN HILL FARM,
A RUINED FARMHOUSE

FOLLOW SIGNPOST
AROUND FIELD

UNDER
ELECTRICITY
CABLES

C2C
SIGN

TRUCK
STOP
CAFE

TOILET

EXELBY
SERVICES

72

C2C
SIGN

VERY FAST &
DANGEROUS DUAL
CARRIAGEWAY

TRAILBLAZER

0
0

¼ mile

500m

APPROX SCALE

70

From the bridge crossing the Wiske outside the village you can see the outline of the Cleveland Hills – our next destination – in the distance. Unfortunately, you still have half the Vale of Mowbray to cross before you get there, much of it, as before, on roads, including this first section to **Oaktree Hill**, a string of houses lining the A167.

Despite the noise of the road, *Lovesome Hill Farm* (☎ 01609 772311, ☐ www.lovesomehillfarm.co.uk; 1S/4D/1F) has been highly praised by some walkers for the quality of its accommodation and the opportunity it offers to stay on a 165-acre working farm complete with pigs, cattle and sheep. As well as the **B&B**, with rates starting at £30 per night, the farm also has a **bunkhouse barn** (the farm can supply you with duvets and pillows) that sleeps 10 people for just £8 per person, or you can **camp** for just £4. The farm lies about 200m to the north of the Coast to Coast route.

Opposite the white Oak Tree Farm, a rough track cuts across to White House Farm (Map 69) and on, across Deighton Lane and via a second farm track, to **Moor House**.

Negotiating more farms, a rail track and a beck or two, you emerge at a **truck stop café** (Map 71) by the busy A19. Campers should note that the service station here is the only place on the route leading to the North York Moors where provisions can be bought. Crossing the road with extreme care, you arrive, around 3½ to 4 hours after leaving Danby Wiske, at Ingleby Cross.

INGLEBY CROSS & INGLEBY ARNCLIFFE   MAP 72, p195

Sandwiched between two busy 'A' roads, Ingleby Cross and its Siamese twin Ingleby Arncliffe are actually surprisingly peaceful places. Ingleby Cross – little more than the tail-end dangling from its larger neighbour – is named after the war memorial at its heart. The only service of any interest to the walker is the **post office** (open Mon-Wed mornings only), situated in the Blue Bell Inn (see column opposite).

If you've walked from Danby Wiske and have time to kill, spend it visiting English Heritage's Mount Grace Priory, the best of the ruined abbeys on the Coast to Coast (see the box on p196).

Where to stay and eat

In **Ingleby Arncliffe**, *Elstavale* (☎ 01609 882302, ☐ http://uk.geocities.com/cl sta_vale; 2D or T) is conveniently situated on the path and offers B&B starting at £23. *Somerset House Farm* (☎ 01609 882555,

☐ www.somersethousefarm.co.uk; 4T/1D) charges £30 per person with a £5 single supplement. They are creating more rooms and hope to have them available in 2008; they also do packed lunches (£5) and laundry (£5 per load). To find it, at the T-junction by the water tower turn right, and it's the last house on the left before you hit the A19 again.

Monk's House (☎ 01609 882294; 1S/1D) is a more convenient option right on the coast path. It's an ancient building (400-600 years old is the owners' estimation) with mullion windows. Accommodation consists of just one double and one tiny single room, with the toilet downstairs; rates are £25.

The Blue Bell Inn (☎ 01609 882272, ☐ www.the-blue-bell-inn.co.uk; 2S/2T/1D en suite) in the centre of **Ingleby Cross** serves very good bar meals (Sun-Fri noon-2pm, 6-9pm) and has real ales and open fires. You can also **camp** in the field out the back for £3 including shower; breakfast is available in the mornings. B&B starts from £25 in the double, £26 in a twin, £28 single. By 2008 they hope to have reinstated their **internet access** for guests.

A mile further along the path, *Park House* (☎ 01609 882899, 🖥 www.park housebb.co.uk; 2D/2T/2F all en suite), describes itself as a Walkers' B&B and strives hard to live up to the description too. It's really rather sublime, newly refurbished with a lovely lounge and grounds as well as a **laundry service** (£5 per load) and access

to the owner's computer so you can check your **email**. They also provide **lifts** to Ingleby if you want to eat out – though you can have an evening meal here too. Rates in the B&B are £25, with a £5 single supplement.

Should you find that all accommodation has been booked in Ingleby Arncliffe and Ingleby Cross walk on to Osmotherley (see p197) for more options including the nearest youth hostel and campsite.

STAGE 11: INGLEBY CROSS TO BLAKEY RIDGE   MAPS 72-81

Introduction

At **23 miles (37km, 8¹/₄hr)**, this is another stage that many walkers prefer to split into two. Unfortunately, there is no accommodation on the route that allows you to do this easily, thus placing you on the horns of a dilemma: split the walk in two, leaving the trail at **Clay Bank Top** to divert to one of the nearby villages such as Great Broughton to the north or Urra to the south? Or attempt the long march to Blakey Ridge in one go and to hell with the blisters? One argument in favour of the first option is that dividing the stage does, of course, allow for a more leisurely walk. On the next day, having returned to Clay Bank Top from your accommodation, you can then walk beyond Blakey Moor to Glaisdale and even further, so you needn't lose that much time overall. Providing you book your accommodation in advance, the B&Bs at Great Broughton, Urra and the other nearby villages are more than happy to pick you up at Clay Bank Top and deposit you back again the next morning. In my experience, most people seem to choose this alternative.

The second option also has its plus points, however. For one thing, though the first half of this walk is hard, the second half, when you are beginning to tire, is flat and straightforward once you have climbed up Urra Moor as you follow the course of a dismantled railway. And secondly, the destination, the Lion Inn at Blakey, is one of the more memorable places on the route, an atmospheric, isolated haven stranded on a windswept moor.

Thus our advice is as follows: if you are feeling fit and can get a room at Blakey Ridge (see p205; not easy because apart from the pub there is only one other B&B), grab it and attempt the 23 miles in one day. But if not, don't feel too upset, for the B&Bs near Clay Bank Top are fine.

One final thing: campers should note that there is **camping** at the excellent Lord Stones Café (see p200), where it's free, and that the Lion Inn at Blakey Ridge also has a (very windy) campsite.

As for the walk itself, this stage takes us into the third national park on our route, the **Yorkshire Moors National Park**. Depending on the weather, this stage could be a joyful one as you skip merrily up and down the moors, stopping

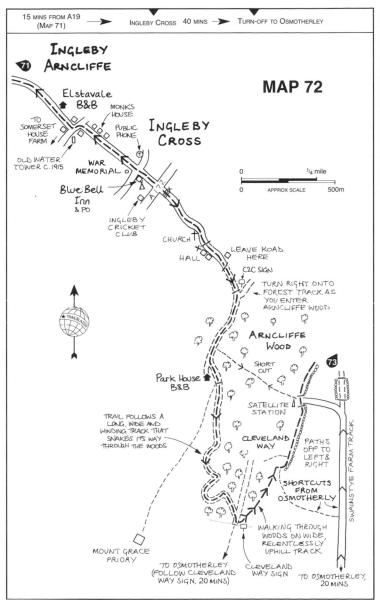

15 MINS FROM A19 (Map 71) ⟶   INGLEBY CROSS   40 MINS ⟶ TURN-OFF TO OSMOTHERLEY

INGLEBY ARNCLIFFE

71

MAP 72

Elstavale B&B

MONK'S HOUSE

INGLEBY CROSS

TO SOMERSET HOUSE FARM

PUBLIC PHONE

OLD WATER TOWER C.1915

WAR MEMORIAL

Blue Bell Inn & PO

INGLEBY CRICKET CLUB

CHURCH

HALL

LEAVE ROAD HERE

C2C SIGN

TURN RIGHT ONTO FOREST TRACK AS YOU ENTER ARNCLIFFE WOOD

★ TRAILBLAZER

ARNCLIFFE WOOD

73

SHORT CUT

Park House B&B

SATELLITE STATION

TRAIL FOLLOWS A LONG, WIDE AND WINDING TRACK THAT SNAKES ITS WAY THROUGH THE WOODS

CLEVELAND WAY

PATHS OFF TO LEFT & RIGHT

SHORTCUTS FROM OSMOTHERLY

SWAINSTYE FARM TRACK

WALKING THROUGH WOODS ON WIDE, RELENTLESSLY UPHILL TRACK

MOUNT GRACE PRIORY

TO OSMOTHERLEY (FOLLOW CLEVELAND WAY SIGN, 20 MINS)

CLEVELAND WAY SIGN

TO OSMOTHERLEY, 20 MINS

0   ¼ mile
0   APPROX SCALE   500m

❏ Mount Grace Priory

When a heritage site advertises itself by saying that it has one of the most remarkable medieval drainage systems in the country, you'd be forgiven for thinking that there's not much point in visiting. But you'd be wrong: the Priory of Mount Grace is the perfect place to potter about for an afternoon if you've taken the short hike from Danby Wiske in the morning and are wondering what to do with yourself for the rest of the day.

The best way to reach the priory is to continue on the Coast to Coast from Ingleby Cross, taking the right-hand fork just after the turn-off for Park House.

The priory is open daily 10am-6pm and charges an **entrance fee** of £4/3 adult/concessions; don't be tempted to duck out of paying, even though the path from the Coast to Coast trail brings you out at the gate at the back of the priory, while the ticket office is by the front.

Mount Grace Priory was built by the **Carthusian** order, a very ascetic sect founded in 1084 by St Bruno, a canon of the Cathedral Church of Rheims. He established a religious community that settled at La Grande Chartreuse near Grenoble, from which we get the name Carthusian (and also the word for all Carthusian monasteries, which are known as charterhouses). St Bruno and his followers saw the world as inherently wicked. For this reason they lived as hermits, so as not to be distracted by the temptations on offer. The monastic order that evolved from this community followed much the same principles. The prior was the only person in the monastery allowed access to the outside world, while each monk lived an essentially solitary existence, eating his meals alone and spending much of his life in his cell. The monk's day was fairly hard, rising at 5.45am and returning to bed only at 2.30am the next morning following a day spent mainly in prayer or contemplation.

Mount Grace Priory, founded in 1398, had 25 cells in total. We have two main people to thank for the preservation of the monastery. James Strangways bought the land from the government in 1540, immediately following the priory's dissolution on December 18, 1539, yet did not destroy the church as required by law at that time. Instead he let it stand as it was, intact save for the roof, possibly because his parents and grandparents had all been buried on the site. More than two centuries later, in 1899, Sir Lowthian Bell bought the adjoining 17th-century house, and during the course of his 30-year residency did some restoration to the priory, including the first attempt to rebuild cell number 8.

The priory today, though definitely a ruin, is an absorbing one, and one that clearly shows in its foundations the basic layout of the place. The restoration of **cell number 8** also makes clear that, for their time, these cells were remarkably comfortable, built on two floors with cabinets, a loom, a small bed, water closet and a small garden.

And the **drainage system**? Well with latrines fitted and clean water piped into every cell, the water supply and drainage system were indeed ahead of their time. Little of the system remains today save for the channels in which the water flowed all around the priory.

only to admire the iridescent plumage of the pheasant, sniff the gorse, gaze at the heather that turns the moor into a variegated sea of colour, or savour the views south to the idyllic valleys of Farndale or north to the industrial glories of Teeside. Or it could be a miserable, rain-soaked, shelterless trudge through the mud with all views obscured by an enveloping, bone-chilling white mist. Let's hope it's the former.

The route

From Ingleby Cross the walk begins with a climb up past the **church** (note the triple-decker pulpit and purple box pews) and on, above the village, to **Arncliffe Wood**, where the path takes a sharpish turn to the south.

Having passed the turn-off for Park House (see Map 72, p195), and the nearby junction with the path to **Mount Grace Priory** (see box opposite), at the southernmost point of the wood a hairpin bend brings the path onto the Cleveland Way, which you'll follow for almost the entire way to Blakey Moor. (The Cleveland Way, incidentally, is well signposted, so orientation should not be a problem on this stage.) Those wishing to visit Osmotherley should turn off south here through the gate.

OSMOTHERLEY   OFF MAP 73, p178

Though a 20-minute walk off the Coast to Coast trail, Osmotherley is a delight and energetic walkers may want to visit even if they're not staying there. In the centre stands a **market cross** and a **barter table**, believed to be the same one from which John Wesley preached. Indeed, in Chapel Yard you can find what is believed to be the oldest practising **Methodist chapel**, constructed in 1754.

Another sight is **Thompson's**, a shop that has been in the same family since 1786 – and looks it! And finally there's the church, **St Peter's**, which is said to have been built on Saxon foundations.

The most distinctive thing about Osmotherley, however, is its beautiful stone terraced cottages, built for the workers who laboured at the flax mill, now *Osmotherley Youth Hostel* (☎ 0870 770 5982, osmotherley@yha.org.uk; 72 beds; £14) at the top end of the village; turn left when you hit the road, rather than right down the hill into town. The hostel serves meals, is licensed and also has a TV and games room. Just before the hostel, *Cote Ghyll Caravan Park* (☎ 01609 883425, ☐ www.coteghyll.com) has **camping** for £6.50, or £7 during school holidays. As its name suggests, its main business is caravans and during the school holidays it can be crammed with kids on holiday running amok, though they do have a few places to pitch a tent on the far side of the site; it is, however, one of the most expensive campsites on our route.

In the village there is a **post office** (Mon, Tue, Thur & Fri 9am-5.30pm, Wed

& Sat 9am-12.30pm) inside the small **shop** (Mon-Sat 8.30am-5.30pm; Sun 9am-5pm) where as well as providing basic provisions they also sell sandwiches (£1.50).

A little further down the hill in the heart of the village is **Osmotherley Walking Shop** (☎ 01609 883818), 4 West End, selling outdoor equipment. At the time of writing it was up for sale, though I've been assured the shop will continue whoever takes it over.

Across the road, the *Queen Catherine* (☎ 01609 883209, ☐ www.queencatherinehotel.co.uk; 2S/1D/2T all en suite), 4 West End, has the most popular bar in town, with live jazz every other Sunday and some great homemade meals (daily 12-2pm and 6-9pm). Rates are £30 per night. The pub is actually named after Henry VIII's wife, Catherine of Aragon, who is believed to have sheltered with monks at the Mount Grace Priory (see box opposite). It is, surprisingly, the only pub named after her in England. The pub is said to be haunted too.

Back up the hill a little way is charming *Vane House* (☎ 01609 883448, ☐ www.vanehouse.co.uk; 3D/4T/1F), 11A North End, with rooms from £32.50 (£40 single occupancy) in high season. Accommodation is also on offer at *The Three Tuns* (☎ 01609 883301, ☐ www.threetunsrestaurant.co.uk; 5D/1T/1F), a restaurant that offers pleasant rooms in the neighbouring Moon House. Rates start at £95/75 for family/double rooms, £55 single occupancy.

For **food**, the *Queen Catherine* has bar meals (12 noon-2.30pm and 6-9pm) including cod for £6.50 and steak for £10.95. The

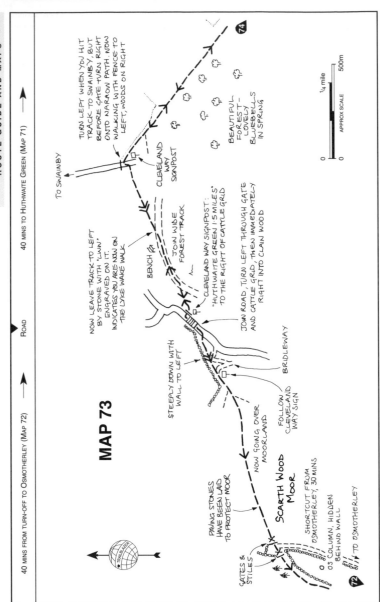

MAP 73

TO SWAINBY

TURN LEFT WHEN YOU HIT TRACK TO SWAINBY, BUT BEFORE GATE TURN RIGHT ONTO NARROW PATH. NOW WALKING WITH FENCE TO LEFT, WOODS ON RIGHT

CLEVELAND WAY SIGNPOST

BEAUTIFUL FOREST - LOVELY BLUEBELLS IN SPRING

¼ mile
APPROX SCALE
0   500m

NOW LEAVE TRACK TO LEFT BY STONE WITH "LWW" ENGRAVED ON IT. INDICATES YOU ARE NOW ON THE LYKE WAKE WALK

BENCH

JOIN WIDE FOREST TRACK

CLEVELAND WAY SIGNPOST: "HUTHWAITE GREEN 1.5 MILES" TO THE RIGHT OF CATTLE GRID

JOIN ROAD, TURN LEFT THROUGH GATE AND CATTLE GRID, THEN IMMEDIATELY RIGHT INTO CLAIN WOOD

STEEPLY DOWN WITH WALL TO LEFT

BRIDLEWAY

FOLLOW CLEVELAND WAY SIGN

NOW GOING OVER MOORLAND

PAVING STONES HAVE BEEN LAID TO PROTECT MOOR

SCARTH WOOD MOOR

SHORTCUT FROM OSMOTHERLEY, 30 MINS

OS COLUMN, HIDDEN BEHIND WALL

TO OSMOTHERLEY

GATES & STILES

TO OSMOTHERLEY

portions are sometimes so big that some trekkers have been known to ask for doggy bags.

Despite the name, *The Golden Lion* (☎ 01609 883526; summer daily 12-3pm, 6-9pm, winter closed Mon & Tue 12-3pm) is more of a smart restaurant than a pub, and is thus slightly more expensive than the Queen Catherine, but it does boast a large menu including a decent selection of gluten-free and vegetarian options.

A third option lies down the road at *The Three Tuns* (see p197), also opposite the Green, which is another surprisingly smart establishment that's more a restaurant than a pub with meals, mainly game and seafood based, served Mon-Sat noon-2.30pm, 5.30-9.30pm, Sun noon-8pm.

For something lighter try *The Coffee Pot* (☎ 01609 883536; daily Mar-Oct 10.30am-5pm Nov-Feb Fri-Sun 10.30am-5pm), a pleasant little café just round the

corner from the walking shop where scones are £1, or just 65p to take away. Its opening hours are basically as above but can vary according to demand or lack of it.

Cheapest of all is *Osmotherley Fish and Chip Shop* (☎ 01609 883557; Apr-Oct Wed 5.30-9pm; Thur 12 noon-2.30pm, 5.30-9pm; Fri-Sat noon-2.30pm, 5-9.30pm; Nov-Mar Thur 5.30-8.30pm, Fri & Sat noon-2.30pm, 5-8.30pm), where it's £4.20 for a large haddock and chips.

To rejoin the trail, you needn't return to the junction with the Cleveland Way, but can take a short-cut up the long Swainstye Farm track (found on the left as you walk from the village towards Cote Ghyll campsite), meeting up with the Cleveland and Coast to Coast paths at the top of Arncliffe Wood (see maps 72-73).

Abbott's No 80/89 **bus** service stops here en route to Stokesley and Northallerton; see pp43-5 for details.

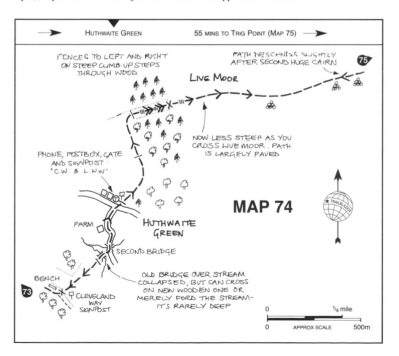

HUTHWAITE GREEN — 55 MINS TO TRIG POINT (MAP 75) →

FENCES TO LEFT AND RIGHT ON STEEP CLIMB UP STEPS THROUGH WOOD

PATH DESCENDS SLIGHTLY AFTER SECOND HUGE CAIRN **75**

LIVE MOOR

NOW LESS STEEP AS YOU CROSS LIVE MOOR. PATH IS LARGELY PAVED

PHONE, POSTBOX, GATE AND SIGNPOST "C.W. & L.W.W"

MAP 74

★ TRAILBLAZER

FARM

HUTHWAITE GREEN

SECOND BRIDGE

OLD BRIDGE OVER STREAM COLLAPSED, BUT CAN CROSS ON NEW WOODEN ONE OR MERELY FORD THE STREAM— IT'S RARELY DEEP

BENCH

73

CLEVELAND WAY SIGNPOST

0 — ¼ mile

0 — APPROX SCALE — 500m

The route continues through Arncliffe Wood, over heather-clad **Scarth Wood Moor**, and joins the Lyke Wake Walk (see box below) in bluebell-carpeted (in spring) **Clain Wood** before joining the road to **Huthwaite Green**.

There is nothing of interest to walkers in this hamlet save, perhaps, a pay-phone, but it is the gateway to a series of moors, a crossing of which now follows. The first is **Live Moor** (Map 74), reached via a steep climb, much of it on steps, beginning from the gate at the eastern end of Huthwaite. Note the first appearance of a number of stone boundary markers along the wayside.

From here the path drops slightly to moor number two, **Carlton Moor** (Map 75), with its gliding club and runway. At the far end of the moor is a trig point and another boundary marker, from where the path drops steeply round a quarry to a road.

Crossing this and its adjacent stile, look for _Lord Stones Café_ (Map 76; ☎ 01642 778227, daily 9am-9pm) hiding next to a small tree plantation to your right. Half underground and tucked away, it's not the easiest café to find, though it is the only one on this stage – and a fine place too – and thus worth discovering, especially if you missed breakfast as they do big bacon butties for £2.

They also have a secret garden where **campers** have been allowed to stay for free, and they would leave the toilet open for their use too! Furthermore,

---

❏ The Lyke Wake Walk

The Lyke Wake Walk, which the Coast to Coast trail joins for part of the stretch across the Yorkshire moors, was the invention of one man. Local farmer and journalist Bill Cowley came up with the idea in 1955 when he claimed that, with the exception of one or two roads that run across the moors, one could walk the entire 40 miles over the North York Moors from east to west (or vice-versa) on heather. Several walkers enthusiastically agreed to see if Mr Cowley was right, and it was agreed that the trail should start on Scarth Wood Moor, near Osmotherley, and finish in Ravenscar. To make the challenge tougher, it was decided that the whole 40 miles should be completed in 24 hours.

The curious name comes from the Lyke Wake Dirge, possibly the oldest verse in the Yorkshire dialect. 'Lyke' was the local term for corpse and the song recounts the passage of the soul through the afterlife. Bill himself became the chief dirger, and handed out black-edged cards to those who successfully completed the challenge. There was also a Wake Club which he founded for those who completed the walk.

Unfortunately, the trail has suffered from hard times recently. Firstly, the popularity of the walk, which saw thousands of people accepting the challenge through the sixties and seventies, led to a fair amount of environmental damage to the moors. These days there are a number of different paths to choose from and the National Park Authority now seeks to limit the damage caused by the walkers. The death of Bill Cowley in 1994 dealt another blow to the trail and the demise of the Lyke Wake Club in 2005 was a further setback.

More recently, however, a new club has been established which aims to continue along much the same lines as the original organization founded by Bill. Details of the club, and the walk which it promotes, can be found at 🖥 www.lykewake.org.

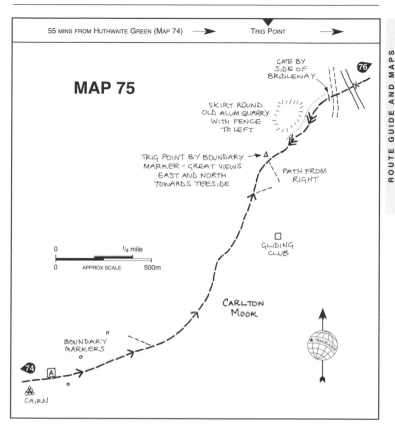

MAP 75

55 MINS FROM HUTHWAITE GREEN (MAP 74) →   TRIG POINT →

GATE BY SIDE OF BRIDLEWAY

76

SKIRT ROUND OLD ALUM QUARRY WITH FENCE TO LEFT

TRIG POINT BY BOUNDARY MARKER – GREAT VIEWS EAST AND NORTH TOWARDS TEESIDE

PATH FROM RIGHT

GLIDING CLUB

0   ¼ mile
0   APPROX SCALE   500m

CARLTON MOOR

BOUNDARY MARKERS

74 A →

CAIRN

★ TRAILBLAZER

they plan to have installed showers by the end of 2007. And all they ask in return for all this is that you patronize their café – which, with its cheap beer and good food, is no great burden! It's also the only place on this stretch where tap water is available.

From here another steep climb follows – this time up to **Cringle Moor** (Map 76), with the superbly situated **Alec Falconer Seat** at the top, from where one can relax and take in the views over the smokestacks of Teeside. Look closely and you can also make out the isolated peak of Roseberry Topping, as well as the monument to Captain Cook (the explorer and navigator) on Easby Moor.

Follow the bends south then east (towards and then away from the summit of Cringle Moor), skirt the cliffs of **Kirby Bank**, then tackle the steep descent.

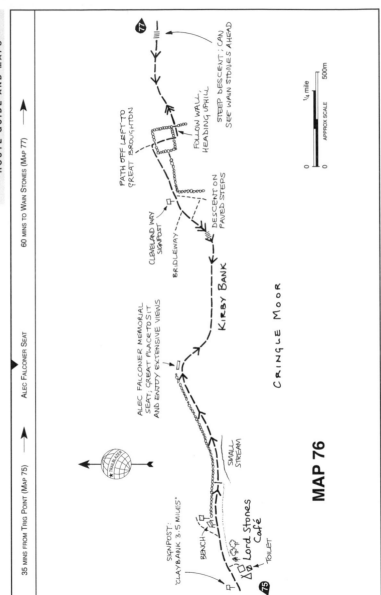

MAP 76

ALEC FALCONER MEMORIAL SEAT; GREAT PLACE TO SIT AND ENJOY EXTENSIVE VIEWS

PATH OFF LEFT TO GREAT BROUGHTON

FOLLOW WALL, HEADING UPHILL

STEEP DESCENT; CAN SEE WAIN STONES AHEAD

CLEVELAND WAY SIGNPOST

BRIDLEWAY

DESCENT ON PAVED STEPS

KIRBY BANK

CRINGLE MOOR

SMALL STREAM

SIGNPOST: "CLAYBANK 3.5 MILES"

BENCH

Lord Stones Café

TOILET

TRAILBLAZER

APPROX SCALE
0   ¼ mile
0   500m

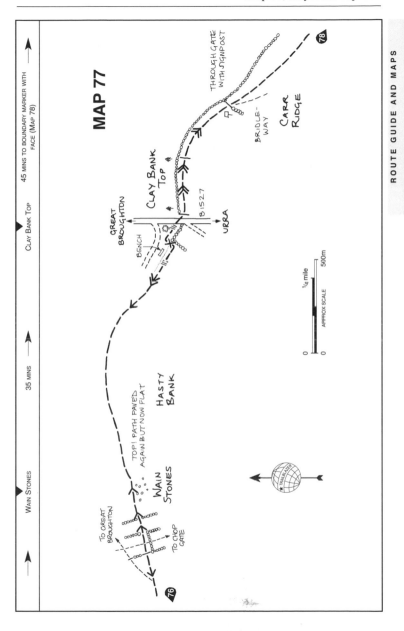

MAP 77

WAIN STONES | 35 MINS | CLAY BANK TOP | 45 MINS TO BOUNDARY MARKER WITH FACE (MAP 78)

Clay Bank Top

Great Broughton

THROUGH GATE WITH SIGNPOST

78

CARR RIDGE

BRIDLE-WAY

B.1527

URRA

BENCH

HASTY BANK

TOP! PATH PAVED AGAIN BUT NOW FLAT

WAIN STONES

TO GREAT BROUGHTON

TO CHOP GATE

76

¼ mile

500m

APPROX SCALE

0

0

TRAILBLAZER

The **Wain Stones** are clearly visible on top of the next moor, the gigantic boulders resembling cake decorations atop **Hasty Bank** (Map 77). If staying at Great Broughton, you may wish to divert from the path on the signposted low-level trail before the climb up to the stones. Otherwise, from the Wain Stones the path continues east to Clay Bank Top and the B1527 and, for those staying in one of the nearby villages, a possible rendezvous with your hosts. Those who are pressing on will doubtless be disappointed that the promise by the signpost of a café down the road at the picnic spot turns out to be an empty one, although a fast-food van occasionally sets up there.

URRA   OFF MAP 77, p203

Accommodation-wise, the nearest place to Clay Bank Top, the point where the B1527 meets the Coast to Coast path, is at Urra. It also happens to be the most recommended.

Maltkiln House (☎ 01642 778216, 🖳 www .maltkiln.co.uk; 1S/1T/1D) lies less than a mile to the south on the road and charges £20-26.

GREAT BROUGHTON
OFF MAP 77, p203

Great Broughton lies two miles to the north of the trail at Clay Bank Top. It boasts several pubs; the walker-friendly *Bay Horse* (☎ 01642 712319), on the High St, is a good choice for both bar meals and more formal two- and three-course meals in their restaurant. Food is served Mon-Sat 11.30am-2pm and 6-9.30pm (12noon-9pm on Sunday).

As far as accommodation goes, almost all B&Bs without exception offer lifts to and from Clay Bank Top, either free or, more likely, for just a couple of quid to cover petrol. Of these, *Ingle Hill* (☎ 01642 712449; 2D/1F) has beautiful gardens and the rooms are en suite and all have TV, though it must be said readers' reviews haven't been entirely positive. The tariff starts at £25.

Wainstone's Hotel (☎ 01642 712268, 🖳 www.wainstoneshotel.co.uk), on Great Broughton High St, is a rather extravagant choice. The 24 en suite rooms are priced from £55 per person for a double or twin and a rather extortionate £84.50 for a single room.

Moors Bus M2 **bus** stops here; see pp43-5 for details.

From Clay Bank Top the penultimate steep climb on the Coast to Coast follows, a tough-ish slog through farmland with the sound of cuckoos from the nearby wood mocking every step. After 20 minutes or so **Carr Ridge**, the top of **Urra Moor**, is reached, and thereafter the going is easy. Initially you follow a wide track over the moor past a **trig point** that lies a little way off the path to your left (Map 78). After then passing a boundary marker with a face clearly etched onto it, you arrive at a junction of paths. It is here that the Cleveland Way finally leaves us as, having passed round a couple of green barriers, you join the disused **Rosedale Ironstone Railway** (Map 79) that used to serve the nearby Rosedale iron mines that opened in 1856.

Passing above the head of pretty **Farndale**, renowned for its daffodils in spring, the track loops south-east and then eastwards towards your destination, the isolated Lion Inn.

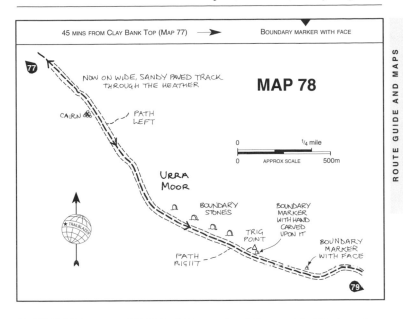

45 MINS FROM CLAY BANK TOP (MAP 77) ⟶ BOUNDARY MARKER WITH FACE

NOW ON WIDE, SANDY PAVED TRACK THROUGH THE HEATHER

MAP 78

CAIRN

PATH LEFT

0   ¼ mile
0   APPROX SCALE   500m

URRA MOOR

BOUNDARY STONES

BOUNDARY MARKER WITH HAND CARVED UPON IT

TRIG POINT

BOUNDARY MARKER WITH FACE

PATH RIGHT

★ TRAILBLAZER

ROUTE GUIDE AND MAPS

BLAKEY RIDGE   MAP 81, p209

For everybody, be they walkers or drivers, Blakey Ridge *is* the *Lion Inn* (☎ 01751 417320, 🖳 www.lionblakey.co.uk; 1T/8D/ 4F), the fourth highest inn in Britain (the highest, the Tan Inn, lies near Keld) and one of the most charming on our route.

The inn is nothing much to look at on the outside. Indeed, it's rather disappointing for those expecting something more rustic. But inside, with its dark time-worn exposed beams and open fires, it looks like the inn dating back to at least 1553 that it claims to be. It's quite charming and with B&B from £19 per person for the twin, £35 for a double with shared bathroom (rising to £38 for the honeymoon suite with four-poster bed), good value too.

The **food**, served at the bar or in the restaurant (daily 12noon-10pm), is tailor-made for walkers, being hearty and tasty. Most dishes, which include a sumptuous steak and Guinness pie, come in at about £8.50.

Camping is allowed in the adjacent field and costs £2.50 and there are showers inside that are accessible when the pub is open. The publican now insists that campers book their pitch in advance, a measure designed to help prevent undesirables who have caused problems recently. Ignore, however, the notices saying that camping is forbidden at weekends – again, it is a measure designed to prevent louts, for walkers are always welcome. Note, too, that there's not much shelter from the wind up there.

Across the road from the inn is the very smart *High Blakey House* (☎ 01751 417186, 🖳 www.highblakeyhouse.co.uk; 1D/2D or T), one of the best positioned B&Bs on the whole route; only one room is en suite. Rates start at £34 per person.

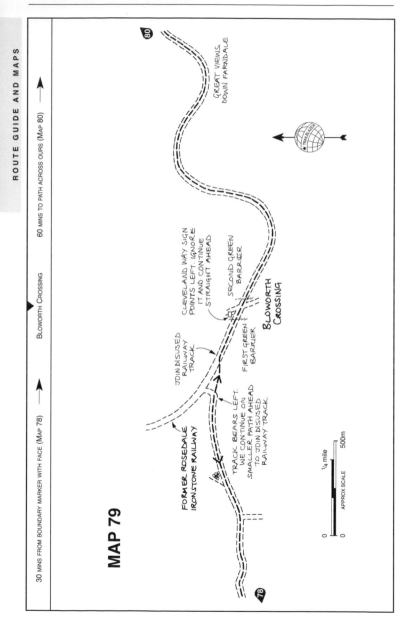

MAP 79

FORMER ROSEDALE IRONSTONE RAILWAY

JOIN DISUSED RAILWAY TRACK

TRACK BEARS LEFT. WE CONTINUE ON SMALLER PATH AHEAD TO JOIN DISUSED RAILWAY TRACK

CLEVELAND WAY SIGN POINTS LEFT. IGNORE IT AND CONTINUE STRAIGHT AHEAD

SECOND GREEN BARRIER

FIRST GREEN BARRIER

BLOWORTH CROSSING

GREAT VIEWS DOWN FARNDALE

TRAIL BLAZER

¼ mile

APPROX SCALE

0

0   500m

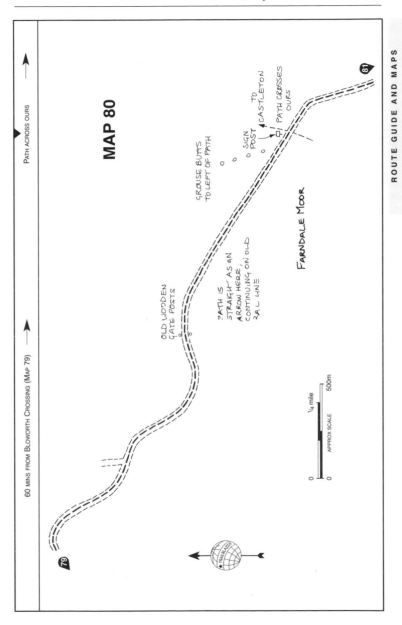

MAP 80

PATH ACROSS OURS

60 MINS FROM BLOWORTH CROSSING (MAP 79)

OLD WOODEN GATE POSTS

PATH IS STRAIGHT AS AN ARROW HERE, CONTINUING ON OLD RAIL LINE

GROUSE BUTTS TO LEFT OF PATH

SIGN POST

TO CASTLETON

PATH CROSSES OURS

FARNDALE MOOR

¼ mile

500m

APPROX SCALE

TRAILBLAZER

STAGE 12: BLAKEY RIDGE TO GROSMONT   MAPS 81-87

Introduction

Those of you who have decided to tackle the walk in reverse, from Robin Hood's Bay to St Bees, believing that the Lakes are the highlight and everything else will pale into comparison, are obviously not familiar with the River Esk.

For many, particularly those who enjoy cosy English villages hidden amongst the finest, gentlest, most bucolic scenery this country has to offer, the **13¹/₂mile (21.5km, 4¹/₂hr)** stroll down the **Esk Valley** from Glaisdale to Grosmont is simply the best section of the walk. For charm, only the lakeland villages of Borrowdale, Grasmere and Patterdale come close to matching the extraordinary beauty of Egton Bridge and Grosmont. While of the places still to come, only Littlebeck village and its accompanying wood bear comparison.

As a final destination on this stage, either Egton Bridge or Grosmont will do. Glaisdale, too, for that matter, though if you do choose Glaisdale this stage will be a very short one, and leave you with a lot to do on the final stage to Robin Hood's Bay. But first you have to get to the valley, and that means getting down off the moors.

The route

The walk begins with a road-walk, following the tarmac north towards **Young Ralph Cross** (off Map 82), which just pokes its head over the horizon as you turn off right onto another road, this one signposted to Rosedale Abbey.

Passing the stumpy white landmark known as **Fat Betty** (off the path to the left), the official path then takes a quick short-cut, crossing a section of the moor to meet up with the wonderfully named **Great Fryup Lane** (Map 83). However, parts of this short-cut are extremely boggy – up to waist-deep, in my experience – and unless you want to end up like the dead sheep that occasionally litter this part of the moor it's probably safer to stick to the roads.

Leaving the road to pass **Trough House**, the path can clearly be made out continuing eastwards round the southern side of Great Fryup Dale. Some keen-eyed trekkers swear that they can see the **North Sea** from just before Trough House, though for most people that particular pleasure will have to wait until the end of **Glaisdale High Moor** where, rejoining the road, the sea is obvious at the far end of the valley.

After a mile of road-walking, Coast-to-Coasters take the rough track along **Glaisdale Rigg** (Map 85) past various standing stones (and a particularly well-made **boundary marker** to the right of the path) and on down to a junction with a number of paths by a small tarn. Passing through farmland, the path descends to the houses of Glaisdale. *(cont'd on p214)*

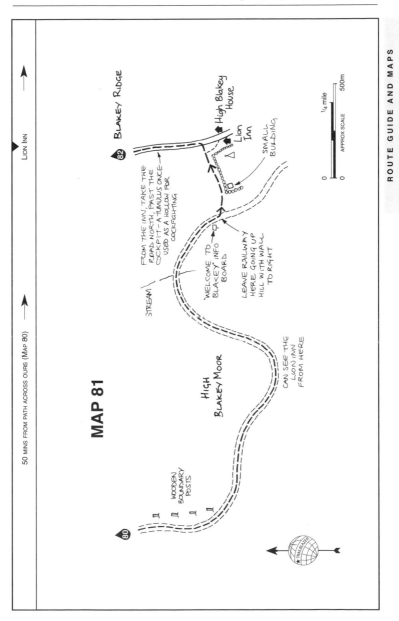

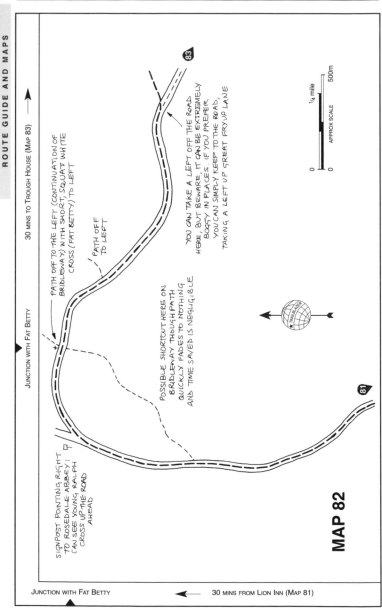

30 MINS TO TROUGH HOUSE (MAP 83) →

JUNCTION WITH FAT BETTY

PATH OFF TO THE LEFT (CONTINUATION OF BRIDLEWAY) WITH SHORT, SQUAT WHITE CROSS (FAT BETTY) TO LEFT

PATH OFF TO LEFT

YOU CAN TAKE A LEFT OFF THE ROAD HERE, BUT BEWARE IT CAN BE EXTREMELY BOGGY IN PLACES. IF YOU PREFER, YOU CAN SIMPLY KEEP TO THE ROAD, TAKING A LEFT UP GREAT FRYUP LANE

83

81

APPROX SCALE

0   ¼ mile

0   500m

TRAILBLAZER

POSSIBLE SHORTCUT HERE ON BRIDLEWAY THOUGH PATH QUICKLY FADES TO NOTHING AND TIME SAVED IS NEGLIGIBLE

SIGNPOST POINTING RIGHT TO ROSEDALE ABBEY; CAN SEE YOUNG RALPH CROSS UP THE ROAD AHEAD

MAP 82

JUNCTION WITH FAT BETTY

← 30 MINS FROM LION INN (MAP 81)

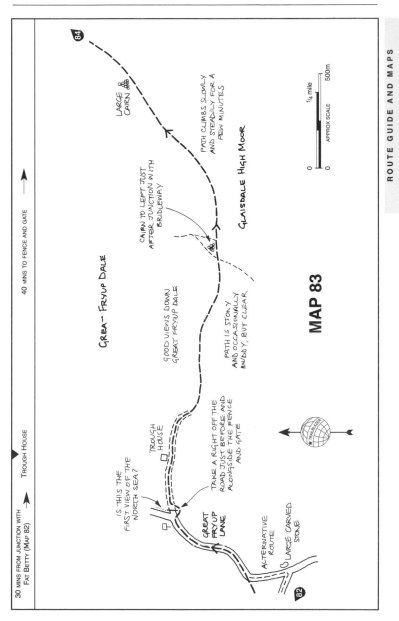

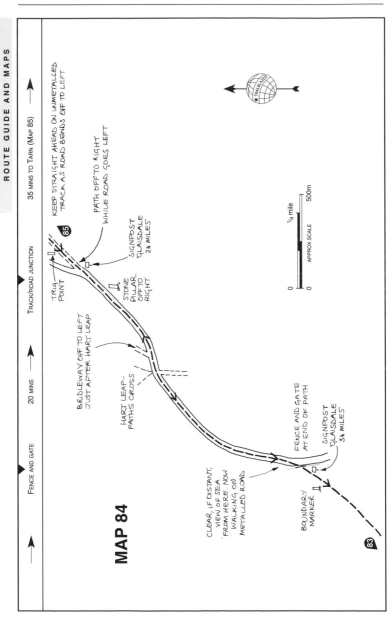

FENCE AND GATE

20 MINS

TRACK/ROAD JUNCTION

35 MINS TO TARN (MAP 85)

MAP 84

CLEAR, IF DISTANT, VIEW OF SEA FROM HERE. NOW WALKING ON METALLED ROAD

HART LEAP - PATHS CROSS

BRIDLEWAY OFF TO LEFT JUST AFTER HART LEAP

TRIG POINT

STONE PILLAR OFF TO RIGHT

KEEP STRAIGHT AHEAD ON UNMETALLED TRACK AS ROAD BENDS OFF TO LEFT

PATH OFF TO RIGHT WHILE ROAD GOES LEFT

SIGNPOST 'GLAISDALE 2¾ MILES'

FENCE AND GATE AT END OF PATH

SIGNPOST 'GLAISDALE 3¾ MILES'

BOUNDARY MARKER

83

85

¼ mile

500m

APPROX SCALE

0

0

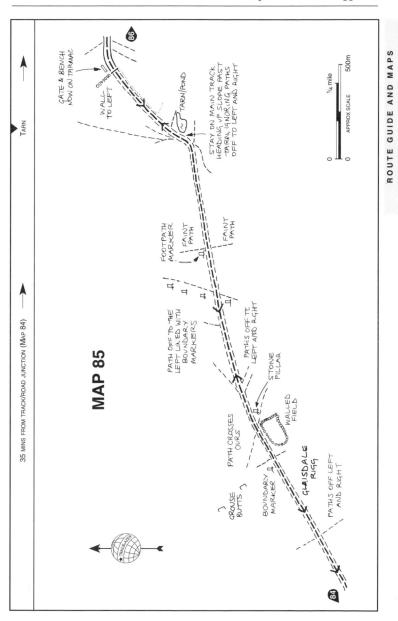

35 MINS FROM TRACK/ROAD JUNCTION (MAP 84)

TARN

MAP 85

GATE & BENCH NOW ON TARMAC

WALL TO LEFT

TARN/POND

STAY ON MAIN TRACK HEADING UP SLOPE PAST TARN, IGNORING PATHS OFF TO LEFT AND RIGHT

FOOTPATH MARKER

FAINT PATH

FAINT PATH

PATH OFF TO THE LEFT LINED WITH BOUNDARY MARKERS

PATHS OFF TO LEFT AND RIGHT

STONE PILLAR

WALLED FIELD

PATH CROSSES OURS

GROUSE BUTTS

BOUNDARY MARKER

GLAISDALE RIGG

PATHS OFF LEFT AND RIGHT

TRAILBLAZER

0   APPROX SCALE   500m

0   ¼ mile

GLAISDALE   MAP 86, opposite

The village of Glaisdale sprawls across its lofty perch overlooking the Esk Valley. The terraced houses that are a feature of the town were originally built to house the ironstone workers in the iron mines of the late 19th century. The **Robinson Institute** is a village hall that also acts as a small theatre.

The late 18th-century **Church of St Thomas the Apostle**, near the upper end of Glaisdale, is notable for its 16th-century wooden font cover and communion table. (Don't be fooled by the '1585' date stone in the side of the steps leading to the tower, for this is from an earlier chapel.)

The church also contains a picture of Thomas Ferris, the beggar made famous in Glaisdale's other main sight, the **Beggar's Bridge** at the other end of the village. In the 17th century, Ferris, a humble pauper, was courting the daughter of the wealthy local squire. In order to win her hand Ferris thought he needed to improve his standing in the community so with this in mind he struck upon a plan to set sail from Whitby and seek his fortune on the high seas. The night before he put this plan into action, however, Ferris went to visit his beloved who lived across the river. Unfortunately, the river happened to be swollen at the time due to heavy rain and Ferris's dreams of a romantic farewell were dashed. The story, however, does have a happy ending: Thomas returned from his adventures on the sea a wealthy man and married his sweetheart, and with some of his fortune made the Beggar's Bridge so that any other young lovers from the neighbourhood would not, in future, suffer the same torment as Ferris did that night.

As for facilities, the **shop** (Mon-Sat 7am-6pm, Sun 9am-2pm) is also home to the **post office** (Mon, Tue, Thur and Fri 8.30am-12.30pm, 1.30-5.30pm, Wed and Sat morning only). There is also a public phone, and a public toilet near the station.

Where to stay and eat

Down near the train station, *The Arncliffe Arms* (☎ 01947 897555; 2D/2T en suite) charges £29, or £35 for single occupancy. It also does food Mon-Sat 12 noon-2pm and 6-8.45pm; Sun 6-8pm only.

Ashley House (☎ 01947 897656; 2S/2D) is at the top of the hill above the Arncliffe Arms. B&B starts from £22.50 here. No pets are allowed.

A quarter of a mile from the path is the award-winning 17th-century *Red House Farm* (☎ 01947 897242, 🖳 www.redhouse farm.com; 2D/1F). Once a working farm and still the home of a number of farm animals, it is often cited as one of the best farm accommodations in the country – and with the farmhouse containing many of its original features it certainly is very, very beautiful. Dogs are welcome but note that they will be stabled and will not be allowed in the house. B&B is from £32.50 per person.

At the very end of the village, *Beggar's Bridge* (☎ 01947 897409, 🖳 www.beggarsbridge.co.uk; 2D en suite) lies just above the eponymous bridge across the tracks from the railway station. Costs are £25 per person, or £35 single occupancy.

Transport (see also pp43-5)

M and D's **Bus** No 99 travels up and down the Esk Valley from Lealholm to Whitby 4-5/day, Mon-Sat.

Trains run between the same destinations via Glaisdale four times a day.

From Glaisdale, enter the woods near **Beggar's Bridge** and continue walking through this idyllic setting along the river until the path winds up to a road, where you should take a left down the hill and into Egton Bridge.

❑ **Important note – walking times**
Unless otherwise specified, **all times in this book refer only to the time spent walking**. You will need to add 20-30% to allow for rests, photography, checking the map, drinking water etc. When planning the day's hike count on 5-7 hours' actual walking.

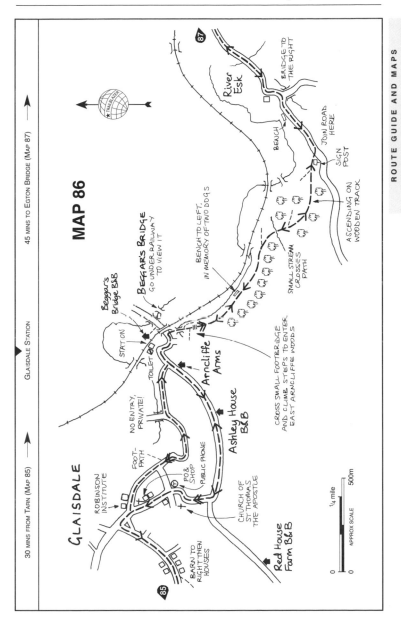

30 MINS FROM TARN (MAP 85) →   GLAISDALE STATION   45 MINS TO EGTON BRIDGE (MAP 87) →

MAP 86

GLAISDALE

Robinson Institute

Foot-path

NO ENTRY, PRIVATE!

P.O & Shop

Public Phone

Church of St Thomas the Apostle

Red House Farm B&B

Barn to right then houses

85

Ashley House B&B

Arncliffe Arms

Station

Toilet

Beggar's Bridge B&B

BEGGAR'S BRIDGE
GO UNDER RAILWAY TO VIEW IT

BENCH TO LEFT, IN MEMORY OF TWO DOGS

CROSS SMALL FOOTBRIDGE AND CLIMB STEPS TO ENTER EAST ARNCLIFFE WOODS

SMALL STREAM CROSSES PATH

ASCENDING ON WOODEN TRACK

SIGN POST

JOIN ROAD HERE

BEACH

River Esk

BRIDGE TO THE RIGHT

87

TRAILBLAZER

¼ mile
APPROX SCALE
0 .... 500m
0 ....

EGTON BRIDGE   MAP 87, opposite

A strong competitor for the accolade of prettiest village on the Coast to Coast, Egton Bridge is a delight, a village of grand houses surrounding an uninhabited island sitting in the middle of the Esk. Everything about the place is charming, from the bridge itself – a 1990s' copy of the original 18th-century structure washed away in a flood in 1930 – to the stepping stones that lead across to the island and the gigantic mature trees that fringe the village.

The Catholic **St Hedda's Church**, too, is incredibly grand given the tiny size of the village. On the exterior are a series of friezes while inside, behind glass to the right of the altar, are the relics of Nicholas Postgate, a local Catholic priest and martyr hung, drawn and quartered for continuing to practise his faith in 1679. See box below for details about St Hedda himself.

Where to stay and eat

It would be a surprise if somewhere as gorgeous as Egton Bridge didn't have decent accommodation, and the village doesn't disappoint. The *Horseshoe Hotel* (☎ 01947 895245, 4D/2T), right on the walk at the start of the village, fulfils every expectation of a country inn, with an expansive beer garden, a variety of local ales and a snug

interior. Meals are typically around the £8.50 mark and are served daily noon-2pm and 7-9pm. B&B in the double/twin rooms is from £30 per person, and from £35-40 for single occupancy.

A little way to the west of the village *Broom House* (☎ 01947 895279, 🖳 www.egton-bridge.co.uk; 5D/1F) lies hidden behind its own orchard. A 19th-century farmhouse with plenty of exposed beams and other charming rural features; they charge £33.50-35.50 per night.

Above the station, *Postgate Inn* (☎ 01947 895241, 🖳 www.postgateinn.com; 2D/1F) is another top choice with food available daily (light lunches 12-2.30pm, snacks 2.30-6.30pm, meals 6.30-9pm) in season (out of season the hours depend on the weather), and B&B for £34.50 per person in the double, £45 single occupancy. To find it, head up the hill from the church.

Transport (see also pp43-5)

Four to five **trains** per day (Mon-Sat) travel in each direction between Whitby and Middlesbrough via Egton Bridge; the Sunday service (5/day) only operates between June and September. In addition, M&D's **bus** No 99 travels from Whitby up the Esk Valley to Glaisdale and Lealholm and back 4-5/day Mon-Sat.

The next mile or so from Egton Bridge to Grosmont takes you past the impossibly elegant **Egton Manor** along an old toll road (the original toll charges are still written on a board hanging from **Toll Cottage**, halfway

---

❏ Saint Hedda

The seventh-century British saint, Hedda, crops up a few times on the Coast to Coast walk, even though he is these days more closely associated with Winchester. He began his Episcopal career at Whitby Abbey (the remains of which can be seen on the last day of the walk, though it's not actually on the path), where he was educated and became a monk, rising to become abbot.

His big break came in 676AD when he was consecrated as the Bishop of Wessex by Saint Theodore of Tarsus, at that time the Archbishop of Canterbury. He ruled over the diocese for thirty years, during which time he moved the see from Dorchester to Winchester and became chief advisor to King Ina, one of three kings whom he served under. Described by the Venerable Bede as 'a good and just man, who in carrying out his duties was guided rather than by an inborn love of virtue than by what he had read in books', he died in 705AD and is buried at Winchester Cathedral.

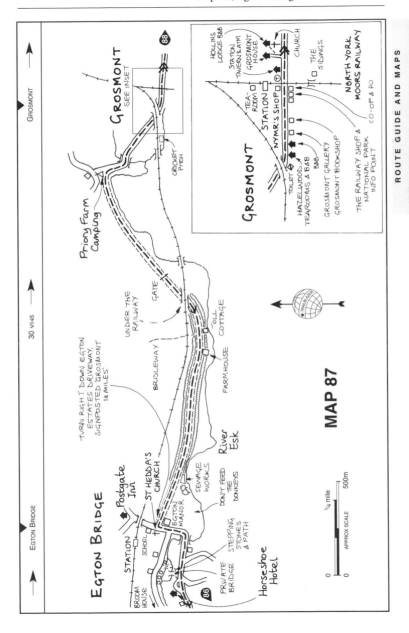

along). It's an easy walk now, taking you under the railway and along by the Esk to Grosmont.

GROSMONT   MAP 87, p217

Tourists and trainspotters alike flock to Grosmont. The steam engines of the privately run **North York Moors Railway** run for only 18 miles (29km) between here and Pickering, but it's quite a sight watching the trains huff and puff into action. If they seem a touch familiar it is because the railway is regularly used by film crews and in the past has featured in such films as *Brideshead Revisited* and, most famously, the first *Harry Potter* movie.

Rail buffs who still aren't sated can visit the nearby **shop** selling all manner of train-related stuff, including any number of model railways.

It's definitely worth waiting to see at least one train in motion before leaving Grosmont, and while you're waiting you can take the alleyway leading through a long train tunnel to the **sidings and loco sheds**, which offer a bit of an insight into what it takes to keep these trains on track. The tunnel is, in fact, one of the oldest train tunnels in the world, one that used to serve George Stephenson's horse-drawn railway. It was during the digging of these tunnels that large amounts of ironstone were uncovered, leading to the start of the ironstone mining industry in the Esk Valley.

As for the rest of Grosmont, it's a pleasant one-street village that boomed on the back of the ironstone industry and has most of the essentials a trekker needs: a **store, pub** (the Station Tavern, of course!), a **jazz café** (in Grosmont Gallery; sandwiches from £2.50; daily 11am-5.30pm), two **tearooms** (one on the station platform and one as part of Hazelwood B&B) and a few small and pleasant B&Bs.

The **Co-op** (Mon-Fri 7.30am-5.30pm; Sat 8am-5.30pm, Sun 9am-5.30pm) is one of the oldest community-run village shops in the country and is also home to the **post office** (Mon-Fri 9am-12noon).

There's a church, too, with a boulder of Shap granite outside the west door, deposited here by a glacier back in the Ice Age. The Station Tavern has an **ATM**, the last on the trail, charging £1.50.

Where to stay and eat

Priory Farm (☎ 01947 895324) sits at the very start of the village and offers **camping** for just £3 per person and there is a convenient 'camping room', a small room in the farmhouse with a toilet and kettle, left open for campers.

Hazelwood (☎ 01947 895292, ☐ www.hazelwoodhouse.net; 1S/1D/1T or F; no pets) is a family-run place at the bottom of the village with a **tearoom** (daily Easter to Oct) attached. B&B is just £27 here.

Grosmont House (☎ 01947 895539, ☐ www.grosmonthouse.co.uk; 3D/2T/1F) is a delightful place tucked away behind the Station Tavern, whose gardens have wonderful views over the railway. Rates are £32 for walkers whether staying in an en suite room or not, £35 single occupancy (though this will not be en suite). Food is available only if you pre-book (even if you're not staying there) and is worth it: the fresh lobster salad they serve here is said to be awesome.

The *Station Tavern* (☎ 01947 895060, ☐ www.tunnelinn.co.uk; food served daily Easter to late Oct 12 noon-2.45pm, 7-8.45pm; on request out of season) serves pub grub on enormous plates and has become something of a venue for spontaneous C2C banquets before people go their separate ways at Robin Hood's Bay. They also do B&B (1S/1D/1F) from £25 to £30.

Hollins Lodge (☎ 01947 895443, 0779 255 2742, ☐ www.bedandbreakfastnorkshire.co.uk; 1D/1D or T) is a new place tucked away at the back of Grosmont. Accommodation is provided in a separate building to the main house in two huge spruce en suite rooms. Rates are £30 per person.

With advance notice some B&Bs provide evening meals.

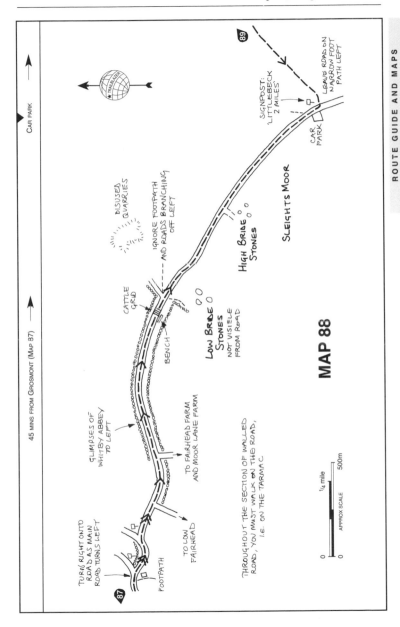

45 MINS FROM GROSMONT (MAP 87)

CAR PARK

TURN RIGHT ONTO
ROAD AS MAIN
ROAD TURNS LEFT

GLIMPSES OF
WHITBY ABBEY
TO LEFT

DISUSED
QUARRIES

IGNORE FOOTPATH
AND ROADS BRANCHING
OFF LEFT

CATTLE
GRID

BENCH

LOW BRIDE
STONES
NOT VISIBLE
FROM ROAD

HIGH BRIDE
STONES

SLEIGHTS MOOR

SIGNPOST:
'LITTLEBECK
2 MILES'

CAR
PARK

LEAVE ROAD ON
NARROW FOOT
PATH LEFT

89

TO FAIRHEAD FARM
AND MOOR LANE FARM

TO LOW
FAIRHEAD

FOOTPATH

87

THROUGHOUT THE SECTION OF WALLED
ROAD, YOU MUST WALK ON THE ROAD,
I.E. ON THE TARMAC.

MAP 88

APPROX SCALE

¼ mile

500m

0

0

TRAILBLAZER

ROUTE GUIDE AND MAPS

Transport (see also pp43-5)

The **steam train** (☎ 01751 472508, 💻 www.nymr.co.uk) to Pickering leaves Grosmont between four and eight times a day depending on the season. The journey takes an hour and ten minutes; an adult return from Grosmont costs £14, a single £11; children are half price.

Some of the trains are drawn by a diesel engine rather than a steam engine, so if you want that authentic chuff-chuff sound on your journey check the timetable to see which services involve the steam engine.

Regular **trains** go to Whitby (5/day; 20 mins) and to Middlesbrough (4/day; 70 mins), Mon-Sat; Sunday 4/day June to Sep. M&D's **Bus** No 99 also travels to Whitby 4-5/day, Mon-Sat; 15 mins) from the railway station.

STAGE 13: GROSMONT TO ROBIN HOOD'S BAY   MAPS 87-95

Introduction

And so we come to the last stage. But don't be fooled into thinking this is a mere formality as the giant climb out of Grosmont will soon demonstrate. It's a long last leg, just under **15½ miles (25km, 6hr)** in total, with enough ups and downs to ensure that you arrive in Robin Hood's Bay suitably dishevelled. The scenery is largely similar to that which has gone before – namely moorland and, in an echo of the first leg, a few miles of cliff-top walking down the coast. The biggest and most pleasant surprise, however, is Little Beck Wood, a narrow belt of the most heavenly woodland in Yorkshire.

The route

First, there's the climb up to **Sleights Moor**, part of the intriguingly named Eskdaleside Cum Ugglebarnby. With views initially down to **Whitby Abbey** to your left, you pass the **High Bride Stones** – five ancient standing monoliths – to the right of the road. (Incidentally, the confusing jumble of the Low Bride Stones stand just below them on a terrace, to your right as you passed over the cattle grid.)

Opposite the car park turn onto the path to the left (currently signposted to 'Littlebeck') and follow it down to the meeting with the A169. Turning left and walking along the busy road for a few hundred metres, a gate opposite heralds the start of the path down through more heather to Littlebeck.

LITTLEBECK   MAP 89, opposite

Yet another tiny hamlet with a lengthy past, it's hard to imagine the picturesque rural idyll that is Littlebeck today was actually once the centre of the alum-mining industry in the 17th to 19th centuries. Alum, by the way, is used in dyeing as well as being added to leather to make it supple. One hundred tons of shale would be produced in order to extract one ton of alum, so it seems incredible that there aren't more scars in the surrounding land.

Littlebeck has one other minor claim to fame as the home of master woodcarver Thomas Whittaker (his house, now called **Woodcarver's Cottage**, is on the bend above Old Mill). Whittaker would 'sign' every piece of furniture he made with a gnome, in German folklore the oak tree's guardian.

Above the cottage is **Kelp House**, where kelp, used in the processing of alum, was stored.

(cont'd on p226)

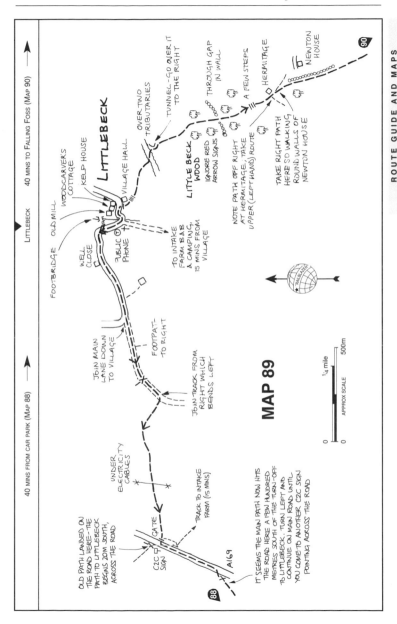

40 MINS FROM CAR PARK (MAP 88) →

LITTLEBECK

40 MINS TO FALLING FOSS (MAP 90) →

LITTLEBECK

TUNNEL - GO OVER IT TO THE RIGHT

THROUGH GAP IN WALL

NEWTON HOUSE

90

A FEW STEPS

HERMITAGE

WOODCARVERS COTTAGE

KELP HOUSE

OVER TWO TRIBUTARIES

VILLAGE HALL

FOOTBRIDGE

OLD MILL

LITTLE BECK WOOD

IGNORE RED ARROW SIGNS

WELL CLOSE

PUBLIC PHONE

NOTE PATH OFF RIGHT AT HERMITAGE, TAKE UPPER (LEFT HAND) ROUTE

TO INTAKE FARM B&B & CAMPING, 15 MINS FROM VILLAGE

TAKE RIGHT PATH HERE SO WALKING ROUND WALLS OF NEWTON HOUSE

JOIN MAIN LANE DOWN TO VILLAGE

FOOTPATH TO RIGHT

JOIN TRACK FROM RIGHT WHICH BENDS LEFT

MAP 89

¼ mile

0   APPROX SCALE   500m

UNDER ELECTRICITY CABLES

TRACK TO INTAKE FARM (15 MINS)

C2C SIGN

GATE

A169

88

OLD PATH LANDED ON THE ROAD HERE - THE PATH TO LITTLEBECK BEGINS 20M SOUTH, ACROSS THE ROAD

IT SEEMS THE MAIN PATH NOW HITS THE ROAD HERE A FEW HUNDRED METRES SOUTH OF THE TURN-OFF TO LITTLEBECK; TURN LEFT AND CONTINUE ON MAIN ROAD UNTIL YOU COME TO ANOTHER C2C SIGN POINTING ACROSS THE ROAD

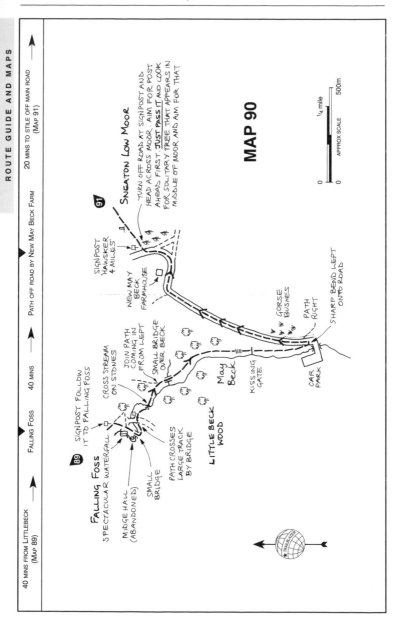

40 MINS FROM LITTLEBECK (MAP 89) — FALLING FOSS — 40 MINS — PATH OFF ROAD BY NEW MAY BECK FARM — 20 MINS TO STILE OFF MAIN ROAD (MAP 91)

MAP 90

0 ¼ mile
0 500m
APPROX SCALE

SNEATON LOW MOOR

TURN OFF ROAD AT SIGNPOST AND HEAD ACROSS MOOR. AIM FOR POST AHEAD FIRST. *JUST PASS IT* AND LOOK FOR SOLITARY TREE THAT APPEARS IN MIDDLE OF MOOR, AND AIM FOR THAT

91

SIGNPOST 'HAWSKER 4 MILES'.

NEW MAY BECK FARMHOUSE

FALLING FOSS
SPECTACULAR WATERFALL

89

SIGNPOST FOLLOW IT TO FALLING FOSS

CROSS STREAM ON STONES

JOIN PATH COMING IN FROM LEFT

SMALL BRIDGE OVER BECK

MIDGE HALL (ABANDONED)

SMALL BRIDGE

PATH CROSSES LARGE TRACK BY BRIDGE

LITTLE BECK WOOD

May Beck

KISSING GATE

GORSE BUSHES

PATH RIGHT

SHARP BEND LEFT ONTO ROAD

CAR PARK

TRAILBLAZER

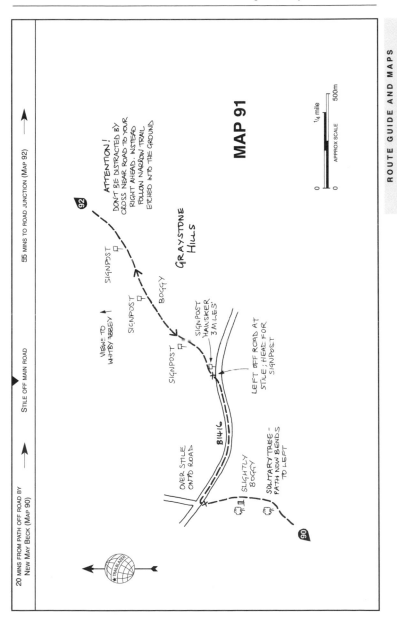

20 MINS FROM PATH OFF ROAD BY NEW MAY BECK (MAP 90) →

STILE OFF MAIN ROAD

55 MINS TO ROAD JUNCTION (MAP 92) →

MAP 91

¼ mile
500m

0   APPROX SCALE

92

SIGNPOST

VIEWS TO WHITBY ABBEY ↑

SIGNPOST

BOGGY

GRAYSTONE HILLS

SIGNPOST

SIGNPOST "HAWSKER 3 MILES"

LEFT OFF ROAD AT STILE; HEAD FOR SIGNPOST

ATTENTION! DON'T BE DISTRACTED BY CROSS NEAR ROAD TO YOUR RIGHT AHEAD. INSTEAD FOLLOW NARROW TRAIL ETCHED INTO THE GROUND

B1416

OVER STILE ONTO ROAD

SLIGHTLY BOGGY

SOLITARY TREE - PATH NOW BENDS TO LEFT

90

TRAILBLAZER

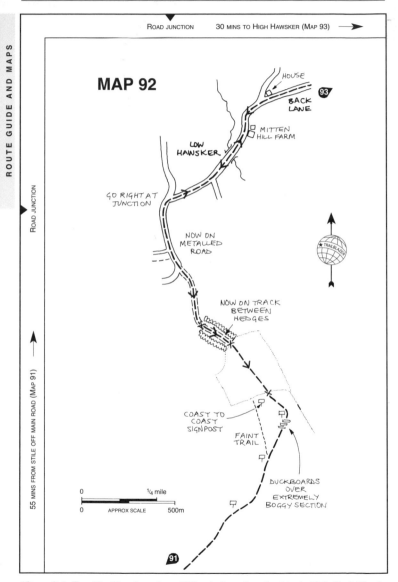

ROUTE GUIDE AND MAPS

ROAD JUNCTION   30 MINS TO HIGH HAWSKER (MAP 93) ⟶

MAP 92

HOUSE

93

BACK LANE

MITTEN HILL FARM

LOW HAWSKER

ROAD JUNCTION

GO RIGHT AT JUNCTION

NOW ON METALLED ROAD

NOW ON TRACK BETWEEN HEDGES

★ TRAILBLAZER

COAST TO COAST SIGNPOST

FAINT TRAIL

DUCKBOARDS OVER EXTREMELY BOGGY SECTION

55 MINS FROM STILE OFF MAIN ROAD (MAP 91)

0   ¼ mile

0   APPROX SCALE   500m

91

(Opposite) Top: The Hermitage (see p226), a hollowed out boulder in Little Beck Woods.
Bottom: The North York Moors Railway at Grosmont (see p220).

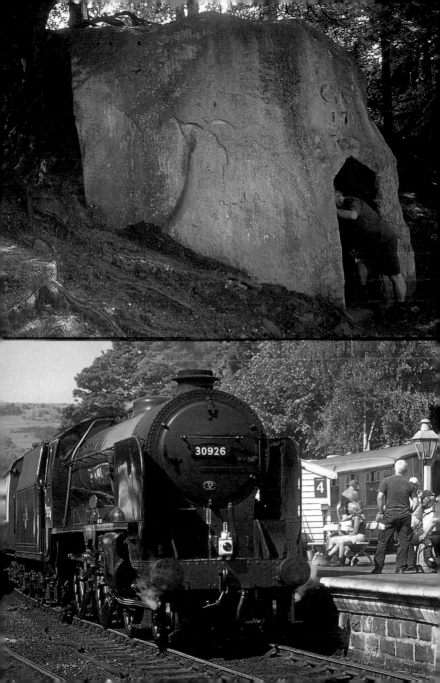

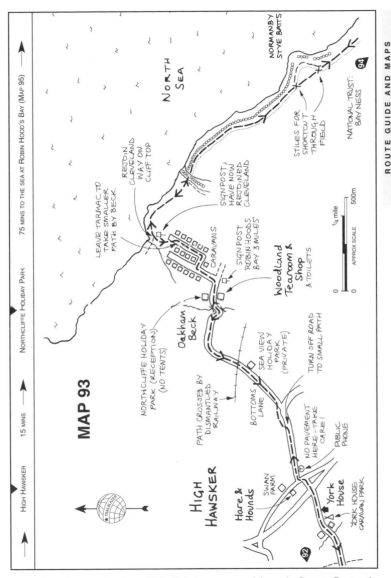

MAP 93

75 MINS TO THE SEA AT ROBIN HOOD'S BAY (MAP 95)

NORTHCLIFFE HOLIDAY PARK

15 MINS

HIGH HAWSKER

NORTH SEA

NORMANBY STYE BATTS

RETD ON CLEVELAND WAY ON CLIFF TOP

LEAVE TARMAC TO TAKE SMALLER PATH BY BECK

SIGNPOST; HAVE NOW RETD ON CLEVELAND

STILES FOR SHORTCUT THROUGH FIELD

NATIONAL TRUST: BAY NESS

CARAVANS

SIGNPOST 'ROBIN HOODS BAY 3 MILES'

Woodland Tearoom & Shop & TOILETS

Oakham Beck

NORTHCLIFFE HOLIDAY PARK (RECEPTION) (NO TENTS)

SEA VIEW HOLIDAY PARK (PRIVATE)

TURN OFF ROAD TO SMALL PATH

PATH CROSSED BY DISMANTLED RAILWAY

BOTTOMS LANE

NO PAVEMENT HERE - TAKE CARE!

PUBLIC PHONE

HIGH HAWSKER

SWAN FARM

Hare & Hounds

York House

YORK HOUSE CARAVAN PARK

½ mile

0   500m

APPROX SCALE

(Opposite) Top: A curlew (see p63) in flight is a common sight on the Coast to Coast path. **Middle**: A most welcome sight for weary walkers: Robin Hood's Bay. **Bottom**: The Horseshoe (plus appropriate visitor), an inn on the edge of idyllic Egton Bridge (see p216).

(cont'd from p220) Fifteen minutes from the centre of the village is **Intake Farm** (☎ 01947 810273, 🖳 intakefarm@farming .co.uk; 2D/1T/1F) where B&B is from £22.50 (£27.50 single or en suite); they also provide **camping** out the back for £4 and can do an evening meal (£15 for three courses) and a packed lunch.

This place gets recommended time and again by readers, largely thanks to the generosity and friendliness of the owners; the kind of generosity that can mean a huge slab of chocolate cake on arrival, for example. Indeed, it's probably only its location just a few hours from the end of the trail that prevents it from being even more popular. Whilst you can reach it from the centre of the village, it's quicker to join the track to the right (south) of the Coast to Coast path heading off from the A169, which takes you via High and Low Quebec Farm to Intake.

Pretty as Littlebeck is, it's nothing when compared to the incredible beauty that awaits in **Little Beck Wood**. This really is a stunning 65 acres of woodland, filled with oak trees, deer, badgers, foxes and birdlife galore. There are also a couple of man-made features to see on the way including, best of all, the **Hermitage**, a boulder hollowed out to form a small cave. Above the entrance is etched the year 1790.

More delights await as the path from the Hermitage takes you to **Falling Foss** (Map 90), a 30m-high waterfall, and the abandoned **Midge Hall**. In front is a small wooden bridge which you should go over, and a second, larger bridge which you walk towards but not across, heading along the signposted path beside **May Beck** instead. This will eventually bring you to a car park at the southern extremity of the wood, from where you turn back north and walk along the road above the valley you've just walked through.

A traverse of two moors and a little road walking are all that now stand between you and the coast. Just before the coast the path passes through **Low Hawsker** (Map 92) and **High Hawsker** (Map 93).

HIGH HAWSKER   MAP 93, p225
The **Hare & Hounds** (☎ 01947 880453) serves hot meals as well as ploughmans and sandwiches (daily 12 noon-2pm and 6.30-9pm). **York House Hotel** (☎ 01947 880314, 3D/3T) offers B&B for £29 (£38 for a single). There's a **campsite**, **York House Caravan Park** (☎ 01947 880354; pitches £4.50), next to the hotel.

From Hawsker, your eastward progression continues down past Sea View and Northcliffe holiday parks (both private) and the **Woodland Tearoom and Shop** (Map 93; Mon-Thur 9am-2pm, Fri 9am-2pm and 4.30-10pm, Sat 9am-10pm, Sun 9am-4pm), where you can get last-minute energy for the final stretch.

And so you come to the final leg, a reunion with the Cleveland Way and a walk along the cliffs leading into Robin Hood's Bay. It's a straightforward though slightly wearying march, particularly if the wind is blowing in strongly off the North Sea. Though the beach at Robin Hood's Bay appears approximately half an hour before it is actually reached, the village itself, tucked away

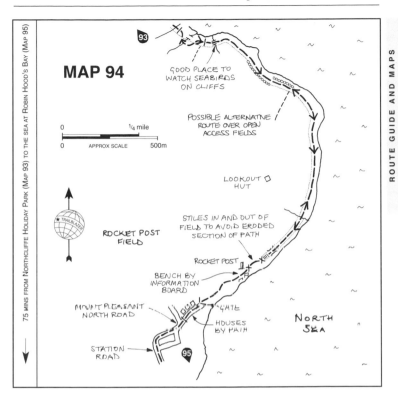

Text labels within the map:

93

MAP 94

GOOD PLACE TO WATCH SEABIRDS ON CLIFFS

POSSIBLE ALTERNATIVE ROUTE OVER OPEN ACCESS FIELDS

0 ¼ mile

0 APPROX SCALE 500m

LOOKOUT HUT

★ TRAILBLAZER

ROCKET POST FIELD

STILES IN AND OUT OF FIELD TO AVOID ERODED SECTION OF PATH

ROCKET POST

BENCH BY INFORMATION BOARD

MOUNT PLEASANT NORTH ROAD

GATE

HOUSES BY PATH

NORTH SEA

STATION ROAD

95

75 MINS FROM NORTHCLIFFE HOLIDAY PARK (MAP 93) TO THE SEA AT ROBIN HOOD'S BAY (MAP 95)

and sheltered by the headland, hides from trekkers until the very last moment.

But soon enough, having passed a **coastguard station** and **Rocket Post Field** (Map 94) – with the post that coastguards used to aim their rescue rockets at for practice – you join Mount Pleasant North Road at the top end of Robin Hood's Bay. Take a left at the end of the road here, and follow it down, down, down to the bay.

All that remains for you to do now is to dip your toes in the sea (or, as most people do, the puddles of seawater by the Bay Hotel), then celebrate your achievement in the nearby Wainwright's Bar (open high days and holidays only) at the Bay Hotel, not forgetting to sign their book to record your success.

And that's it. The walk is over. Congratulations: you've walked the width of England, a total of 191$\frac{1}{2}$ miles (307km), which is certainly something to tell the grandchildren. But there's still one question left unanswered: What are you going to do for an encore?

ROUTE GUIDE AND MAPS

ROBIN HOOD'S BAY   MAP 95, p231

Robin Hood's Bay is the perfect place to finish, a quaint, cosy little fishing (and, once upon a time, smuggling) village that is entirely in keeping with the picturesque theme of the walk.

Though fishing has declined since its heyday in the 19th century, there has been a revival thanks to its crab grounds, said to be one of the best in the north. The bay can also boast the highest sea wall in Britain, 12m high.

The old town huddles around the slipway. It's an amazing place: row after row of terraced, stone cottages arranged haphazardly uphill from the bay with plenty of twisting interconnecting alleyways and paths to explore. Within there are a number of pubs to celebrate in – a few of them serving decent meals – and tearooms where you can wallow in cream teas to your heart's content. There are gift, souvenir and antique shops aplenty as well, and a **museum** (July-Aug Sun-Fri noon-4pm).

And what is the connection with Robin Hood, you're probably wondering? Who knows? And after all the effort and energy you've expended over the past fortnight or so to get here – who honestly cares?

Services

The **Old Coastguard Station Visitor Centre** sits right by the end of the trail (supposedly June-Sep daily 10am-5pm, April, May & Oct, weekends only, 10am-5pm, Nov-Mar, weekends only, 11am-4pm) seems to be struggling to meet its posted opening hours, though the official tourist information **website** (⌨ www.robin-hoods-bay.co.uk) has plenty of useful information.

There's no cashpoint either, though the **post office and general store** (Mon-Fri 9am-5.30pm, Sat 9am-12.30pm) will do cashback if you spend a minimum of £5.

Where to stay

There are two good **campsites**: the first, *Middlewood Farm Holiday Park* (☎ 01947 880414, ⌨ www.middlewoodfarm.com), has been described by one happy camper as the best site on the entire route and it's certainly a smart and efficient operation. Facilities include a laundry room and some of the finest bathrooms on an English campsite. They even, for £1, offer the chance for you to take a bath! Currently, it costs £6 to stay.

To find Middlewood, from the end of the walk by the Bay Hotel head west past the chippy and keep going for ten minutes along the path.

Its rival, *Hooks House Farm* (☎ 01947 880283, ⌨ www.hookshousefarm .co.uk), is only *slightly* inferior facility-wise and is 50p cheaper at £5.50 per adult. Its location, however, a stiff ten-minute walk up the hill from where the path enters the village, is a drawback.

Boggle Hole Youth Hostel (☎ 0870 770 5704, ⌨ bogglehole@yha.org.uk; 80 beds; £14) is a picturesque former corn mill located in a ravine known as Boggle Hole, about a mile or so further south from the village and reachable either along the shore or the road inland. The hostel is open 24 hours, serves meals and has a bar.

❏ **The rescue of** *The Visitor*

A small memorial just above the old village celebrates the heroic rescue of the brig, *The Visitor*, which ran aground off Robin Hood's Bay during a storm in 1881. With the village's small lifeboat unable to help in such rough seas, the villagers summoned help from Whitby. That night, the lifeboat from Whitby was dragged over the snow to Robin Hood's Bay, a distance of some 8 miles (13km). Sometimes the snowdrifts were up to 2m deep and it took 200 men to clear a path for the lifeboat. Yet having arrived at the bay it managed to launch safely and by some miracle all the crew of *The Visitor* were saved.

Back in Robin Hood's Bay, at the top of the village is **Thackwood** (☎ 01947 880858, 🖳 www.thackwood.co.uk, 2D/1T en suite), the first B&B you see as the trail comes into town, which charges £65, or £40 single occupancy.

This is followed by **Northcliff** (☎ 01947 880481, 🖳 www.north-cliff.co.uk; 2D/1T all en suite) also on Mount Pleasant North Rd, a Victorian villa where every room comes with TV. Rates are from £27.50 per person (£25 if staying more than one night), £32 single occupancy.

On the same street is the **Manning Tree** (☎ 01947 881042, 🖳 www.manningtreebnb.co.uk; 1T/2D) with a similar standard of accommodation; rates also from £27.50 per person in a double, £36 single.

On Mount Pleasant South Rd there is more of the same with the pick of the bunch **Lee-Side** (☎ 01947 881143; 1T/2D) with rooms starting at £27.50 per person, and **Streonshalh** (☎ 01947 881065, 🖳 www .streonshalh.co.uk; 2S/5D or T all en suite), costing from £27.50, £37 in the single.

Ahead, on the road junction with Whitby Rd, is the **Grosvenor Hotel** (☎ 01947 880320, 🖳 www.thegrosvenor.info; 10 en suite rooms) with B&B from £30, while around the corner, **The Villa** (☎ 01947 881043, 🖳 www.thevillarhb.co.uk; 1S/D/1T) is another Victorian property, though one that has no en suite bedrooms – a deliberate decision to retain the period features of the property such as the cast-iron fireplaces and the servant bells. That doesn't mean there's no room for a few mod-cons, however, including internet access and flat-screen TVs in the rooms. Rates are £60 or £45 for the single.

Opposite and even older, **North Ings** (☎ 01947 880064, 🖳 www.northings.co .uk; 4D/1T) dates back to 1730 and boasts five rooms with wi-fi internet access and flat-screen TVs. Rates start at £50 for single occupancy, or £30 per person in a twin/double room.

Below, a whole string of B&Bs on Station Rd leads down towards the old village. They're all pretty similar. There are

beds for £30 per person at **The Wayfarer** (☎ 01947 880240; 3D/1D or T/1F, all en suite).

The elegant **West Royd** (☎ 01947 880678, 🖳 westroyd@btinternet.com) comes next, built in 1897 and maintaining its Victorian charm. Rates again start at £30 per person.

This is followed by **Devon House** (☎ 01947 880197, 🖳 www.devonhouserhb .freeserve.co.uk; 4D all en suite) charging £30; **Clarence Dene** (☎ 01947 880478, 🖳 www.clarencedene.com; 2D/1F), charging from £30, or £40 single occupancy; and **Birtley House** (☎ 01947 880566, 🖳 www .birtleyhousebedandbreakfast.co.uk; 3D/1T all en suite), charging the same.

Below these comes **Victoria Hotel** (☎ 01947 880205, 🖳 www.thevictoriahotel .info; 10T or D, all en suite) where all rooms come with TV, hairdryer and radio alarm clock. Rates are £40, or £50 for single occupancy. Take the alleyway next to the Victoria and it leads onto a road with fantastic views down to the old town. This is where you'll find **Raven House** (☎ 01947 880444, 🖳 http:// ravenhouse.rhbay .co.uk), which more than one reader has recommended. Edwardian rather than Victorian, all the rooms enjoy great panoramas as well as en suite bathrooms and a TV. Rates start at £30.

In the **old village**, most of the accommodation has been given over to holiday apartments for those intending to stay for a week or more. One that isn't, behind the old Muir Lea Stores along an alleyway known as The Bolts, is **Upside Down Cottage** (☎ 01947 880564, 🖳 upsidedowncottage@bt internet.com; 1S/1T/1D), charging £30 per person.

Not far from the Dolphin Inn is the delightful **Ingleby House** (☎ 01947 880887, 🖳 www.inglebyhouse.com; 4D en suite) whose main business is holiday apartments, though they can be rented out on a short-term basis too; note, however, that you can't book single-night stays in advance. A charming place where the rates vary from £50 in the pine room up to £80 and include a light DIY breakfast.

Finally, right by the sea is the *Bay Hotel* (☎ 01947 880278; 4D/1D or T en suite), occupying the prime location in the village, with a great restaurant and a bar named after the author of the Coast to Coast. It sells various memorabilia of the walk including keyrings, certificates, T-shirts and fridge magnets. Rates start at £60 per room, or £50 single occupancy.

The Boathouse Bistro (☎ 01947 880099, 🖳 www.boathouserhb.co.uk; 4D/1T/1F all en suite), The Dock, charges from £32.50 per person (£50 single occupancy).

Where to eat

For takeaway sandwiches you could do a lot worse than visit *Pickwick's Picnics* (open from mid-Feb to end Oct, 9.30am-5.30pm), with sandwiches around £2.50 for 2-3 fillings.

There are plenty of good tea rooms to relax in should you arrive early and need to while away the afternoon. Near the seafront is *Bramblewick*. Further up the hill, *Swell* (10am-3.30pm, to 4 or 5pm in summer), in the heart of the old-town alleyways, is the smartest place though, disappointingly, our cream tea came with synthetic, 'squirty' cream from an aerosol can.

For evening dining, it's hard to look beyond *Bay Hotel* (daily 12 noon-2pm, 6.30-9pm) or the *Victoria Hotel* (daily 12 noon-2pm, 6-9pm, no bar meals Sunday evening), both of which do some great bar meals. However, at the time of writing, *The Wayfarer* was planning to open a restaurant (daily in summer 6-10pm, Tue-Sun in the low season); booking is advisable.

A less obvious place to eat is the *Dolphin Inn* (food served noon-2pm, 6.30-8.30pm), though they do good crab and local fish dishes, as well as boasting a good range of real ales and regular live music sessions.

There's also a **chippy** (Mon & Wed noon-4pm; Tue & Thu noon-7.30pm; Fri & Sat noon-8.30pm; Sun noon-7pm) near the front by Boathouse Bistro.

Transport (see also pp43-5)

Arriva's **buses** Nos 56/X56 travel between Scarborough and Whitby via Robin Hood's Bay (1/hour Mon-Sat, 5/day Sunday); it takes 20 mins to Whitby and 40 mins to Scarborough. A single fare to Whitby is £2.80.

In the other direction the Nos 56/X56 go to Middlesbrough (90 mins; 10/day Mon-Sat and 8/day on Sundays/bank holidays).

If you prefer to get a **taxi**, call Bay Taxis on ☎ 01947 880603.

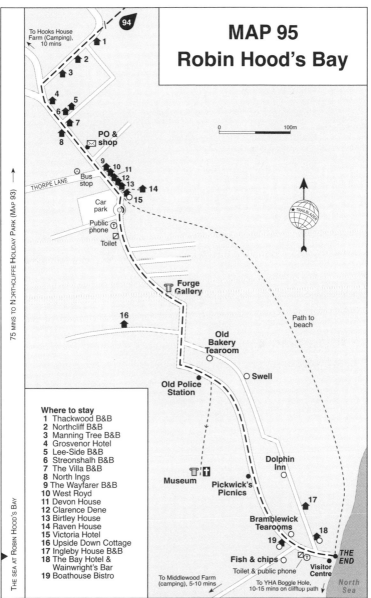

MAP 95
Robin Hood's Bay

94

To Hooks House Farm (Camping), 10 mins

PO & shop

THORPE LANE

Bus stop

Car park

Public phone

Toilet

0   100m

★ TRAILBLAZER

Forge Gallery

16

Path to beach

Old Bakery Tearoom

Old Police Station

Swell

Museum

Pickwick's Picnics

Dolphin Inn

17

Bramblewick Tearooms

18

19

Fish & chips

Toilet & public phone

Visitor Centre

THE END

North Sea

To Middlewood Farm (camping), 5-10 mins

To YHA Boggle Hole, 10-15 mins on clifftop path

75 MINS TO NORTHCLIFFE HOLIDAY PARK (MAP 93)

THE SEA AT ROBIN HOOD'S BAY

Where to stay
1 Thackwood B&B
2 Northcliff B&B
3 Manning Tree B&B
4 Grosvenor Hotel
5 Lee-Side B&B
6 Streonshalh B&B
7 The Villa B&B
8 North Ings
9 The Wayfarer B&B
10 West Royd
11 Devon House
12 Clarence Dene
13 Birtley House
14 Raven House
15 Victoria Hotel
16 Upside Down Cottage
17 Ingleby House B&B
18 The Bay Hotel & Wainwright's Bar
19 Boathouse Bistro

Trail map key

Walking track	Bridge	Forest/wood
Minor track	Fence	Boggy ground
4WD track	Stone wall	Building
Road	Hedge	Accommodation
Steps	Water	Campsite
Slope	Sand	Church
Steep slope	Stones	Public toilet
Stile	Stream	Public telephone
Gate	River	Map continuation

Town plan key

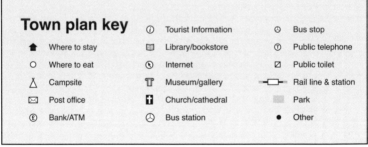

Where to stay	Tourist Information	Bus stop
Where to eat	Library/bookstore	Public telephone
Campsite	Internet	Public toilet
Post office	Museum/gallery	Rail line & station
Bank/ATM	Church/cathedral	Park
	Bus station	Other

INDEX

Page references in bold type refer to maps

TRAILBLAZER GUIDES – TITLE LIST

Adventure Cycle-Touring Handbook	1st edn out now
Adventure Motorcycling Handbook	5th edn out now
Australia by Rail	5th edn out now
Azerbaijan	3rd edn out now
The Blues Highway – New Orleans to Chicago	2nd edn out now
China Rail Handbook	1st edn mid 2008
Coast to Coast (British Walking Guide)	3rd edn out now
Cornwall Coast Path (British Walking Guide)	2nd edn out now
Corsica Trekking – GR20	1st edn early 2008
Dolomites Trekking – AV1 & AV2	2nd edn out now
Inca Trail, Cusco & Machu Picchu	3rd edn out now
Indian Rail Handbook	1st edn mid 2008
Hadrian's Wall Walk (British Walking Guide)	1st edn out now
Himalaya by Bike – a route and planning guide	1st edn mid 2008
Japan by Rail	2nd edn out now
Kilimanjaro – the trekking guide (includes Mt Meru)	2nd edn out now
Mediterranean Handbook	1st edn out now
Nepal Mountaineering Guide	1st edn mid 2008
New Zealand – The Great Walks	1st edn out now
North Downs Way (British Walking Guide)	1st edn out now
Norway's Arctic Highway	1st edn out now
Offa's Dyke Path (British Walking Guide)	2nd edn out now
Pembrokeshire Coast Path (British Walking Guide)	2nd edn out now
Pennine Way (British Walking Guide)	1st edn out now
The Ridgeway (British Walking Guide)	1st edn out now
Siberian BAM Guide – rail, rivers & road	2nd edn out now
The Silk Roads – a route and planning guide	2nd edn out now
Sahara Overland – a route and planning guide	2nd edn out now
Sahara Abenteuerhandbuch (German edition)	1st edn out now
Scottish Highlands – The Hillwalking Guide	1st edn out now
South Downs Way (British Walking Guide)	2nd edn out now
South-East Asia – The Graphic Guide	1st edn out now
Tibet Overland – mountain biking & jeep touring	1st edn out now
Tour de Mont Blanc	1st edn May 2008
Trans-Canada Rail Guide	4th edn out now
Trans-Siberian Handbook	7th edn out now
Trekking in the Annapurna Region	4th edn out now
Trekking in the Everest Region	5th edn mid 2008
Trekking in Corsica	1st edn out now
Trekking in Ladakh	3rd edn out now
Trekking in the Pyrenees	3rd edn out now
The Walkers' Haute Route – Mont Blanc to Matterhorn	1st edn Apr 2008
West Highland Way (British Walking Guide)	2nd edn out now

www.trailblazer-guides.com

TREKKING GUIDES
Europe
Corsica Trekking – GR20
Dolomites Trekking – AV1 & AV2
Scottish Highlands – The Hillwalking Guide
Tour de Mont Blanc
Trekking in the Pyrenees
Walker's Haute Route: Mt Blanc to Matterhorn

Africa
Kilimanjaro

South America
Inca Trail, Cusco & Machu Picchu

Australasia
New Zealand – The Great Walks

Asia
Trekking in the Annapurna Region
Trekking in the Everest Region
Trekking in Ladakh
Nepal Mountaineering Guide

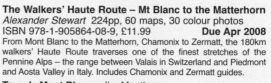

The Walkers' Haute Route – Mt Blanc to the Matterhorn
Alexander Stewart 224pp, 60 maps, 30 colour photos
ISBN 978-1-905864-08-9, £11.99 **Due Apr 2008**
From Mont Blanc to the Matterhorn, Chamonix to Zermatt, the 180km walkers' Haute Route traverses one of the finest stretches of the Pennine Alps – the range between Valais in Switzerland and Piedmont and Aosta Valley in Italy. Includes Chamonix and Zermatt guides.

Tour de Mont Blanc *Jim Manthorpe*
1st edition, 224pp, 60 maps, 30 colour photos
ISBN 978-1-905864-12-6, £11.99 **Due May 2008**
At 4807m (15,771ft), Mont Blanc is the highest mountain in western Europe, and one of the most famous mountains in the world. The trail (105 miles, 168km) that circumnavigates the massif, passing through France, Italy and Switzerland, is the most popular long distance walk in Europe. Includes Chamonix and Courmayeur guides.

Scottish Highlands – The Hillwalking Guide
1st edition, Jim Manthorpe 312pp, 86 maps 40 photos
ISBN 978-1-873756-84-3, £11.99
This guide covers 60 day-hikes in the following areas: ● Loch Lomond, the Trossachs and Southern Highlands ● Glen Coe and Ben Nevis ● Central Highlands ● Cairngorms and Eastern Highlands ● Western Highlands ● North-West Highlands ● The Far North ● The Islands. Plus: 3- to 4-day hikes linking some regions.

New Zealand – The Great Walks *Alexander Stewart*
1st edition, 272pp, 60 maps, 40 colour photos
ISBN 978-1-873756-78-2, £11.99
New Zealand is a wilderness paradise of incredibly beautiful landscapes. There is no better way to experience it than on one of the nine designated Great Walks, the country's premier walking tracks which provide outstanding hiking opportunities for people at all levels of fitness. Also includes detailed guides to Auckland, Wellington, National Park Village, Taumaranui, Nelson, Queenstown, Te Anau and Oban.

Kilimanjaro: the trekking guide to Africa's highest mountain
Henry Stedman, 2nd edition, 320pp, 40 maps, 30 photos
ISBN 978-1-873756-97-1, £11.99
At 19,340ft the world's tallest freestanding mountain, Kilimanjaro is one of the most popular destinations for hikers visiting Africa. It's possible to walk up to the summit: no technical skills are necessary. Includes town guides to Nairobi and Dar-Es-Salaam, excursions in the region and a detailed colour guide to flora and fauna. **Includes Mount Meru.**   *'Stedman's wonderfully down-to-earth, practical guide to the mountain'.* **Longitude Books**

Himalaya by Bike – a route & planning guide
Laura Stone 336pp, 28 colour & 50 B&W photos, 60 maps
ISBN 978 1 905864 04 1, *1st edn,* £14.99, – due mid 2008
An all-in-one guide for Himalayan cycle-touring. Covers the Himalayan regions of Pakistan, Tibet, India, Nepal and Sikkim with detailed km-by-km guides to main routes including the Karakoram Highway and the Friendship Highway. Plus: town and city guides.

Adventure Motorcycling Handbook – a route & planning
guide *Chris Scott, 5th edn,* 288pp, 28 colour, 100 B&W photos
ISBN 978 1 873756 80 5, £12.99
Every red-blooded motor-cyclist dreams of making the Big Trip – this book shows you how. Top ten overland machines, choosing a destination, bike preparation, documentation and shipping, route outlines. Plus – ten first-hand accounts of epic biking adventures worldwide.
   'The first thing we did was buy the Adventure Motorcycling Handbook*'*
         Ewan McGregor, *The Long Way Round*

Adventure Cycle-Touring Handbook – a route & planning
guide *Stephen Lord,* 320pp, 28 colour & 100 B&W photos
ISBN 978 1 873756 89 8, *1st edition,* £13.99
New guide for anyone planning (or dreaming) about taking their bicycle on a long-distance adventure. This comprehensive manual will make that dream a reality whether it's cycling in Tibet or pedalling from Patagonia to Alaska. Part 1 covers Practicalities; Part 2 includes Route outlines; and Part 3 has Tales from the Saddle.
   'The definitive guide to how, where, why and what to do on a cycle expedition' **Adventure Travel**

Tibet Overland – a route & planning guide *Kym McConnell*
1st edition, 224pp, 16pp colour maps
ISBN 978 1 873756 41 6, £12.99
Featuring 16pp of full colour mapping based on satellite photographs, this is a guide for mountain bikers and other road users in Tibet. Includes detailed information on over 9000km of overland routes across the world's highest and largest plateau. Includes Lhasa–Kathmandu route and the route to Everest North Base Camp. '*... a wealth of advice...*' **HH The Dalai Lama**

Trekking in Ladakh *Charlie Loram*
3rd edition, 288 pages, 75 maps, 24 colour photos
ISBN 978 1 873756 75 1, £12.99
Fully revised and extended 3rd edition of Charlie Loram's practical guide to trekking in this spectacular Himalayan region of India. Includes 75 detailed walking maps, guides to Leh, Manali and Delhi plus information on getting to Ladakh.
      'Extensive ... and well researched'. **Climber Magazine**

Trans-Siberian Handbook *Bryn Thomas*
7th edition, 448pp, 60 maps, 40 colour photos
ISBN 978 1 873756 94 2, £13.99
First edition short-listed for the **Thomas Cook Guidebook Awards**. New seventh edition of the most popular guide to the world's longest rail journey. How to arrange a trip, plus a km-by-km guide to the routes. Updated and expanded to include extra information on travelling independently in Russia. New mapping.
   'The best guidebook is Bryn Thomas's "Trans-Siberian Handbook"
         The Independent

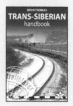

TRAILBLAZER'S LONG-DISTANCE PATH (LDP) WALKING GUIDES

We've applied to destinations which are closer to home Trailblazer's proven formula for publishing definitive route guides for adventurous travellers. Britain's network of long-distance trails enables the walker to explore some of the finest landscapes in the country's best walking areas and they are an obvious starting point for this series. These are guides that are user-friendly, practical, informative and environmentally sensitive.

● Unique mapping features
In many walking guidebooks the reader has to read a route description then try to relate it to the map. Our guides are much easier to use because walking directions, tricky junctions, places to stay and eat, points of interest and walking times are all written onto the maps themselves in the places to which they apply. With their uncluttered clarity, these are not general-purpose maps but fully edited maps **drawn by walkers for walkers**.

● Largest-scale walking maps
At a scale of just under 1:20,000 (8cm or 3^1/$_8$ inches to one mile) the maps in these guides are bigger than even the most detailed British walking maps currently available in the shops.

● Not just a trail guide – includes where to stay, where to eat and public transport
Our guidebooks are a complete guide, not just a trail guide. They include: what to see, where to stay (pubs, hotels, B&Bs, campsites, bunkhouses, hostels), where to eat. There is detailed public transport information for all access points to each trail so there are itineraries for all walkers, both for hiking the route in its entirety and for day walks.

West Highland Way *Charlie Loram* ISBN 978-1-873756-90-4, £9.99
2nd edition, 192pp, 53 maps, 10 town plans, 40 colour photos

Pennine Way *Ed de la Billière & Keith Carter* ISBN 978-1-873756-57-7, £9.99
1st edition, 256pp, 135 maps & town plans, 40 colour photos

Coast to Coast *Henry Stedman* ISBN 978-1-905864-09-6, £9.99
3rd edition, 240pp, 109 maps & town plans, 40 colour photos

Pembrokeshire Coast Path *Jim Manthorpe* ISBN 978-1-905864-03-4, £9.99
2nd edition, 208pp, 96 maps & town plans, 40 colour photos

Offa's Dyke Path *Keith Carter* ISBN 978-1-905864-06-5, £9.99
2nd edition, 208pp, 88 maps & town plans, 40 colour photos

South Downs Way *Jim Manthorpe* ISBN 978-1-873756-95-9, £9.99
2nd edition, 192pp, 60 maps & town plans, 40 colour photos

Hadrian's Wall Path *Henry Stedman* ISBN 978-1-873756-85-0, £9.99
1st edition, 192pp, 60 maps & town plans, 40 colour photos

North Downs Way *John Curtin* ISBN 978-1-873756-96-6, £9.99
1st edition, 192pp, 60 maps & town plans, 40 colour photos

The Ridgeway *Nick Hill* ISBN 978-1-873756-88-1, £9.99
1st edition, 192pp, 53 maps & town plans, 40 colour photos

Cornwall Coast Path *Edith Schofield* ISBN 978-1-873756-93-5, £9.99
2nd edition, 224pp, 112 maps & town plans, 40 colour photos

> '*The same attention to detail that distinguishes its other guides has been brought to bear here*'. **The Sunday Times**

TRAILBLAZER
British Walking Guides

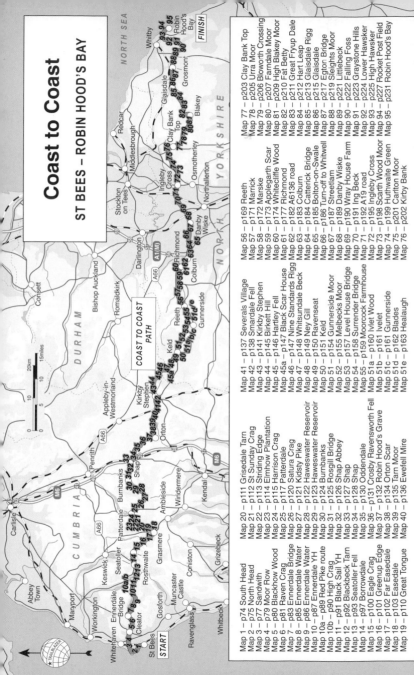

Coast to Coast

ST BEES – ROBIN HOOD'S BAY

COAST TO COAST PATH